Indian Dances

Marc Alexander

Krishna Rao and Chandrabhaga Devi in Dasi Attam
(Bharata Natyam)

INDIAN DANCES
Their History and Growth

RINA SINGHA
and
REGINALD MASSEY

GEORGE BRAZILLER
New York

GV
1693
.S553
1967x

Copyright © 1967 by Rina Singha and Reginald Massey

First American Edition

All rights reserved

For information address the publisher:
George Braziller, Inc.
One Park Avenue, New York 16, N.Y.

Library of Congress Catalog Card Number: 67-20736

Printed in Great Britain

CONTENTS

Acknowledgements   page 13
Introduction   17

Part One
DASI ATTAM (BHARATA NATYAM)

1. History of Dasi Attam — 31
2. Technical Terms and Movements of Dasi Attam — 39
3. A Dasi Attam Performance — 44
4. The Devadasis, the servants of the gods — 51
5. Kuchipudi — 62
6. Bhagvata Mela Nataka — 68
7. Kuravanji — 73

Part Two
KATHAKALI

8. History of Kathakali — 79
9. Features of Kathakali Technique and Training — 92
10. Make-up, Costume, Head-dress and Jewellery of Kathakali — 99
11. The Dance-drama and Its Stories — 108
12. Mohini Attam — 114
13. Ottan Tullal — 117
14. Yakshagana — 121

Part Three
KATHAK

15. History of Kathak — 125
16. The Technique of Kathak — 139

Contents

17.	A Kathak Performance	*page* 149
18.	Kathak Training	155
19.	The Ras Lila of Braj	165

Part Four
MANIPURI DANCE

20.	Manipuri Dance	171
21.	Manipuri Technique and Music	180
22.	Lai Haroba and Ras Lila	184
23.	Other Dances	190
24.	Sattra Dances of Assam	194

Part Five
ODISSI AND OTHER STYLES

25.	Odissi	201
26.	Santiniketan	207
27.	Uday Shankar and his Dance	210
	Appendix: Gurus and Dancers	214
	Bibliography	237
	Glossary	240
	Index	245

ILLUSTRATIONS

Krishna Rao and Chandrabhaga Devi in Dasi Attam (Bharata Natyam) *frontispiece*

Part One: *Dasi Attam (Bharata Natyam)*

Bas-reliefs from the gateways to the temple at Chidambaram:	
A dancer, with musicians, in a pose no longer in use	*facing page* 32
A pose still in use	32
Krishna Rao as Shiva Nataraj, the god of the dance	32
Mudras representing 'fish' and 'tortoise'	33
A bee hovers over an open lotus	33
Basic Dasi Attam foot position	33
The basic Kathakali stance	33
Ram Gopal as Shiva the Hunter	48
Krishna Rao and Chandrabhaga Devi demonstrate the nritya aspect of Dasi Attam: the god Krishna begs Radha's forgiveness	49
The nritta aspect of Dasi Attam	49

Part Two: *Kathakali*

A paccha character	80
Nritta movement	80
Preparation for a performance	81
A Kathakali performance in its traditional setting	81
Krishnan Kutty demonstrates the Kathakali expressions for the 9 rasas: love, humour, grief, anger, heroism, terror, disgust, wonder and serenity	96
A Mohini Attam pose	97

Part Three: *Kathak*

Rina Singha in a thumri pose	128
Rina Singha in *Mughal Miniatures*	128
Uma Sharma reaches the *sum*, at the climax of a movement	129
Radha waits for Krishna but ... a sakhi tells her ... he is dancing with another	144

Illustrations

The dancer in the role of the kalahantarita nayika — the woman
    grieving for her departed lover   *facing page* 145
Partap Pawar and Tirath Ajmani in a Kathak duet   145

Parts Four and Five: *Manipuri, Odissi and Other Styles*

Radha and Krishna in Vrindaban, interpreted by Manipuri dancers
    Thambal Yaima and Bihari Sharma   176
The Pung Cholom   177
Ranjana and Darshana Jhaveri dance a Manipuri nritta movement   177
Uday Shankar   192
Sonal Mansingh in an Odissi pose   192
Indrani Rehman dances an item in Odissi style   193

ACKNOWLEDGEMENTS

The authors wish to acknowledge the help given by the following persons and organizations in the preparation of this book:

Charles Bindon; E. M. Hatt; E. Upendar Reddy; Fernau Hall; Greenwich Public Libraries, London; India House Library, London; India Office Library, London; India Tourist Office, Toronto; Jamila Massey; Julienne Lewis; Khalid T. Ahmed; Marc Alexander; Margaret Henderson; Naseem Khan; Suhasini Ramaswamy; Syed Hassan Ali; Syed Mumtaz Ali; Thambal Yaima; U.K. Chandrabhaga Devi; U.S. Krishna Rao.

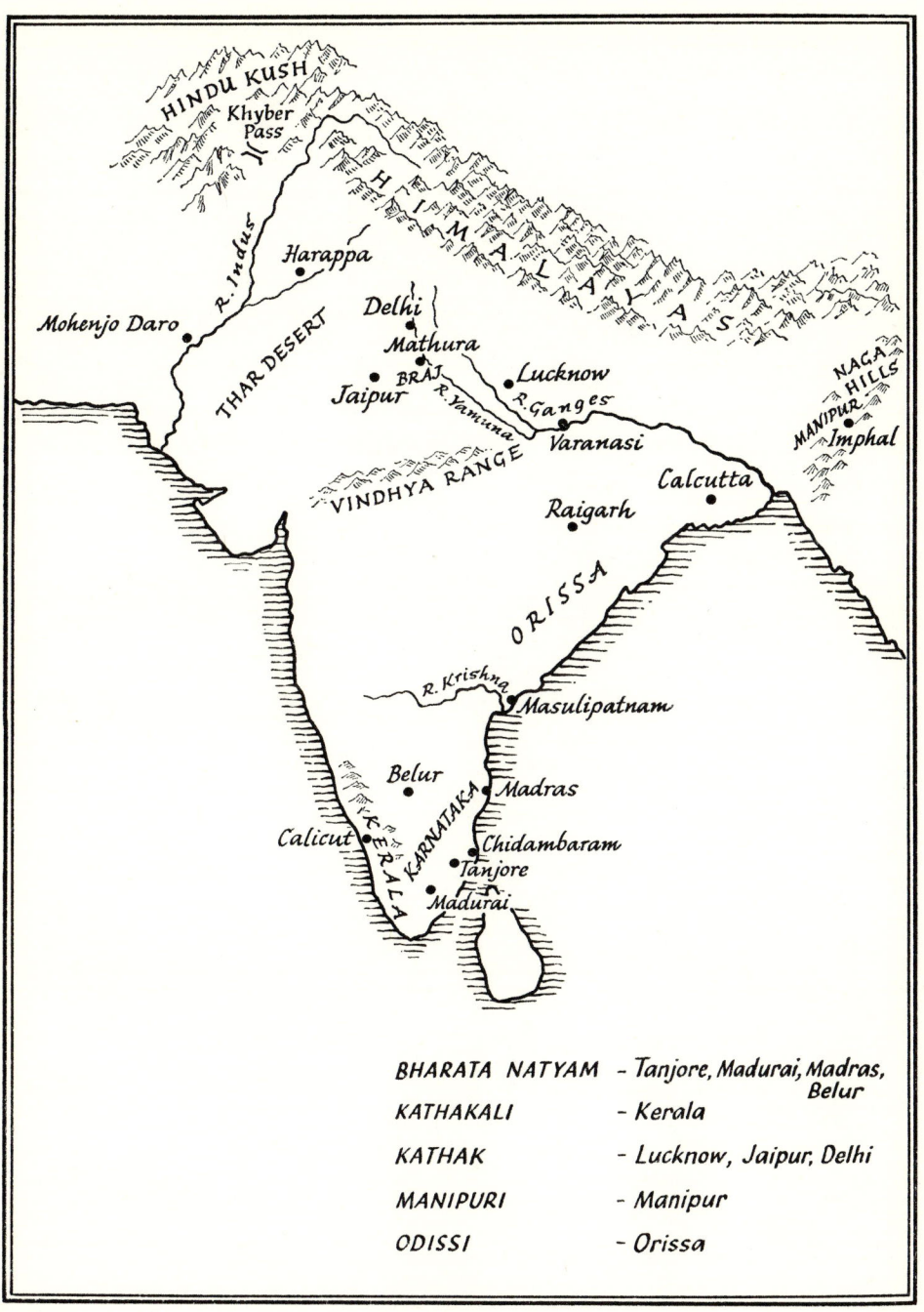

The main centres of classical dancing in the
India-Pakistan subcontinent

INTRODUCTION

Man is not alone in wanting to dance. Many birds and animals appear to dance at some time or other: the peacock and the lyre-bird for instance are famous for it. Like them, man also has probably danced from the earliest stages of evolution. He experiences pleasure as well as satisfaction in rhythmical movement, since this exercises his body and, at the same time, releases inner tensions. Moreover it can induce hypnotic trances. This may have led to the belief that dance has magical powers, and so it came to be used in early cults and rites for propitiating the gods and driving away evil spirits. By dancing man expressed himself in a way which he conceived as the post powerful and eloquent of the means at this disposal. He celebrated by dancing, he gained courage by dancing and often, like the birds and animals around him, he courted with the help of dance.

Dance is found among all men whether in primitive or advanced societies. Its functions vary in these societies from religion to pure entertainment. So in all probability, dance goes back as far as man himself but its styles and forms are many — some very new, or at least seemingly so, and others of great antiquity.

Indian dancing, even in its classical styles, is one of the most ancient forms still surviving. It has of course altered, but its basic elements would appear to be much as they were over two thousand years ago.

The earliest civilizations discovered in the Indian subcontinent are those of Mohenjo Daro and Harappa in the Indus valley, and are dated at about 6000 B.C. It would appear that by that time dance had achieved a considerable measure of discipline and it is likely, but not certain, that it was connected with religion. In any case it must have played a part of some importance in society, for one of the finds at Mohenjo Daro was a beautiful little statuette of a dancing girl. Not surprisingly however, almost nothing is known of the dance technique of this early period.

Introduction

Around 2000 B.C., the Aryans came to the subcontinent through the passes in the North-West. They were a fair-skinned race whereas the indigenous inhabitants were dark. They were a close-knit society of people and were easily able to subjugate the Dravidians. So as to establish themselves permanently, they set about organizing a new order by instituting the caste system which was initially based largely on colour. The Sanskrit word *varna* means both caste and colour. At the same time they introduced their own culture and religion and in turn adapted some indigenous customs and even gods. This was made easier by the fact that they settled down with the intention of co-existing with the original inhabitants of their new homeland.

The caste system would never have survived so long, had it not been accepted by all. Military pressure could not have sustained it. Although caste was a form of segregation or apartheid, it was worked out in such great detail and so interlocked with religious, social and economic conditions that it operated without creating any tensions. It brought about a division of labour in a way which eliminated the need for slavery, and consequently this institution never existed in ancient India. Part of the success of the caste system lay in its great diversity. Apartheid as it is practised today is crude by comparison because it entails the use of force, increases tension, and ignores the realities of contemporary conditions.

The caste system allowed for many gradations in the social scale and each had a vast spread. A certain amount of social intercourse was permissible between adjacent castes and in rare cases it was possible, though difficult, to step one stage higher in the caste structure. The scale went up gradually through many sub-castes and yet all were members of the same body politic. The Brahmins were the intellectuals and the head of this body. The Kshatriyas were the arms, the military caste which defended the whole. The Vaishyas were merchants who provided for physical needs and were likened to the stomach. Last of all came the Shudras who did manual labour and were compared with the feet of the body. The sub-castes within each of these four main castes were related to professions or occupations. For example, there were sub-castes of physicians, archers, money-lenders and cobblers. In the arts there were certain castes which specialized in music, in painting and in dancing. All of these functioned as hereditary guilds.

The caste system is now breaking up because the conditions

Introduction

which brought it into being and sustained it, no longer exist. Discrimination on the basis of caste has been made a legal offence, but the idea has penetrated deep into the consciousness of the people and will take time to die out completely.

The Aryans produced great scholars who studied everything in a scientific manner. Strangely enough, they never wrote any histories; instead all subjects, including history, were clothed in the garb of mythology and given religious sanction by being associated with the gods. They had a great pantheon of gods and goddesses, each of whom was responsible for some aspect of life. There were various degrees of gods as well as demons and there are stories of constant battles between the two in which the gods are always victorious.

Religious sanction always makes ideas much more invulnerable, and so legends grew around the history of the Aryans and their coming into India, beginning with the *Rig-Veda* and culminating in the two epics of the *Ramayana* and the *Mahabharata*. All learning was embodied in books called *shastras*. Each shastra covers its subject in detail and represents obviously, not the sudden inspiration of a single man, but the accumulation of a tradition codified in one volume, sometimes by one whose name is known, sometimes by a person or persons whose names are not recorded. In the same way, the works of Homer could not have been produced out of the void of a barbaric society, but represent the acme of a long tradition of culture.

Brahmin teachers considered that the highest knowledge was not suited for all men and were anxious to pass it on only to those who were worthy of it and capable of using it with discrimination. This meant that such knowledge was preserved exclusively for the Brahmins themselves. To make quite sure that it would not fall into the wrong hands it was expressed in allegorical terms and complicated verses or *mantras* which had to be interpreted by experts, rather like the Greek oracles and the books by mediaeval alchemists and astrologers. Thus the Brahmins became the intellectual leaders of society and the custodians of religion.

The sacred scriptures consisted of the four principal vedas — the *Rig-Veda*, the *Yajur-Veda*, the *Sam-Veda* and the *Atharva-Veda*, and several minor ones. These, together with the two epics and the various *Puranas* or legends concerning the gods, have a close connection with the classical dance. There was, of course, a shastra for dance and drama and the respect for these arts was such that some regarded the *Bharata Natya Shastra* as the fifth veda.

When the sage Bharata was asked by his fellows to explain the origins of this veda, he replied that after the Golden Age and during the Silver Age the people of the world had strayed from a righteous path, and become subject to greed, jealousy and anger, so that 'their happiness mixed with sorrow'. The gods then asked Brahma, the Great Father, to devise a fifth veda which could be seen as well as heard and which would belong to all the people, since the shudras were forbidden to listen to recitations of the four vedas. Brahma therefore, agreed to create a fifth veda which would induce 'duty, wealth, as well as fame, and contain good counsel . . .', which would be 'enriched by the teaching of all the scriptures and give a review of all arts and crafts'. So he took recitation from the *Rig-Veda*, song from the *Sam-Veda*, histrionic representation from the *Yajur-Veda* and the sentiments from the *Atharva-Veda*, and with a combination of these created the new *Natya-Veda*.

Brahma then asked the god Indra to teach it to the other gods and give a performance according to its principles. But Indra said that the gods were unable to do this since they would neither understand it nor interpret it skilfully enough. He suggested instead, that the sages were better fitted for the task. Brahma, therefore, taught the veda to Bharata and asked him to make ready a drama. Bharata in turn instructed his hundred 'sons', by which is probably meant men who followed him in becoming authorities on music, dance and drama. They then prepared for a performance. Brahma asked Bharata to include the graceful style in his play, but the sage said that this style was unsuited to men. So Brahma created from his mind *apsaras* or nymphs for this purpose. The drama was finally staged during the Banner Festival of Indra which was held in honour of his victory over the enemies of the gods and which was itself the subject of the performance. The gods were extremely pleased and rewarded the players with many gifts. However, certain demons who had sneaked in took offence at the dramatization of their defeat and saw to it that the actors lost their memories and their powers of speech and movement. Indra divined what had happened and, taking up the finest banner staff, battered all these demons to death. He then gave this staff, or Jarjara, to the players for their protection. But other demons came and continued to harass the actors until Brahma advised Bharata to build a playhouse.

Introduction

This done, its various parts were protected by different deities. All the actors and actresses too were given patron deities to protect them. Brahma himself protected the middle of the stage and this is why flowers are symbolically scattered on it at the beginning of every performance.

Brahma also tried to reason with the demons and spoke to them saying, that they were not the only ones to be shown to disadvantage in drama, but that drama would show all manner of people, gods, as well as demons, in every condition. 'There is no wise maxim, no learning, no art or craft, no device, no action that is not found in the drama'. It would instruct as well as entertain. Every man would find in it something of relevance to himself.

In Hindu drama, therefore, expression was achieved through music and dancing, as well as through acting, so that a play could be a combination of opera, ballet, and drama, in which one of these was given more prominence than the others. The *Natya Shastra* examines in detail every conceivable aspect of production: the ideal playhouse, metrics, prosody, diction, types of characters and appropriate costumes and make-up, intonation, the representation of sentiments, emotional and other states, style in acting, movements of every limb, the setting and construction of a play, conventions of time and place, and even the canons of criticism and assessment. It also deals with music, both vocal and instrumental. These instructions apply equally to acting and dancing for the two professions were combined. An indication of this is the fact that the word for drama, Nataka, derives from the word meaning 'dance'.

The date and authorship of the *Bharata Natya Shastra* are both in dispute. The book has been variously dated from the 2nd century B.C. to the 3rd century A.D., but there is even less certainty about the author. 'Bharata' originally meant a dancer-actor so that the title could mean simply 'A Shastra on Drama for the Dancer-Actor'. On the other hand 'Bharata' is also a name, and so it is possible that the title means 'A Shastra on Drama by Bharata'. However, for practical purposes, whatever his real name might have been, the sage of the *Natya Shastra* is called Bharata.

The dance gurus based their teaching on this treatise but it was handed down to their *chelas* (disciples) practically and by word of mouth. In any case, they reserved the most precious secrets of their art for selected chelas only who, in their turn, guarded them carefully, so that it was extremely difficult for outsiders to make a study of the

Introduction

subject. European Sanskritists knew of the *Natya Shastra* from references to it in other books but believed that all manuscripts had been lost. It was only in the latter half of the last century that, while working on a mediaeval work on drama, Hall came across a manuscript of the *Natya Shastra*. This led to others being discovered and much work was done by the German Heymann, and by the Frenchmen Regnaud, Grosset and Lévi. In 1894 Pandits Shivadatta and Kashinath Pandurang Parab brought out the original Sanskrit text. Further interest was aroused in the early part of this century, by the discovery of a commentary by Abhinava Gupta. In 1950 Manomohan Ghosh made the first translation of the *Natya Shastra* into English, which was complete except for the part devoted to music. This was a major work of scholarship and original research.

A subject as rich and complex as Indian dancing has several aspects. Just as the precisely cut facets of a rare diamond combine to reveal its myriad beauties so, with Indian dancing, its full beauty is revealed only when all its many aspects are united in perfect balance. In order therefore to be able to appreciate this balance, it is necessary to have some idea of its constituent parts.

Dance was classified as either *margi* or *desi*. That which was sacred to the gods and danced for them was margi, while the dance for the pleasure of humans was desi. It was further defined as either *tandav* or *lasya* in character.

Tandav was first danced by the god Shiva, Lord of the Dance, who then conveyed this art to mortals through his disciple Tandu. Shiva is the symbol of procreation and it is because of this that tandav is often regarded as a male dance. To assume this, however, is to limit its field. Tandav covers all dance which expresses actions and feelings with strength and vigour, whether danced by men or women. When it is danced without facial expression it is called Prekashani tandav, and when it includes facial expression it becomes Bahurupa tandav. There are seven generally accepted types of this tandav said to have been danced by Shiva:

Ananda, expressing joy.
Sandhya, the evening tandav.
Uma, the tandav he danced with his consort Uma.
Gauri, the tandav he danced with his consort Gauri.
Kalika, which he danced when he slew the demon Kalika.

Introduction

Tripura, which he danced when he slew the demon Tripura.

Samhara, his dance of death which symbolizes the release of the soul from the prison of Maya or illusion.

Lasya is that element of the dance which is graceful and delicate and expresses emotions on a gentle level. It is usually associated with the dance of women because Parvati, the consort of Shiva, taught it to Usha, the daughter of the sage Bana, who then passed on the art to the women of India. However, since love is the predominant sentiment in lasya, it is also danced by men when their dance expresses this sentiment. For example, Krishna's dance with the *gopees* (milkmaids) is in lasya.

There are three main components, *natya*, *nritta*, and *nritya*, which together with their subsidiaries make up the classical dance.

Natya is the dramatic element of a stage performance. There are three main points of resemblance between natya and classical Greek drama. Bharata defines natya as 'a mimicry of the exploits of gods, *asuras* (demons), kings, as well as of householders of this world'. This is very similar to Aristotle's description of tragedy as 'an imitation of some action that is important, entire and of a proper magnitude'. In both cases there is a purpose beyond pure entertainment. For the Greeks, tragedy effected 'through pity and terror, the correction and refinement of such passions', the Natya Shastra maintains that drama will teach and, in addition, 'give courage, amusement, as well as counsel'. Aristotle's drama comprised fable, manners, diction, sentiments, music and decoration. Bharata also enumerates six parts namely decoration, postures, gestures, words, representation of temperaments and music.

Here the similarity ends, for to the Greeks tragedy was the highest form of drama, and tragedy in the Greek sense did not exist in Hindu drama.

In Greek drama the emphasis was on hearing, hence Aristotle was primarily concerned with the fable or plot and the poetry in which this would be expressed. For the Hindus the impact was mainly visual and so Bharata gives detailed attention to the manner of presentation.

Unlike Aristotle, Bharata does not forbid the representation of violent action, even death, on the stage, provided always that it is shown with control and beauty, however terrible.

Hindu drama was not bound by the unities of either time or place quite as strictly as was Greek drama and its idea of the unity of

Introduction

action too was somewhat different. The aim was rather, towards a general unity of impression.

Nritta is the rhythmic movement of the body in dance. It does not set out to express a mood or sentiment or tell a story and therefore uses no facial expression. It visualizes and reproduces music and rhythm by means of abstract gestures of the body and hands and by extensive and precise use of footwork.

Nritya is that element of the dance which 'suggests *ras* (sentiment) and *bhava* (mood)'. Both ras and bhava are conveyed through facial expressions and appropriate gestures. The most important book on nritya is the *Abhinaya Darpanam* of Nandikeshvara, who is thought to have lived in the 2nd century A.D. As with Bharata, his identity is difficult to ascertain. On the subject of nritya, there are some differences between these two authors on points of detail, but the general outline is the same in both books.

Nritta then, is concerned solely with rhythmic movement in dancing and is therefore loosely termed 'pure dance'. The object of both natya and nritya on the other hand, is to depict ideas, themes, moods and sentiments. This they do by using *abhinaya*, which derives from the Sanskrit 'abhi' meaning towards, and 'ni' meaning to carry. The word thus signifies 'a carrying to the spectators'. The practice of abhinaya involves four techniques. These are known as *angik, vachik, aharya* and *satvik*.

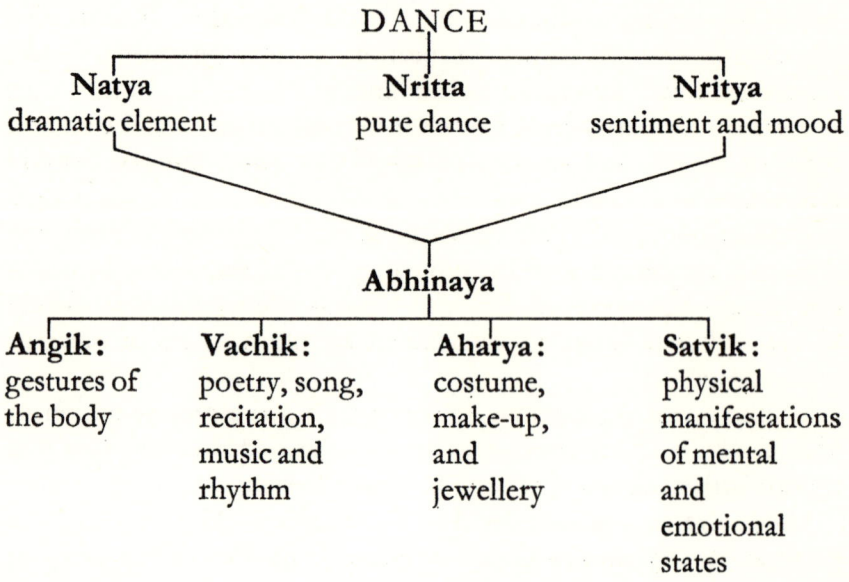

DANCE

Natya	**Nritta**	**Nritya**
dramatic element	pure dance	sentiment and mood

Abhinaya

Angik:	**Vachik:**	**Aharya:**	**Satvik:**
gestures of the body	poetry, song, recitation, music and rhythm	costume, make-up, and jewellery	physical manifestations of mental and emotional states

Introduction

Angik abhinaya is the term used for all gestures of the body and comes from the Sanskrit word 'ang' which means body. The analysis of the various gestures in the *Natya Shastra* is truly remarkable. There are thirteen gestures for the head, thirty-six glances, seven movements for the eyeballs, nine for the eyelids and seven for the eyebrows. The nose, the cheeks, the lower lip, each have six gestures and the chin has seven. There are nine gestures for the neck. The *hastas*, hand gestures, are sixty-seven in number. Twenty-four of these are for one hand, thirteen for both hands, and thirty are nritta hastas, belonging to the realm of pure dance. Hence these thirty are used exclusively in dancing, whereas the others may also be used in drama. There are three movements for the belly and five each for the chest, waist, sides, thighs, calves and feet.

Besides these there are thirty-two *charis*, which are movements for one foot and include the calf and thigh.

There are four ideal postures of the body in movement. Ragini Devi, the dancer and critic, describes them admirably as 'the deviations of the body from the central plumbline, or equipoise of the figure. These bends are called *abhanga* (slightly bent), *samabhanga* (equally bent) i.e. equilibrium, *atibhanga* (greatly bent), and *tribhanga* (thrice bent).'

A unit of dance which includes the postures of the body, and hand and foot movements, is called a *karana*. There are one hundred and eight of these, all of which are carved into the four gateways of the great temple of Chidambaram in South India.

The vachik aspect of abhinaya deals with the dancer's use of poetry, song, recitation, music and rhythm. The *Natya Shastra* specifies certain tempos for particular sentiments, as for instance, 'In the comic and erotic sentiments the speech tempo should be medium, in the pathetic slow and in other sentiments a quick tempo is appropriate.'

Aharya abhinaya covers the use of costume, make-up and jewellery. There are special provisions for the appearance of every type of character, so that the race, caste, social status and sex of any character is at once obvious. For example, goddesses had green costumes and their ornaments were of lapis lazuli and pearls. The demonesses had black costumes with sapphires in their hair. These conventions were necessary because no stage sets were used in Hindu dance or drama.

Satvik abhinaya represents physical manifestations of various

Introduction

mental and emotional states. These are paralysis, perspiration, hair standing on end, change of voice, trembling, change of colour, weeping and fainting. Now in real life these manifestations are produced involuntarily, but the dancer, using satvik abhinaya, has to induce them voluntarily. This means supreme control of the mind, so that the dancer can not only turn the tap on, so to speak, but is also able to turn it off at will.

The *Natya Shastra* also enumerates eight rasas, which are sentiments or emotional states. Associated with each of these is a presiding deity and a colour:

Name of Ras	Nearest equivalent	Deity	Colour
Shringar	Love	Vishnu	Light green
Hasya	Humour	Pramatha	White
Karuna	Pathos	Yama	Ash
Rudra	Anger	Rudra	Red
Vir	Heroism	Indra	Light orange
Bhayanaka	Terror	Kala	Black
Bibhatsa	Disgust	Shiva as Mahakala	Blue
Adbhuta	Wonder	Brahma	Yellow

Some later authorities mention a ninth ras, Shanta or serenity. The presiding deity here is Narayana and the colour is the white of the lightly fragrant kunda flower.

Nandikeshvara gives this hint as to how a dancer or actor might attempt to evoke ras,

> 'Where the hand goes, there also should go the eyes,
> Where the eyes go, there should go the mind.
> Where the mind goes bhava should follow,
> And where bhava goes, there ras arises.'

Introduction

Since all the gurus based their teaching on the same shastras and because of the close link between religion and dance, the style of dancing must originally have been much the same throughout the land. But as the knowledge was passed from teacher to pupil it changed a little in transmission to suit the circumstances of the dancers and the customs of a particular area. People in a large country like India vary a great deal in habit, custom, temperament and language, and because of this dance took on a distinct character in each region. Dance terms acquired different meanings in different language areas and sometimes different words came to be used to indicate the same thing.

We have already said that castes were subdivided according to occupation and this applied to dancers as well. The type of people in each dancing caste also considerably influenced the form of the art.

In the extreme South for example, dancing girls were dedicated to serve the gods and it was they who preserved the tradition. Their dance was therefore feminine and suited to solo performances in the temple and later, the court. In the South-West the dancers were generally warriors of the Nayar caste and, quite naturally, their dance was masculine and emphasized the bhayanaka and vir rasas (the emotions of terror and valour). In the North it was the cultured patrons who were largely responsible for the elegance and allusiveness of the dance style. In the North-East the people are gentle and restrained by nature and this is reflected in the soft and delicate movements of their dance.

By the latter half of the last century dancing had generally come to be regarded with reservation. This feeling intensified into hostility. There are many reasons for this which stem chiefly from the decline of aristocratic patronage and the consequent fall in the status and reputation of the dancers. There was also in India at about this time an upsurge of Victorian middle-class morality which sapped the creative energies of the people. It was only the efforts of anti-philistines like Tagore, Vallathol, Menaka, E. Krishna Iyer, Rukmini Devi and Uday Shankar and the inspiration of Western dancers like Pavlova, that finally led to the resuscitation of this ancient art form.

Today, although dancing has been firmly reinstated, gurus and dancers are faced with the task of extending and enlarging the classical repertoire to include subjects which will be relevant and

Introduction

meaningful to the mid-twentieth century. Blind orthodoxy endangers authenticity. The classics must, and always will be a source of inspiration and instruction, but even these cannot come to life without being informed with the integrity of contemporary creative experience. Experiment and innovation are essential to the survival of a tradition. Bharata himself was aware of this and in our own time Tagore has written, 'There are no bounds to the depths or to the expansion of any art which, like dancing, is the expression of life's urge.... Genius is defined in our language as the power that unfolds ever new possibilities in the revelation of beauty and truth.... Greatness, in all its manifestations, has discontent for its guide....'

PART ONE

Dasi Attam
(Bharata Natyam)

I
History of Dasi Attam

The home of Dasi Attam is in the South, in the area covered by the States of Madras, Andhra and Mysore. Like all the other classical dances of India, Dasi Attam too has its roots in the *Natya Shastra* of Bharata. It derives its name from its chief exponents in ancient times who were the devadasis or women in the service of the gods, and so Dasi Attam means 'the dance of the devadasis'. Relatively recently the term 'Bharata Natyam' has come into general use for the dance hitherto known as Dasi Attam. This change may well have been made in an attempt to dissociate the art from the devadasis who had come to be regarded as disreputable practitioners. The words 'Bharata Natyam' mean 'Dance according to the principles of Bharata', a term that could, indeed, apply to any of the chief schools of classical dance in India, since all of them are based essentially upon Bharata's work.

The most southerly parts of India have, throughout the history of that subcontinent, been the least affected by foreign influences, that is, with the exception of Aryan influences which were profound. This is due chiefly to the geography of that area, for it is divided off from the North by the vast plateau of the Deccan and the mountain ranges and forests of Central India. Invaders came always through the passes in the mountains far away in the North-West, and traders came to the western shores of India. So it is in the south of India where the largest numbers of the pre-Aryan inhabitants of the country are found. This is because the Aryans who came to the South had not come as invaders, but were pioneer settlers who had gradually filtered in, while others had come as missionaries. They were thus far outnumbered in their new homeland, and in order to preserve their identity they had confined themselves strictly to their own society, and built up a rigid caste system. Since they were both learned and wealthy, they very soon became considerable landowners, and thus superior to the indigenous population both educationally and economically.

In order to retain this superiority they applied the caste system extremely strictly and allowed no inter-marriage with the Dravidians. At the same time they applied the rules of their society in such a way that in time these came to be accepted generally as the mores of their adopted country. The Dravidians were separate but nevertheless indispensable units of society. Each caste had its duties, which were essential to the well-being of all. Mixing of the castes would blur the clear definition of these duties, and this would lead to a disruption of the smooth running of the community as a whole. Since religion too was bound up with this idea of society, as it was with feudal society in Europe, Aryan beliefs and with them Aryan culture were also gradually introduced, until the majority of the people of South India became Shaivite Hindus, for Shiva was the god of the Aryan Brahmins. He was the creator, the preserver, and the destroyer, and also Lord of the Dance.

The famous figure of Shiva as Nataraj (Lord of the Dance) shows the dynamic aspect of this god and embodies all his attributes. In his right hand he holds the *damru* (small drum), the symbol of creation. The idea of creation by means of sound has its roots in the belief that there are two kinds of sound, the struck and the unstruck. The struck is audible to us since it is a vibration of air, but the unstruck is a vibration of ether and inaudible to us. In the same way, with the Pythagorean theory, the music of the spheres could not normally be heard by humans. Whereas the sound we hear dies away, the other 'forms permanent numerical patterns which lie at the very root of the world's existence'. It is 'the principle of all manifestation and the basis of all substance'. Shiva the creator then, holds a symbol of sound in his right hand. Balancing this on the other side, his left hand holds the fire of destruction. His other right hand is held in an attitude of reassurance — he will give protection — and his second left hand, with the arm held straight across the body, points to the left foot, which is raised in benediction and grants bliss to all who come to him. His right foot rests on a demon of evil which he has defeated. The Nataraj is an exquisite study of balance and symmetry, of movement and at the same time of stillness. To Rodin it represented the highest sculptural concept of body movement known to the world.

Bas-reliefs from the gateways to the temple at Chidambaram.
(*left*) A dancer, with musicians, in a pose no longer in use.
(*right*) A pose still in use.

Marc Alexander

Krishna Rao
as Shiva Nataraj,
the god of the dance

Marc Alexander

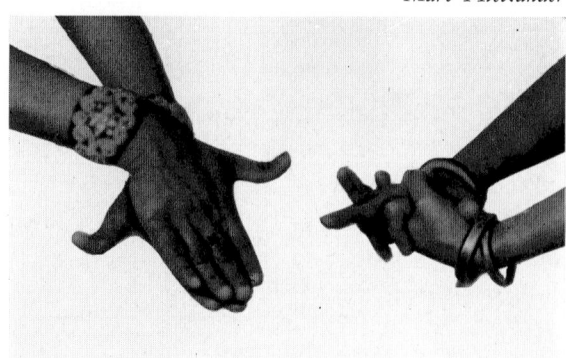

Marc Alexander

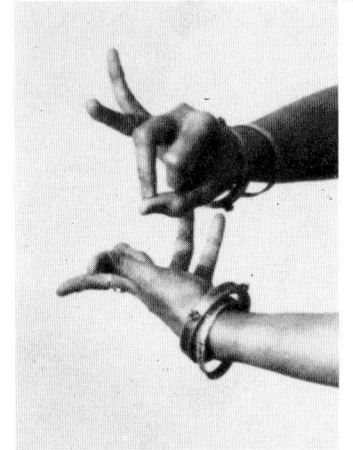

Mudras representing 'fish' and 'tortoise'

A bee hovers over an open lotus

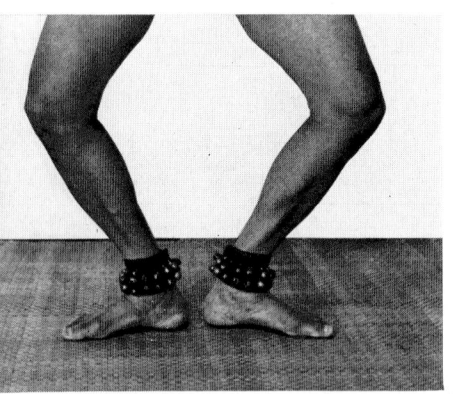

Basic Dasi Attam foot position

The basic Kathakali stance

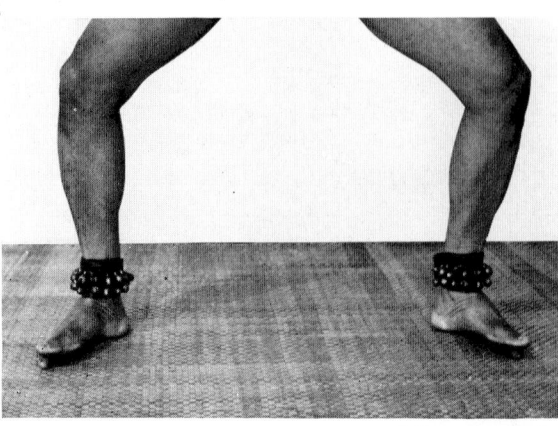

Marc Alexander

Marc Alexander

History of Dasi Attam

That the original Dravidian inhabitants of the subcontinent were already fond of the arts, dancing included, is now proved by the excavations of pre-Aryan sites and the discovery of dances which were purely Dravidian in origin, such as the tullals and devil dances of Kerala, and the dances of the aboriginal hill tribes. So with the aryanization of India, dance naturally continued to play an important part in the lives of these people, especially as it was so closely connected with religion.

There are numerous other representations of Shiva in the temples which display his different aspects singly. His static and generative aspect is worshipped in the form of a phallic symbol or lingam. This is a short column rounded at the top and mounted on a decorative plinth. Offerings of flowers and sweetmeats are placed at the base by the *pujarees* (worshippers).

Of the many temples dedicated to Shiva in South India, several date from the revival of Brahminism which came after the great Buddhist period. Buddhism had started in the North as a puritanical faith, not greatly interested in employing the arts to its service. Temple dancing was, however, regarded as particularly unnecessary, especially in view of the fact that some devadasis performed services of an immoral nature in addition to their temple duties. The kingdom of Ashoka, the great Buddhist, had covered almost the whole of the subcontinent, but even then the southern tip was not under his rule. Buddhism, therefore, never really captured the popular imagination in this area, as it did in the North, and the gods continued to be served as they had always been — the devadasis continued to dance for them with the same perfection and devotion as ever before.

Buddhism, unlike Hinduism, was a proselytizing religion and spread to the countries to the east and north-east of India where it took much more permanent root. With it also of course, went the culture of India, its painting, its sculpture and its dance. In these countries it was adapted to suit the genius of each people. The dance particularly, was bound to be affected by this transference. Without the shastraic literature which kept it alive and gave it the basis upon which it could develop, its form gradually petrified, its *mudras* (hand gestures) lost meaning and dropped out of use. Now, although still very beautiful, the dances of Bali and Cambodia bear only a superficial resemblance to the Dasi Attam which was their initial inspiration. In the theatre and dance of Japan there are now only traces which connect them with the dance of India.

As with most religions which begin with severe simplicity so it was with Buddhism. When it became firmly established, its austerities were relaxed one by one and its temples too were adorned with statues and paintings. Eventually, the Lord Buddha was accepted as one of the ten *avatars* or incarnations of Vishnu and Buddhism was thus absorbed into Hinduism.

The reassertion of Brahminism and its concrete expression in the form of magnificent temples, meant, of course, that the devadasis were more than ever in demand for service in these temples. Large numbers of them were attached to each one. The temples themselves were highly ornate structures, every possible surface profusely and painstakingly decorated with friezes, bas-reliefs and sculptures, not only of gods and goddesses and their exploits, but with figures of the heavenly nymphs or apsaras and their dance. The most famous of these temples dedicated to Shiva is that of Chidambaram in South India. On the four gateways of this are carved the 108 *karanas* or postures of the body in dance, which are described in the *Natya Shastra*.

A number of these are still in use, although the more acrobatic ones are no longer seen.

Throughout this time South India had been more or less left to itself, while the North had seen invasion after invasion. The Greeks, the Bactrians, the Scythians, the Kushans, the Huns and all the succeeding powers to the north and north-west had come in their turn.

In the twelfth century came the rise of Vaishnavism. It spread from the North and had an immediate appeal wherever it went. People turned to it as a more comprehensible expression of their faith and many temples were dedicated to it.

Because of constant upheavals and consequent re-adjustments, the people in the North rarely had the leisure to build enduring temples. The influx of influences was varied, some were artistically enriching while others totally inimical to artistic development. On the other hand the South, free from the fear and destruction of war, had both the time and the means to give rein to artistic expression. Their temples were abiding anchors which kept their religion as well as their arts from floundering. Since they were permanent, those attached to them had a firm and unbroken tradition. This applies especially to dance, where the temples were not only

History of Dasi Attam

enduring records of the art, but also supported a living tradition in the persons of the devadasis and their musicians called *nattuvanars*.

Of the Vaishnavite temples those at Belur and Halebid have an important significance for the history of Dasi Attam. They are of course decorated with sculptures of Vishnu and the many stories and legends about him, but they also keep alive for ever the name of a very remarkable queen. This royal lady, Queen Santala, is said to have been the greatest of dancers, and it was in these temples that she danced. Sculptures depicting her are among the most beautiful there, and have been a constant source of inspiration to succeeding generations of dancers.

As in the North, so Vaishnavism enriched the poetry, the music and the dance of the South. And since the god Krishna was one of Vishnu's avatars Dasi Attam added to its repertoire a new store of songs and stories based on Krishna's love for Radha.

With the Muslim invasions in the twelfth and thirteenth centuries, Hinduism was again under stress in the North, and even in the South the Hoysala power was destroyed and the Pandyan kingdom was reduced to its former limits. This disruption, however, did not last very long and certainly did not have any very great or lasting ill-effects on Dasi Attam, for a century or so later the South was again re-united under the Vijayanagar Empire. This was a period of great splendour and extravagance. Vijayanagar flourished and Dasi Attam, through the devadasis, was at its height. The Muslim rulers to the north of the powerful Empire were under constant threat from it, and it was not until a confederacy of the Sultans of the Deccan destroyed it in the middle of the sixteenth century that Vijayanagar finally fell. Although much of the richness and splendour were undoubtedly gone for ever, the threat to Hinduism and its dance in particular was by no means overwhelming; for the Deccani Sultans themselves were great patrons of the arts. Consequently Dasi Attam went to their courts as well, and it is at this time that terms from Muslim usage like 'salamu' and 'tillana' were added to Dasi Attam. Both of these are adaptations of Persian words. In this way Dasi Attam started on a new phase of secularization, for up to this time the secular functions of the devadasis had always been performed among Hindus. They had danced for the king or highly placed patrons, they had helped in the celebrations of domestic festivities and taken part in religious functions. Now with the Muslims in power, even tolerant Muslims, some modifications were inevitable. The changes were not drastic and amounted to somewhat more emphasis on pure dance and, where abhinaya or expression was concerned, a greater use of love songs which could be interpreted in both human and divine terms.

Even during the height of the Mughal Empire, when it stretched into Mysore and Karnataka, the continuity of tradition in the South was not disrupted. Such struggles as had arisen, had been largely dynastic and comparatively short and had not greatly altered the manner of living. Pressures from outside had not been strong enough to leave very profound marks. Social and religious life had been integrated and the caste system had been a stabilizing factor, the effects of which are still stronger there than anywhere else in India, even though officially the system itself no longer exists. The South Indians have, therefore, always been attracted to and occupied with aesthetic and intellectual pursuits, and in all they do, they exhibit a certain solid and definitive quality. Why is it then, that they should have allowed so beautiful an art as Dasi Attam, to all but die out? The blame cannot rest on any one cause, it was rather, an unfortunate combination of factors which led to the general decline.

By the last half of the nineteenth century the devadasis, once highly valued members of society, were falling into disrepute. They were already a caste unto themselves and by the end of the century this caste had come to be thought of as low. Because many of them prostituted themselves, their dance too lost the spiritual and devotional quality which made it great, and therefore also lost the following it once had. The Dasi Attam which a hundred years ago had been defined anew by the four brothers Chinniyah, Punniah, Vadivelu and Shivanandan of Tanjore came to be known fifty years later as 'Tanjore Nautch'. Shaivism itself, under the impact of the new materialistic machine age had lost its religious fervour and its forms were reduced to mere ritual, so its dance also no longer aroused the same interest. British rule brought with it, not only the machine age but also Christianity. The missionaries who first came to India were not encouraged by the British Government, but nevertheless they came. They set up printing presses, hospitals and schools, and preached that all men are equal under God. They worked with the poor and the outcast, and converted many. This was the first real challenge to the caste system in South India. Even the lowliest saw that given the opportunity, he could better himself.

History of Dasi Attam

The Hebraic faiths, Judaism, Christianity and Islam have never connected religion with dance. Music, sculpture, painting, architecture, literature and even drama had all been used by the Church, but dancing was something only the pagans employed in connection with worship. It was beyond the conception of the Victorian Christian to imagine that faith could be expressed through so immodest and voluptuous a medium as the 'nautch dance'. They were of course right so far as the 'nautch dance' was concerned, the idea was indeed impious — but Dasi Attam was not 'nautch'. To ladies who were used to quiet English parishes and tea on Sunday with the vicar, who were single-mindedly dedicated to the idea of service, these exotic movements must all have seemed alike: when Radha danced her longing for Krishna they found it hard to see this as an expression of the soul's longing for God — and dancers had such a bad reputation. They felt it their duty to do all they could to stamp out the practice. They were not alone and would never have succeeded so well if they had been. The Indians themselves had lost sight of the true nature and value of their heritage and allowed it to deteriorate. This was probably partly due to their eagerness to precipitate themselves into the 'modern age' and partly perhaps because they were dazzled by the new western culture. It all seemed so much better than their own, besides it was so much easier to 'get on' if they could meet European culture on its own terms.

By the beginning of this century dance survived in only a few obscure places. However Rabindranath Tagore, Uday Shankar and Menaka had already begun to try and revive interest in the dances of the North. In the South, E. Krishna Iyer decided to reawaken the interest of his countrymen in the real Dasi Attam. Eventually he was joined in his efforts by others. There were discussions in magazines and newspapers as to the merits and disadvantages of the dance. Public interest was aroused and in the early thirties some of those who had nursed Dasi Attam through its period of disgrace, were able to perform again in public. Yet even now the dance was still in the hands of its traditional custodians.

Rukmini Devi was the first great dancer of South India who was not a devadasi, and who, since she was from a respectable Brahmin family, opened the way for the future. After her, many other high caste families allowed their daughters to take up dancing as a profession. Shanta, Kamala, and Kausalya formed the nucleus of the new movement.

Dasi Attam

This new-found acceptability is a long-delayed echo of the status of dancing in earlier times. Queen Santala herself danced in the black marble-pillared halls of the temples at Halebid and Belur nine hundred years ago, and so became the inspiration of dancers of the future. Now, once again dancing has become respectable, so much so that it is an essential social accomplishment which everyone is flocking to acquire. This can be regarded as a healthy trend since it has aroused a consciousness of the dance, and so given Bharata Natyam a wider field of appreciation both at home and abroad, and in addition given recognition and employment to the old nattuvanars. But there is, unfortunately, a danger that the art may become diffused by being so freely handled by amateurs. In recent years the mushrooming of 'Academies', 'Schools', 'Colleges', 'Institutes' and 'Societies' run by teachers of doubtful quality, is a serious threat to the true Bharata Natyam and its devotees. However, the exodus of the dance from the temple to the theatre and the home is in harmony with the spirit of the times in which we live.

2

Technical Terms and Movements of Dasi Attam

Dasi Attam embodies all three aspects of Indian classical dancing, namely nritta, nritya and natya (i.e. pure dance, dance embodying an expressive mood and dance containing a dramatic element).

Allarippu, which opens every performance is a pure dance piece. It neither expresses any emotion nor tells a story, but is nevertheless, highly symbolic in its intent. The word allarippu itself derives from the Telugu 'alarimpu', which means 'to decorate with flowers'. Some of the movements do indeed suggest that the dancer scatters flowers in honour of the deity and the stage, but the use of the word may be purely figurative, for the dance also shows the gradual flowering or opening out of the dancer's body in readiness for the recital which follows. This section, since it is the very first item in the performance, is also used as a form of invocation to the deity and greeting to the audience. There are, in effect, three degrees of greetings in the allarippu, first to the deity, then to the learned among the audience, and lastly to the rest of the audience. The second greeting must have been incorporated when the devadasis went out of the temples, and added to their duties by dancing for patrons as well.

The allarippu also serves much the same purpose as an overture, in that it gives an indication of what is to follow in the rest of the performance. It includes some of the basic positions of Dasi Attam, particularly the ones from which all the *adavus*, the dance units, flow. Since the allarippu uses mainly simple positions, the field is left fairly clear for future elaborations according to the capacity of the performer.

Dasi Attam as the very name implies, should only be danced by women. In the South Indian treatise on dancing, *Natanathi Vadya Ranjanam*, male dancers of Dasi Attam are compared with widows

Dasi Attam

as harbingers of evil and bad luck. But in spite of this injunction, the dance does have its tandav aspect — that of masculine strength — as well as the lasya aspect of feminine grace. Moreover, some early temples show sculptures of male dancers, which would seem to indicate that men danced it, at least before it became the almost exclusive preserve of women, the devadasis, and came to be called Dasi Attam after them.

The dance celebrates Shiva as Ardha Nari Nateswara, or that form in which he manifests himself as half man and half woman, a being complete and absolute; for like Zeus, Shiva too produced an offspring from his thigh, symbolizing that a god need have no other vessel to carry his seed.

In Dasi Attam therefore, the right side represents the masculine, tandav, and the left the feminine, lasya. It is because of this that every action on the right must be mirrored on the left.

Originally, when the dance was restricted to the temple, the basic movement of the dance was forwards. The devadasi approached the image of the god gradually as the dance progressed. When however, the dance left the temple, certain changes in direction were inevitable. At the palace of a king or a prince, the audience would almost certainly have been seated all around the dancer, either at the same level or on low platforms covered with sumptuous cushions. The same basic situation would, of course, obtain all down the social scale. Consequently, actions had to be repeated in all four directions, but the overall movement was essentially towards the patron. With the advent of the proscenium stage there had to be yet another adjustment. The circle of the audience was now cut down to only an arc, and so the centre back of the stage became the point from which the dancer's movements radiated. Thus, at the end of each section within the dance, the dancer takes a few highly stylized paces back to the starting point, turning slightly to the right and left alternately at each step. It is from this point on the stage that every item proceeds.

There are moments in a Dasi Attam performance when the nattuvanar, recites certain syllables in particular rhythmic patterns. These are purely dance syllables and have no other meaning, and are known as *sollukuttus*. The nattuvanar beats out the rhythm of the syllables on his small brass cymbals and the dancer duplicates them with the bells on her ankles.

Bharata described 108 dance units comprising positions of the

Technical Terms and Movements of Dasi Attam

body, the movement of the feet and legs and gestures of the hands. He called these basic units *karanas*, but also said that as tastes altered, dance-masters and choreographers would invent others. A permanent visual record of all these karanas adorns the four gopurams or gateways of the great temple at Chidambaram. This temple is dedicated to Shiva Nataraj and legend has it that the god himself laid the foundation of the temple. It was in fact begun around A.D. 600 and added to by various dynasties of kings. The dance poses are carved in bas-reliefs of twenty-one by twenty inches. Around each tablet of the eastern and western gopurams are Sanskrit verses describing the karanas. The dancer is always a woman with two musicians, one on either side of her, who are given less prominence by being made half her size. Some of the karanas show a delicacy both subtle and elegant, while others require an extraordinary flexibility of the whole body, found today only among gymnasts or yogis. Although these karanas depict a woman dancer, her dance itself is tandav. Indeed one position, that in which the leg is raised vertically above the head, would be considered decidedly immodest in a woman, as the story of the dance contest between Shiva and Parvati illustrates. For it was by using this position that Shiva finally forced Parvati to retire in embarrassment and concede victory to him. So it is still a mystery why a woman dancer should be shown in this position at Chidambaram. Although a large number of the positions in these karanas are still used in Dasi Attam, many of them, including the one that so disconcerted Shiva's consort, have fallen out of use.

Just as in Bharata's time the basic unit of dance was the karana, so it is generally agreed that today this unit is the *adavu*, which seems to have evolved from the karana. There are various schools of Bharata Natyam and each has its own canons with regard to the adavu. One school, for example, insists that the heels should be about three to four inches apart when the feet are in their primary position. Another school takes the opposite view, that the heels should be in contact. Likewise, there are different views about hand movements. The principles of Bharata, nevertheless, underlie the teachings and assumptions of every important school.

The adavus are a part of the nritta aspect of Dasi Attam. There are about fifteen groups of them with types within each group. Dancers do not usually admit how many adavus they have mastered, for this is a professional secret, but it is estimated that the average dancer must be able to execute over forty types, and the best over seventy.

A short, brilliant succession of adavus is known as a *tirmana*. The word means 'conclusion', and a tirmana is used to conclude a section of dance or highlight a portion in the middle, or even, sometimes, at the beginning.

The adavus are combined in the tirmanas with complex rhythm patterns known as *jatis*. Jatis are a combination of long and short syllables. There are five types of jatis, based on 3, 4, 5, 7 and 9 beats. Tisra jati is the first type and has the syllables ta-ki-ta. The second type, the chaturasra, of four beats is ta-ka-dhi-mi. The third, khanda jati, has five beats which are ta-ka ta-ki-ta. The seven beats of the misra jati are ta-ka-dhi-mi ta-ki-ta. The fifth type which has nine beats ta-ka-dhi-mi ta-ka ta-ki-ta, is the sankirna jati.

The syllables of a jati are vocal representations of the sounds which the dancer has to produce from her ankle bells by striking the stage with her feet. She can do this by bringing her foot down flat or striking only with the heel or toe.

Jatis played on the drums are known as *chollus*.

The piece of pure dance where jatis are given full play, is known as a *jatiswaram*. Here the jati is combined with *swara*, which means literally 'musical sound'. The swara, sung in a raga or musical mode, is set to the measure of the jati. It is not usual to repeat a jati, but a dancer may include as many jatis as she wishes. A *swarajati* too is a blend of swara and jatis, but here the swara is rather more in evidence.

Another nritta item is the *tillana*, which is usually the penultimate section of the performance. It clearly originated in the North and was perhaps finally absorbed into Dasi Attam during the seventeenth century when Mughal influence extended from Delhi to Tanjore. Some of the ragas to which it is danced, such as Kafi, Behag and Todi, are a regular feature of Hindustani music. The tillana balances the allarippu at the other end of the scale, for where one gives the skeleton on which the dance is built, the other displays the complete form adorned with all the refinements of grace and beauty.

The *shabdam* is the first section of the performance which introduces abhinaya, or the interpretation of words by means of mime and gesture, but these passages are interspersed with pure dance. A shabdam is a song, often in Telugu, in praise of a god or king,

Technical Terms and Movements of Dasi Attam

and is sung in raga Khamboji or in ragmalikas. It is usually quite short and the prevailing mood is generally devotional or erotic love. Frequently, however, the element of love allows for either interpretation, and it was probably because of this that the shabdam was regarded as particularly suitable for performance in the Muslim courts of South India, and indeed was so popular there. This popularity in the Muslim courts, has left its mark on the shabdam in the form of the 'salamu' or Muslim salutation, which comes at the end of the piece. Later on, however, the name was changed to '*charnam*' which is also the last part of a poem.

The item in Dasi Attam where abhinaya really comes into its own is the *padam*. Padas are love lyrics which cover every conceivable aspect of love from the mystic and divine to the earthly and profane, but as is usual with such poetry even the most sacred can be and sometimes is, given a superficial and entirely secular interpretation. Most of the padas danced are in Tamil, Telugu or Sanskrit, although they have all developed into poems of seven lines from short Sanskrit verses called *slokas*. A number of them were set to music by some of the best-known musicians of South India. Bharata intended the padas to be sung by the dancer herself, but not all dancers do this today, although some may occasionally join in with the musician or even take over the singing. The emphasis in a padam is on the words of the poem, and in order to allow the fullest interpretation through abhinaya, the movement of the dance is slow.

A balanced combination of all the elements of Dasi Attam is seen in the *varnam*, which precedes the padams. This is the most complex item in the performance, and alternates between nritta and nritya. The melody is rendered to the words of the song as well as to swaras or sol-fa syllables. The prevailing mood is love.

3

A Dasi Attam Performance

As we have seen, the introductory piece of the Dasi Attam performance is always the allarippu. A dancer may begin the recital with her feet together, body leaning slightly forward and palms joined above her head. Indians always use joined palms for the namashkar, that is, when they greet anyone, but the position in which they are held indicates the status of the person greeted. When, as in this first position, they are held above the head, the greeting can only be addressed to a deity or a person who is deeply venerated. The custom is also found in areas where Hindu influence has been marked, for instance, at his coronation the King of Sikkim was greeted in this way by his subjects. The first action of the dancer then, is to salute the deity. As the music begins, she glides her neck in subtle movement from side to side. Her eyes follow the neck in a triangular movement — up, right, left, and back to normal. This is repeated a few times and then the shoulders and hands join the movements of the eyes and neck. This combination is known as *rechakas*. The dancer's face lights up with joy and there is almost a smile on her lips, which flickers briefly into life at moments of emphasis.

This gliding of the neck from side to side, indicates deep pleasure and, in a modified form, is a part of the natural vocabulary of gesture of Indians in general; since they, in common with the Latins, make abundant use of gesture to support speech.

Throughout the allarippu no accompanying song is used, and the only vocal accompaniment employed, is in the form of dance syllables or *sollukuttus*. Each sequence is executed at slow, double and quadruple time. The next phase of the allarippu constitutes the salutation to the learned in the audience, though in former times it would have been addressed to the patron or the special guests. The

A Dasi Attam Performance

palms are again joined, but this time they are held in front of the face. Again, other beautiful movements of dance follow. In the last phase the dancer takes up a half-kneeling position, the knee never quite touching the ground, and from here greets the whole audience, to the right, to the left and in front.

We saw earlier, that the allarippu introduces as it were, the recital which is to follow and shows some of the basic positions of Dasi Attam. The chief among these is one where the dancer stands with knees bent and with feet at an angle of about 120°. The arms are held on a level with the shoulders and parallel to the ground. The elbows are slightly bent and the hands are held so that the fingers bend up backwards. There are many slight variations to this position, for instance the knees may be bent even further so that the dancer is almost sitting, or the hands may be held in front of the chest with the fingers in other specified positions, or the left arm may be extended to the side and the right held in front of the chest, both palms up and the head turned so that the eyes are on the left hand. It is from such positions that the adavus flow and, as with ballet, dancers must learn to achieve them with ease and maintain them comfortably.

After the allarippu comes the jatiswaram, which is again an item consisting entirely of pure dance. The rhythmic patterns are of paramount importance here, for the success of a jati depends entirely upon the interplay between, and the accomplishment of, both dancer and drummer. Between them these two create dynamic variations to the accompaniment of the vocal passages of swaras and sollukuttus. The dancer begins with feet together and the back of her wrists resting on her hips and marks time with her foot before beginning a jati. The jatis to be danced are never pre-arranged between dancer and drummer and the speed with which each apprehends the other's intentions indicates an almost uncanny rapport between the two. The tension is exactly the same as that created between the soloist and drummer during a recital of Indian music. When both performers are of the first order, each seems to challenge the other to a greater display of mastery. It is by no means essential for the dancer and drummer to confine themselves to the same jati, indeed the dynamic tension is much greater when one is counterpointing the other, for both must conclude on precisely the same beat. This obviously indicates great skill, knowledge of time measures and a mathematical ear, and requires lightning calculations on the part of both performers. But the dancer has more than these calculations to think of, because while her feet are occupied with the rhythmic patterns, her body must give abstract expression to the swaras, one beautiful pose melting rapidly into the next. The really expert dancer appears to picturize the music with her arms and body as with her feet she measures and improvises intricate jati patterns. The elements of pure dance movement seen in the allarippu are here greatly added to and elaborated.

The two items up to this point have been of pure dance only. The next introduces nritya for the first time. The shabdam opens with a pure dance piece in the form of a tirmana and then goes on to an interpretation of the *sahitya,* the literary content, and the actual words of the song which follows. The abhinaya at this stage is not very elaborate, for this is merely a brief introduction to it, and gives a foretaste of what is to come later in the performance. The sahitya is, however, interrupted occasionally by tirmanas which form an interlude. The possibility of a double meaning in the words of a shabdam is quite clear from the following example, which is in fact addressed to Shiva.

'O Thou, Beautiful One, Favoured of the Goddess of Fortune, praised at all times by those learned in the arts, Giver of plenty, to Thee I bow.
When I wait for Thee, who alone art my guide, is it fair that Thou shouldst favour another with Thy presence?
O Great Lord, I tremble with love and devotion for Thee.
I cannot bear the flowery arrows of Manmatha, the god of love. O Thou with the third eye in the middle of Thy forehead, I seek Thy protection and bow to Thee.'

As always the shabdam ends with a salutation.

All the elements of Dasi Attam have now been introduced and next comes what is perhaps the most exacting part of the whole repertoire, for all the elements are now brought into play in a single item, the varnam. The rendering of a varnam calls for all a dancer's virtuosity in nritya. Both alternate throughout the varnam which can last anything from forty-five minutes to over an hour. The music and poetry of the song too have a particularly high quality, so much so that at times they almost vie with the dancer for attention. The varnam opens with a tirmana at single, double and quadruple speeds. Then follows the song which is punctuated by brilliant pure dance pieces. The songs of the varnam are always in some way connected with love and the precise nature of the mood is brought out in the opening statement. For instance, the mood may be one of religious love where the devotee is shown to be in love with the god Shiva. In the rest of the song she describes the torment and anguish she suffers as a result of her devotion to him. Not all the songs are necessarily connected with religious love. They can be purely erotic and these usually involve a *sakhi*, the name used for the confidante of the lovelorn maiden. In ancient times, a third party or go-between seems always to have played an important role in affairs of the heart. These songs usually tell of the maid confessing her love to her sakhi and begging her to arrange a meeting with her lover, or of the sakhi making a plea to the lover on behalf of her friend and telling him of her pitiable state. Sometimes the song is not one of unqualified praise for the lover extolling his beauty and virtues, but one reproaching his unfaithfulness or deriding his taste in the choice of a new love. Another song may tell of a conversation between a mother and her daughter who tends to become too easily involved with strangers.

The dance reaches a climax in the charnam, and although in this, as throughout the varnam, nritta and nritya alternate, it is the nritta which stands out for its beautiful and varied adavus and jatis.

After the speed and excitement of the varnam's conclusion, comes the complete contrast of a number of slow and lyrical padams. A padam has to be slow because it is exclusively abhinaya, interpreting in detail as it does, the words of a song through facial expressions and hand gestures. All padams deal with the theme of love and the dancer is represented as the *nayika* or beloved longing for the *nayaka* or lover. This is an expression of the love and longing of the human soul for union with the divine spirit. Hindus regard love as one of the dominant and root sentiments; the other three being anger, heroism and disgust. This being so, they express their religious longing in the form of an analogy which is at the same time highly expressive and comprehensible to the simplest of souls.

The padam allows for an exhaustive exploration of every possible meaning of a phrase, and each phrase is repeated several times in order that the dancer may interpret every shade of meaning. It follows then, that the greater the understanding of the dancer, the richer the colour she is able to give to any phrase; for example, in the padam which begins with the words . . . 'Krishna come quickly . . .' the dancer can demonstrate the word Krishna in many ways, each time pointing one of his many attributes, qualities, or things associated with him.

We have already seen that the texts of the padams can be given a highly erotic interpretation. Here are two examples chosen at random:

'O friend, why does He hide from sight, the Lord Gopala of Muvapuri, and hidden, cast glances at me?
This is indeed an auspicious day.
Tell Him He will be royally welcome.
O friend am I not His?
When He comes, my behaviour will not be such as to make Him think I am childish.
How can I ever desert Him, He who is full of compassion for me?
Have I ever annoyed Him with talk of others?'

'O Krishna, I am on my way to Mathura to sell buttermilk.
Please let me go!
I shall come in the evening I assure Thee — do not hold so fast my skirt.
This is the King's highway, dally not with me here.
The milkmaids will soon join me; let me go.
O Krishna, I implore Thee, do not tease me now.
Please let go my hand! Why art Thou so impatient?'

Both of these as it happens, concern Krishna, but in some songs the god is not actually named, so the dancer has to indicate the deity through her abhinaya. There was a time, however, when she used to make it quite clear that she was addressing not a god, but a particular member of her audience. Since in a padam a dancer was allowed great freedom of interpretation, she was at liberty to be as flirtatious and as inviting as she wished. Unfortunately, there were many 'patrons' who were highly flattered by this and were only too glad to be the objects of such alluring advances. It was this kind of thing which brought classical dancing into such disrepute, until in the end all dancers were dismissed as indecent and immoral 'nautch girls'.

The meaning of the word love was not confined to its merely romantic aspect. According to the *Natya Shastra* it has two bases —

Houston Rogers

Ram Gopal as Shiva the Hunter

Krishna Rao and Chandrabhaga Devi demonstrate the nritya aspect of Dasi Attam: the god Krishna begs Radha's forgiveness

Marc Alexander

The nritta aspect of Dasi Attam

Marc Alexander

A Dasi Attam Performance

union (sambhoga) and separation (vipralambha). Both, of course, arise from different causes and are to be expressed on the stage accordingly. Sambhoga is to be represented by such actions as clever movements of the eyes, eyebrows, glances, serenity of eyes and face, soft, delicate and graceful movements of the limbs, sweet smiling words and so on. Vipralambha is to be represented by, among other things, languor, anxiety, yearning, indifference, fear and jealousy.

Most padams would come under the second heading and there is a very wide range of them.

One tells of a wife who has been superseded by a new love. It is a very poignant song in which the wife, utterly broken, recalls the happiness of the days when she and her husband lived in perfect love. Yet others, tell of women who are not so resigned, and who vent their anger on the wayward man by taunting him, and by denigrating their rivals, by sarcastic remarks and other displays of jealousy.

There is another beautiful padam in a different vein which, assuming that Ranganatha (Rama), is exhausted after his labours, expresses concern for him, and recounts from the *Ramayana* some of his exploits. Here the dancer has the opportunity of showing her range and versatility.

Padams can be the most interesting part of the whole recital, especially for those who have some idea of the basic content of each one, for if the dancer is truly accomplished she makes the meaning of the words perfectly clear. Bhava, or mood, is common to all men and therefore within the understanding of all. It is something which speaks to the soul and has no need of words. We can all see whether a person is happy or sad without being told in so many words. We can appreciate a padam without necessarily understanding the actual words of the song, just as one can enjoy an opera sung in a foreign language; although in both cases an understanding of the words must needs increase our enjoyment even further.

After the padams comes the tillana. This is a dance of pure joy and the dancer's face and whole body express delight. She is exuberant yet captivatingly feminine, and displays the whole range of the devices of allurement. She is by turns capricious, coy, flirtatious, inviting, and almost mocking in the confidence of her beauty. She performs her intricate jatis with an ease which belies her consummate skill. Each adavu is repeated at two or three speeds and punctuated with scintillating tirmanas. The repetition of the same musical phrase throws into relief the dancer's variations as she combines in delightful harmony the movements of eyes, hands, fingers, neck, shoulders, waist and feet. The sculpturesque quality of Dasi Attam blends, in the tillana, with the fluidity of Kathak, so that one sculpturesque pose melts rapidly into another. It is as if the frozen figures of Belur and Halebid had become vibrant with the sap of youth.

The performance ends on a quiet and serious note with the recitation of a sloka. The recitation is in the form of variations on a melody which is set in a particular raga. There is no rhythmic or musical accompaniment. The dancer expresses the meaning of the fairly simple words through abhinaya, at the same time providing the adjectives, as it were, herself.

4

The Devadasis, the Servants of the Gods

Men have always conceived their gods in anthropomorphic terms and this being so, it was only logical that these gods should be endowed with human frailties. The deities had to be appeased, more often than not through fear of the consequences of omission. So worship has ever involved sacrifices of some kind. Men offered the best of their possessions — the fruits of the field, the fatted calf and even humans. Abraham was prepared to sacrifice the only son of his old age.

The fertility cult seems to have existed in all ancient civilizations. The great Mother Goddess appears under different names, Mylitta, Isis, Ashtoreth, Astarte, Ishtar, Aphrodite, Venus, Bhagvati, Parvati and Ceres to name only a few. The function of these goddesses was reproductive. They ensured the cycle of the seasons which regulated the growth of crops. They were responsible for the increase of the livestock and the perpetuation of the race. The well-being of the city and the countryside depended upon the goodwill of the regional mother goddess.

The reproductive powers of the goddess were embodied in the female sex organs and it must have seemed proper that the gift which would be most acceptable to her, would be the virginity of a girl. This would, in addition, be an auspicious beginning to the girl's ability to bear children, since by being deflowered in honour of the deity, she performed a pious act and thus acquired fertility and prosperity.

Herodotus says of the Assyrians, 'Every woman born in the country must once in her life go and sit down in the precinct of Venus, and there consort with a stranger.... A woman who has once taken her seat is not allowed to return home till one of the strangers throws a silver coin into her lap, and takes her with him beyond the holy ground. When he throws the coin he says these words, "The goddess Mylitta prosper thee." (Venus is called Mylitta by the Assyrians.) The silver coin may be of any size; it cannot be refused, for that is forbidden by law, since once thrown it is sacred. The woman goes with the first man who throws her money and rejects no one. When she has gone with him, and so satisfied the goddess, she returns home, and from that time no gift however great, will prevail with her.... A custom very much like this is also found in Cyprus.'

Herodotus does not say whether these women had to be virgins, but St Augustine tells of a custom in Phoenicia, where the worship of Venus demanded an offering of virginity. Parents offered their daughters to the temple to be prostituted in the service of the goddess. When the fixed period was over the girls were married off and thenceforth led the ordinary life of a housewife.

Young girls and virgins were dedicated to the temples for a variety of reasons. In an account of his visit to Syria, Lucian records that he saw a great temple to Venus at Byblos. Here they performed certain ceremonies in mourning for Adonis, whom they believed to have been killed by a wild boar in their country. Consequently, they beat their breasts and observed mourning as for one who is dead. But the next day they behaved as if he were alive and shaved their heads, in the manner of the Egyptians when Apis died. Those women who were unwilling to sacrifice their hair had, instead, to sell themselves for one day and the money they thus obtained was given to the temple.

Sometimes the sending of girls to the temple had a double aim, namely, that of serving the deity while at the same time earning their marriage portions.

Girls were also dedicated as a result of vows. Strabo gives an instance of this when he says, 'Now Comana is a populous city and is a notable emporium for the people from Armenia; and at the time of the "exoduses" of the goddess, people assemble there from everywhere, from both cities and the country, men together with women, to attend the festival, and there are certain others, also, who in accordance with a vow are always residing there, performing sacrifices in honour of the goddess. And the inhabitants live in luxury, and all the property is planted with vines, and there is a multitude of women who make gain from their persons, most of whom are dedicated to the goddess, for in a way the city is a lesser

The Devadasis, The Servants of the Gods

Corinth.'

Of Corinth itself he says, 'And the temple of Aphrodite was so rich that it owned more than one thousand temple slaves, courtesans, whom both men and women had dedicated to the goddess. And therefore it was also on account of these women that the city was crowded and grew rich....'

There is ample evidence in the writings of Socrates, Apollodorus, Plautus, Arnobius, Justin, and Eusebius which tells of sacred prostitution in the Middle East, West Asia, Greece, Cyprus, Egypt and North Africa. Although comparatively little is known concerning the pre-Aryan Indus Valley civilization, which flourished about the third millennium B.C., it seems likely that dancing played an important part in the lives of these people. Many clay figurines of dancing girls have been excavated from the ancient cities of Mohenjo Daro and Harappa. It is possible that these dancing girls were connected with religious ritual. Professor Mackay says, 'It is still uncertain whether dancing formed a part of the religion of the inhabitants of the Indus Valley, although it is so important a feature of the ritual of certain sects in India today. A scene on a fragment of a faïence amulet showing a man beating a drum and people dancing to the music seems to suggest, from its appearance on a religious symbol, that the dance was a ceremonial one; but this suggestion, of course, cannot at present be verified.... Another amulet from the same city (Harappa) shows the cult-object invariably associated with the Urus-bull, while by the side of it appears a figure which may be of a woman dancing; if this interpretation be correct, the dance must certainly be a religious one. In connection with the subject of ritual dancing allusion must be made to the wonderful figure of a dancing girl found by Rai Bahadur Daya Ram Sahni. The dancer, who from her features is obviously an aboriginal type, may represent the predecessor of the dancing girls (devadasis) who are attached to many temples in modern India.... It is interesting to think that this bronze figure may represent very probably a temple dancer of Mohenjo Daro.'

But there is no evidence to suggest that these dancing girls, whether secular or religious, were in any way connected with prostitution. With the advent of the Aryan invasion of India in about 2000 B.C., and the consequent decline of the Indus Valley civilization, new religious practices were introduced into the subcontinent. The worship of the sun-god Surya (equivalent of

Apollo) demanded the services of girls in the temples to sing and play instruments in honour of the god. In time their function extended to include dancing and sacred prostitution. The *Padmapurana*, which evolved much later with the resurgence of Brahminism, goes so far as to say that the dedication of a number of prostitutes to the temple of Surya is one of the surest ways of gaining Suryaloka, or the heaven of the sun-god. The fact that the gods were accustomed to having celestial nymphs or apsaras dance for them in heaven, would appear to lend divine sanction to this statement. For surely they would require the same devotion on earth that they received in heaven. This recommendation of the Padmapurana was obviously implemented by those dedicated to the worship of Surya, for in the seventh century the celebrated Chinese Buddhist pilgrim Huien Tsang notes a large number of sacred prostitutes at the temple of this god in Multan. Al-Barauni, the Arab historian, also confirms similar practices in India.

The spread of Buddhism seems to have checked, though not altogether abolished, this trend. There are numerous stories in Buddhist literature of how fallen women were reclaimed to a state of grace, and thenceforth led lives of asceticism. This is borne out by the existence of orders of nuns and almswomen, called Bhikshinis, instituted by the Buddha himself.

Both Kautilya, in his *Arthshastra* (circa 300 B.C.), and Vatsayana, in his *Kama Sutra* (circa A.D. 100), talk about courtesans in detail, but neither of them makes any mention of sacred prostitution. The accomplished ladies they talk about were rather like the Greek hetairae. In the case of the *Kama Sutra* particularly, this is a strange omission, as the whole book is devoted to the art of love in all its range and subtlety. It is unlikely, in view of his scientific approach to the subject, that Vatsayana would have left them out due to any scruples of conscience. It may be that technically he would have classified them under religion, and therefore regarded them as irrelevant to his treatise. But in any case, the fact that these two authors say nothing about sacred harlotry, by no means proves that the system could not have existed in India. We have already seen that it existed there before their time and certainly after their time, and that it also existed in Western Asia and North Africa during their own time. Some writers have suggested that because South India had mercantile links with the Eastern Mediterranean during the ninth and tenth centuries, the idea of temple dancers may have

The Devadasis, The Servants of the Gods

come from those lands. But this seems highly unlikely, because the puritanical influence of Islam had already been well established there.

The fourth century A.D. saw the rise of Brahminism. The Laws of Manu laid down the functions of the four castes; the highest of them being the Brahmins or priests, whose persons were holy and who monopolized all learning.

When the great temples were first built in India, dancing girls were attached to them as a matter of course. These not only performed services for the idol, but also provided an additional source of income for the shrine. The ninth and tenth centuries saw the most glorious period of temple architecture and it was at this time that the temples in South India, still famous today, were built. The richness of the decoration of these temples was fittingly complemented by the enchanting forms and matchless dancing of the devadasis, literally servants of god. We know from inscriptions that the Chola king Rajaraja installed four hundred devadasis in his temple at Tanjore. They were housed in luxurious quarters in the four streets surrounding the temple and were granted tax-free lands. Their social status was very high for they attended upon the god himself; they looked after his sanctum and danced before him. Invitations to royal occasions served to enhance this prestige even further. Such a high regard for these women was not surprising, for they had undergone a severe training in music and dance, were skilled in languages and had, moreover, been 'married' to the temple deity. This last ceremony took many forms, varying from region to region.

In the Coimbatore district at least one girl from every family of musicians was selected for temple service. After her dance training at home she was dressed in fine clothes and bedecked with jewels. She was made to stand on a heap of rice, and two devadasis, also standing on heaps of rice, held a folded cloth before her. The girl held the cloth while her dancing master grasped her ankles and moved them up and down in time to music. In the evening she was taken to the temple for the Tali (wedding necklace) tying ceremony. She sat down in front of the idol and the officiating priest gave her flowers and marked her forehead with sandalwood paste. He then tied the tali, which had been lying at the idol's feet, round her neck. Later on, after more training in music and dance, the marriage was consummated by a Brahmin, preferably rich, who represented the idol.

Dasi Attam

Among the Basava sub-caste the girl was married in a similar fashion, but to a khanjar (dagger). This was clearly a phallic symbol representing the lingam of the god Shiva.

At the Suchindram temple in South Travancore, the marriage of the devadasi to the idol was symbolic of the marriage of Parvati to Shiva. The priest lit the sacred fire, recited the mantras (sacred texts), and tied the tali round the girl's neck.

In other parts of India the dancing girls went through marriage ceremonies with trees, swords and flowering plants.

These marriages meant that the devadasi could never be a widow, and so she was considered lucky. Her presence, therefore, on auspicious occasions such as weddings and births was regarded as essential. Whenever possible she made talis for others and sometimes incorporated a bead or two from her own as a special favour.

We have two descriptions of the dancing girls in the kingdom of Vijayanagar from foreigners at the court.

The first is Domingo Paes, who was a member of the Portuguese Embassy. He talks about the idol which has the body of a man and the head of an elephant (obviously Ganesh). This idol was attended by dancing girls who fed it and danced before it, and also dedicated their daughters to it. He says that any high-born man might visit these girls without censure, that they lived in the best quarters of the town and were allowed to sit and even chew betel in the presence of the King's wives. Paes is wide-eyed with wonder at their wealth, especially their jewellery. Seeing them on one particular occasion he writes, 'Who can describe the treasure these women carry on their persons? Collars of gold thickly set with diamonds and rubies and pearls, bracelets also on their arms, jewelled girdles and anklets on their feet.... There are some among them who have had lands presented to them and litters and maidservants without number. One woman in this city is said to possess 100,000 parados, about £25,000, and I can believe this from what I have seen.'

Paes' description is vividly authenticated by murals, which can still be seen, at a temple near Conjeevaram. Fernao Nuniz, a countryman of Paes gives similar descriptions of the institution of devadasis in Vijayanagar.

It is plain then, that these devadasis were women of means. But this was not their only valuable possession. They were highly educated and polished in their manners and so able to provide their patrons with intellectual stimulation. This is the main reason why men of rank and learning resorted to them, as their own wives, being mainly confined to hearth and home, were sadly lacking in these qualities. It was, therefore, the accepted thing for these gentlemen to support such women privately, or to hire them from the temples. Moreover, their association with good luck meant that in time, the presence of dancing girls became more or less obligatory at celebrations of all kinds.

Methwold, who visited the Muslim kingdom of Golconda in the time of Elizabeth I, remarks upon the system of devadasis and their dance training from early childhood. These dancing girls 'whom the lawes of the country do both allow and protect', were invited to formal public functions where 'they danced gratis, but at all other meetings, as circumcisions, weddings, ships' arrivals, or private feasts, they assist, and are paid for their company'.

The institution of dancing girls became therefore, an accepted part of Muslim society. Another Englishman, Mundy, informs us that the Muslims at Agra distinguished among various types of dancing girls and regarded them as distinct from the level of common prostitutes. These dancing girls from Agra, Delhi and Lucknow, known generally as *tavaifs* were not devadasis, but highly sophisticated courtesans and repositories of culture and refinement. The sons of the upper classes were sent to them in order to round off their education. Though most of these tavaifs were professing Muslims and so had no connections with temples, their development obviously owes much to the devadasis. Their accomplishments, particularly in music and dancing, and their marriage to trees and flowering plants, compare exactly with the custom of the temple dancers. In both cases the preservation of classical dancing, particularly in the South, is due in large measure to these women.

A later picture of the life and customs of the South Indians, including of course the devadasis, emerges from an account of the Abbé Dubois at the end of the eighteenth century. He was well qualified to write *Hindu Manners, Customs and Ceremonies*, since he spent thirty years of his life in that country. Talking of the status of women in general, he says that it was not considered seemly for ordinary women to learn to read, sing, or dance. If any of them did by chance acquire any of these skills, far from exhibiting them, they would be ashamed to own up to them. This attitude was fostered by the fact that only dancing girls required the use of these arts.

Later, this was to have a serious effect on the survival of classical dancing and indeed on the education of women in general. It is only comparatively recently that the education of women has become widely accepted.

From the eighteenth century onwards, there was an ambivalent attitude towards the devadasis. On the one hand they were fully accepted, indeed, according to Dr Shortt, they were an asset to the town in which they lived and were at the very centre of Hindu society. The wives of citizens neither saw any harm nor felt any injury when their husbands consorted with devadasis; on the contrary, they thought it perfectly honourable. Yet on the other hand, there was an implied censure in the fact that these very wives did not, for anything in the world, wish to have the accomplishments commonly associated with dancing girls. A possible explanation of this may lie in the structure of the caste system. The devadasis although connected with the temples, were not Brahmins. They formed, as it were, a caste unto themselves. Their way of life was based on matrilineal law. Property passed from mother to daughter although sons were not exempt. In practice the daughters of devadasis, after the requisite training, also became temple dancers. If for some reason such as a physical defect, a girl could not take to her mother's profession, she was married off to someone in her own caste. The sons either became nattuvanars (musicians) and dance masters, or married outside their caste and left the community. There were occasional cases of the sons or daughters of the richest of the devadasis marrying into good Brahmin families.

Many nattuvanars took the surname Pillai or Mudali, which were regarded as respectable adjuncts to Tamil names. These masters have jealously guarded and preserved the art of dance music in spite of a grave danger, at one time, of it being utterly lost. The danger arose because many of them, being illiterate, had no access to the shastraic literature connected with the arts. However, some families tenaciously preserved the theoretical background and set a standard for both the practice and the theory of the music. The great musician Mattuswami Dikshitar and his pupils, the brothers Chinniyah, Punniah, Shivanandan and Vadivelu Pillai deserve particular mention for this work. Their families and their pupils have continued the tradition to the present time.

There were two main divisions of dancing girls, the valangai or right-hand and the idangai or left-hand. The valangai would only

The Devadasis, The Servants of the Gods

dance for or consort with the upper or right-hand castes. The idangai were not selective and were sometimes known as kammaladasis because they catered for the artisans, that is the kammalans or left-hand castes.

No devadasis, however, were allowed to have any dealings with the Untouchables. If they did, they were tried by their own Panchayat or caste court, and if found guilty were excommunicated.

As we have seen, all devadasis were temple dancers, but those who danced at court or for the nobles were called rajadasis and those who danced at weddings and social ceremonies of all kinds were known as alankaradasis. The name sanis was reserved for those in Telugu districts, and in the temple at Vizagapatnam they were called kurmakis. The devadasis also differentiated among themselves on the basis of language. In Southern Travancore the Malayalam-speaking dancers would neither marry into nor even eat with the families of Tamil-speaking devadasis.

Both the South Indian Princely States and the Madras High Court recognized their rights and status. They were legally permitted to adopt daughters from outside their profession or caste. These girls were entitled to their adoptive mothers' inheritance exactly as if they had been real daughters, but these rights were recognized in British India only in those areas which came under the jurisdiction of the Madras High Court. In some Princely States in other parts of India, the rights of temple dancers were also recognized, though in varying degrees from State to State.

The gift of a son from the gods is the greatest boon to an Indian family. If a marriage failed to produce a son, one of the daughters would be 'married' to the temple idol and serve a period there as a devadasi, after which she would return home and be given all the privileges and responsibilities of a son and heir. She would inherit her father's property; and at their death would perform the important religious ritual of applying the torch to the funeral pyres of her mother and father.

As mentioned before, the devadasis were averters of ill-luck, so the duty of performing the Arti ceremony was exclusively theirs. A small diva (oil-lamp) which burnt ghee (clarified butter) was placed on a salver. The subject was either the idol or a person. The devadasi would hold the salver at arm's length up to the subject's forehead, and describe a given number of circles with it. This Arti was performed twice daily for the idol and for anyone else from whom the evil eye or danger had to be averted. People going on a journey or about to encounter danger, in battle for instance, would get a devadasi to perform the Arti. This ritual was also used to avert the evil eye from new brides, pretty children and beloved sons.

Yet another function of the devadasis, which the Abbé Dubois describes, was connected with their reputation for bringing good luck. They were hired to accompany people when they went visiting, and it was considered most improper to go anywhere without a number of these attendant 'good luck charms'.

What appears to have surprised the good abbé most of all was the modesty of these women. He admires their cleanliness and their good taste in clothes, their dignity of deportment and the civility of their language. 'Indeed,' he says, 'they are particularly careful not to expose any part of their body.' He concludes that this probably arises from their sophistication in the art of seduction, the unseen being more tantalizing than the seen.

In 1870 Dr Shortt, a surgeon in South India, read a paper before the Anthropological Society of London, entitled 'The Bayadéres; or Dancing Girls of Southern India'. He describes how these girls started their training from the age of five or thereabouts. Before sunrise they had instruction for an hour each in singing and dancing, and the same again in the afternoon. After three years they were allowed to perform in public, but their training continued throughout their career. He notes several kinds of dancing which the girls were supposed to master. They were paid a token salary by the temple authorities, but their riches were accumulated through the munificence of their admirers. He, like the Abbé Dubois, praises their beauty and their culture and is not at all surprised that so many European officers took them for mistresses.

At the beginning of this century Thurston encountered many devadasis in the temples of Madurai, Conjeevaram and Tanjore, and in his book *Castes and Tribes of Southern India* he gives a detailed description of how a devadasi retired from her profession. 'When a dancing woman becomes too old or diseased, and thus unable to perform her usual temple duties, she applies to the temple authorities for permission to remove her ear-pendants (todus). The ceremony takes place at the palace of the Maharaja. At the appointed spot the officers concerned assemble, and the woman, seated on a wooden plank, proceeds to unhook the pendants, and places them, with a nuzzar (gift) of twelve fanams (coins) on the plank. Directly after this she turns about, and walks away without casting a second glance at the ear ornaments which have been laid down. She becomes immediately a taikkizhavi or old woman, and is supposed to lead a life of retirement and resignation.' The pendants were later returned to her, but she never wore them again.

One of the main reasons why the devadasi system fell into disrepute was that young girls were sometimes abducted to swell the numbers in the temples. This led to a concerted effort on the part of the British Government, the Indian States and some Indian social reformers, to put an end to the system. The Princely States of Mysore and Travancore both stopped the dedication of devadasis in 1910 and 1930 respectively. But in 1927 there were still 200,000 temple prostitutes in the Madras Presidency alone, which was a part of British India. In that same year Gandhi wrote, 'There are, I am sorry to say, many temples in our midst in this country which are no better than brothels.'

Katherine Mayo in her books *Mother India* (1927) and *Slaves of the Gods* (1929) presented a false and one-sided view of Indian society, but succeeded nevertheless in stirring the conscience of many people both in India and abroad. There was a hue and cry against the system but it is difficult to say how far these attempts were successful, since it was not easy to get accurate and consecutive assessments of the numbers of devadasis. In the census of 1931 the point was made that many did not return themselves as such, but regarded themselves as married women by virtue of their 'marriage' to the temple god.

Although there are no devadasis as such in India today, there are many good dancers, dance teachers and musicians who come from the devadasi caste. It is they who are the custodians of the tradition, the discipline and the feeling of reverence for music and dancing, nurtured through hundreds of years. Their approach to these arts has retained an attitude of dedication which only professionalism can engender. Whatever else may have been said about them by well-intentioned puritans, it is undeniable that their art was an integral part of their religion and as such pure and untainted. It is to them that we owe the survival and preservation of one of the oldest classical dance forms in existence today.

5
Kuchipudi

The earliest dance-drama of South India, which unfortunately cannot be dated with certainty, was the *Shiva-Lila Natyam*, which consisted of plays based upon legends about Shiva. By the tenth century, inscriptions prove the existence of other religious dance-dramas which were called Brahma Melas. Later, Vaishnavism made inroads into the traditional Shaivite cults and the worship of the god Vishnu brought into being new art forms and new themes. These were, of course, concerned with Vishnu and his ten avatars. Of the ten the one who attracted most popular devotion, was Krishna; for he, in the *Bhagavad Gita*, introduced a new concept into Indian religious thought, the idea of a personal God. For the poor peasant it was Krishna who made possible the love between God and Man and the bond of devotion one for the other. This gave rise to the Bhagti movement, and the bhagtas who followed its precepts roamed the countryside with its new message of love. These bhagtas, known in Andhra as Bhagvatulus and in Tamil Nad as Bhagvatars, used poetry, song, music and drama for the propagation of their faith and beliefs. In Andhra their dance-drama came to be called Kuchipudi and in Tamil Nad, Bhagvata Mela Nataka.

The first book to refer to these new dance-dramas is the *Machupalli Kaifiat* of 1502. The people of Siddhavattam were suffering great hardship under the local tyrant Gurava Raju. They presented their grievances in the form of a play, ostensibly as entertainment for their king, Immadi Narasa Nayaka. Their diplomacy bore fruit, for we are told that the king read between the lines and liberated his people. Even at the end of the sixteenth century, by which time the mighty kingdom of Vijayanagar had declined, the learned Pandita Radhya Charita remarked on the high standard of the art in South India.

Kuchipudi

Kuchipudi and Bhagvata Mela Nataka have a common origin. Both have Vaishnavite themes and use Telugu, the language of Andhra. Moreover, the dancer-actors in each case are Brahmin men. It seems, nevertheless, that Kuchipudi was the first to evolve. It grew in Andhra, an area comparatively near North India which was the home of Vaishnavism.

Sidhyendra Yogi, a saintly Telugu Brahmin can be called the founder of this dance-drama as we know it today. He was a devotee of Krishna and the lord appeared to him in a darshan or vision and asked him to write a play on the Parijatapaharana. This legend tells of how Krishna was asked by Rukmini, his wife, to obtain for her the Parijata tree from the garden of the god Indra. Krishna, with the help of Narada Muni, the sage, succeeded in getting the tree for Rukmini. Now, Krishna's love Satyabhama, became extremely jealous when she heard of this episode. She taunted Krishna, nagged at him and became more and more sarcastic about the lord's relationship with Rukmini. If he cared for her at all, he would have to prove it by bringing her the tree as well. Krishna had no alternative. He set out for Indra's garden and the quest began. ...

When Sidhyendra Yogi finished the play, he was confronted with the problem of staging it. Nowhere could he find actors who were sufficiently competent to play it or people willing to back him. Eventually, he arrived at Kuchelapuram, the village of his wife's family, which lay on the banks of the river Krishna about twenty miles from the city of Masulipatnam. Here the Brahmins, who were Krishna worshippers, agreed to help him. Young men and boys learnt their parts and their families supported the scheme enthusiastically. It was a great success, and after this the villagers put on the play every year as a part of their religious festivals. The neighbouring villages, Kappatralla, Alampur, Marampali and Mandapetta also took up the idea. In 1675, the Nawab of Golconda, Abdul Hassan Tahnisha, saw a performance of *Parijatapaharana* by the Kuchelapuram Brahmins. He was so impressed that he granted the village and the surrounding lands to the dancers, with the stipulation that the tradition of the dance-dramas should be carried on. This grant was inscribed on copper plate, which was the custom in South India symbolic of authority and perpetuity. This is an interesting example of how a Hindu religious art was not only tolerated, but actually fostered by a Muslim prince.

Through the years Kuchelapuram village came to be called

Dasi Attam

Kuchipudi, and it is this name which attached itself to the dance. Although none of the other villages perform the dance-dramas any longer, Kuchipudi has, in spite of many vicissitudes, carried the tradition down to our own day.

Tirtha Narayan Yati's famous dance-opera *Krishna Lila Tarangini* is a work much favoured by Kuchipudi artistes. It deals with Krishna's life from childhood to marriage. Each part of this work is interspersed with the rhythmic dance syllables known as sollukuttus. Since the *Krishna Lila Tarangini* is a very long dance-opera, it often happens that selected pieces from it are danced or sung as solo performances. A popular item is the very first section, 'Balagopala Tarangam', dealing with the childhood of Krishna. It has five stanzas of poetry set to music, and sollukuttus between each stanza. A very unusual feature of the 'Balagopala Tarangam' is that the artiste has to perform various balancing feats while still dancing. With an ornate brass pot resting on his head, he improvises a few rhythmic patterns within the given time scale, or he may have to do the same thing on the spherical shape of a large earthen pot placed upside down on the ground. This illustrates the high technical virtuosity required of a Kuchipudi dancer.

The greatest contribution towards the abhinaya, or expression, of this dance was made by Kshetrayya of Muvvu, a veritable genius in the writing of padams. He wrote 4500 of them although only 700 are extant and danced today.

The well-known play, *Golla Kalapam* of Ramiah Shastri, and the *kritis* or dance-songs of Thyagaraja are further material used by the Kuchipudi dancers. The kritis of Thyagaraja are addressed to Rama who, like Krishna, was an incarnation of Vishnu. Apart from these, the themes used are the epics and puranas, especially the *Bhagvata Purana* and Jayadeva's *Gita Govinda*. The last work gives the Kuchipudi dancer-actor twenty-four hymns or ashtapadis to interpret through abhinaya. The first ashtapadi is the Dasavatara, very commonly enacted, which gives an account of the ten avatars of Vishnu and their births. After acting out one, the dancer assumes a pose associated with the avatar and pauses before going on to the next. Thus, he starts with Matsya (the fish), the first incarnation, carries on to Kurma (the tortoise), Varaha (the boar), Narasimha (the man-lion), Vamana (the dwarf), Parasurama (the wielder of the axe), Raghurama (Rama), Balarama (Krishna), Buddha (the enlightened one), and last of all Kalki (the horseman of destruction),

Kuchipudi

who is yet to come.

The Kuchipudi artistes are well versed in Telugu and Sanskrit and have an understanding of the literature of dance and music. Since they themselves provide the vocal music, they have to be singers as well.

The nritya elements (representing moods and sentiments) of Kuchipudi are padams, varnams, shabdams and slokas.

Padams are danced in exactly the same manner as in Dasi Attam. The most popular authors of padams are Jayadeva, Thyagaraja, Sarangapani, Kshetrayya and Maganti Subba Rao.

Varnams too are danced as in Dasi Attam.

Although many shabdams are similar to those of Dasi Attam, Kuchipudi has a few special varieties. The Vinayaka Kavita, the Mundaka Shabda and the Abhishekam form part of this group. An abhishekam takes about ten minutes to unfold and describes a deity from birth to glorification. There are abhishekams about Rama, Prahlada, Sita and other important mythological characters.

Slokas are verses which, like shabdams, are rendered in solo abhinaya. They are, however, pure poetry and as in the Thumri Andaaz of the dance-style Kathak, the dancer sits throughout his recitation of them and gives full scope to shringar bhava, the expression of love. How this North Indian influence found its way into the repertoire of Kuchipudi would be an interesting subject for investigation. In the nritta or pure dance part, too, a strong Kathak element can be seen. It is possible that Kuchipudi absorbed these influences during the Mughal period when Andhra was a part of the empire and Kathak at the peak of its popularity.

The pure dance or nritta of Kuchipudi consists of adavus, jatis, jatiswarams, tirmanas and tillanas. These are similar to the nritta of Dasi Attam, but Kuchipudi has one type of pure dance, namely kannakole, not found in Dasi Attam, Bhagvata Mela Nataka or Kuravanji, all of which employ the same basic techniques. The kannakole is mainly footwork. While the musicians play the syllabic beats, the dancer executes patterns within the tal or time-measure (pronounced 'taal'). In the saptatal of the kannakole the dancer improvises variations on seven different tals. This particular technique of footwork is very much like the layakari of Kathak in which the dancers of Jaipur and Lucknow excelled and which we shall discuss later.

The music of Kuchipudi is Karnatic and the chief musician is the

Dasi Attam

nattuvanar who recites the dance syllables, at the same time clapping them out with his hands or playing them on a pair of small brass cymbals. There are three other musicians, a mridangam player, a clarinettist and a violinist.

Each male character wears a *dhoti* (loin-cloth) with a jacket, and jewels and crown if the part requires them. He may also wear a beard and moustache. The female characters, played of course by men, wear the normal sari and choli with false plaits or other more elaborate coiffures. Nowadays the sari is being replaced by the fan-fronted costume worn by Dasi Attam dancers. The facial make-up is quite simple.

Kuchipudi dance-dramas are performed only at night. A temporary open-air stage is constructed in the temple courtyard, but if more people than the courtyard could possibly hold are expected, the stage is put up at the end of a street. In this case the street itself would be the auditorium and the balconies of the houses on either side serve as stalls and private boxes.

The audience begins to congregate hours before the show. Little boys reserve the best places, people talk and gesticulate and babies add to the general clamour. There is, underlying it all, an air of expectancy. The stage has no curtain to be rung up so there is no hint whatsoever that the proceedings are about to begin. Suddenly Hasyagadu appears. Appropriately attired as the Fool, he jumps, staggers, capers and makes faces. His function is to draw attention towards the stage, to make the people settle down and prepare themselves for the good things to come. After his exit there is an invocatory prayer by the artistes off stage. This is usually from the *Gita Govinda* and invokes the blessings of the gods. The musicians led by the nattuvanar, now take their place on one side of the stage. They play a short rhythmic piece on the mridangam and cymbals, and after this the nattuvanar sings a prayer in honour of Balatripurasundari, the goddess of the Kuchipudi temple. He follows this with a long sloka explaining the meaning of the dance-drama, its significance to the lives of the people and their moral duty to listen patiently and learn from it.

The important characters perform an introductory dance called a *daru*. This involves the holding up of a sheet of white cloth by a pair of volunteers. The artiste comes on behind it, showing only his head and feet. He does a few dance movements and when the sheet is whipped dramatically away, he comes forward and dances more elaborately. The audience knows by his gestures whom he represents and he demonstrates his skill at considerable length.

There are many kinds of darus. They are not improvised but form an integral part of Kuchipudi. Later, as the dance-drama progresses, the onlookers are regaled with extemporized snatches of comic relief known as Pagati Veshamu. These come after the longer movements and are more in the nature of intermissions. Much the same thing took place in the mediaeval mystery and miracle plays in England, where it became customary for actors to insert unscheduled slap-stick into didactic religious drama.

Unfortunately, encroaching modernism, in the form of the gas lamp, has now appeared in Kuchipudi. This has destroyed the other-world atmosphere created by the oil-fed divas, the tiny-tongued lights licking into the night. Now we have the incessant hiss of gas and the vigorous pumping of lamps, sometimes during the tenderest part of the drama.

The most important Kuchipudi artistes alive are, Lakshmi Narayana Shastri and Chinta Krishna Murti, both Brahmins from the parent village. The products of a long tradition of the art, they are experts in every sense of the word. Lakshmi Narayana Shastri is very old now, but was in his time, justly famous for his role of Bhama in *Bhama Kalapam*. He has trained some excellent pupils, the famous dancer Balasaraswati being among those whom he instructed in the rendering of padams. It is sad indeed that for many years this master has been neglected by the public and the State.

Chinta Krishna Murti has organized a permanent dance company in the village. Its repertoire includes the classics of Kuchipudi, and when invited, they go on tours of the surrounding villages and towns. However, they too are in a neglected condition and their finances are precarious. The art is being kept alive mainly through the faith of a few people like Murti.

In recent times women too have begun to learn Kuchipudi, but they perform only short extracts from the dance-dramas as solo items. Kuchipudi is therefore better known today through these performances than through the actual dance-dramas which are rarely, if ever, performed outside the local villages.

6

Bhagvata Mela Nataka

The King of Tanjore, Achutappa Nayak (1561–1614), one day inadvertently ate a betel leaf with his left hand. Now, why should this seemingly innocent action have led to the establishment of an important school of dance-drama? A short explanation of the customs of India is here clearly called for. The betel is the heart-shaped leaf of a climbing plant, smaller in size than a man's hand. It has a mildly pungent taste and possesses some medicinal value, especially as a digestive aid. The leaf is thinly coated with a touch of slaked lime and the refined sap of the katha tree, and then folded into a neat triangle containing finely chopped areca nut, cardamum, scents and other herbal preparations. The triangle is secured with a single clove. Very often, in sophisticated circles, the betel or *paan* as it is called, is covered with silver leaf and sprinkled with rose water. Although the paan was chewed after meals to counteract the richness of the food, it later became a social habit, until today, paans are an addiction with some people, particularly with those who take refined tobacco with them. The mouths of such habitués are permanently stained a rich reddish-brown. In the best houses paans are offered to guests on silver salvers with a certain amount of ceremony as in the West one would be offered a choice liqueur.

The paan, however, was only incidental. The real culprit was the left hand. The king should have used the right hand, since the left hand, which performs the duties of personal hygiene, is regarded as unclean. It is probably due to this that the term 'left-hand castes' arose in South India, because these were the low castes which carried out all the menial and unpleasant tasks. Achutappa's conscience was so burdened that he sought ways of expiating his guilt. A gift to the holy Brahmins seemed the best means of expiation. Now, it happened that at this particular time there was a group of Brahmin refugees in Tanjore who had come from Andhra. What is more, among these were some dancers, musicians, and others who were devoted to the religious arts. Since the king was a patron of the arts, here was an eminently suitable opportunity. He therefore granted, about ten miles from the city, a house, a well and a portion of land to each of the 501 families. The king's desire was, that they should continue their cultural activities and develop them. In gratitude the Brahmins named their village Achutapuram, after their royal benefactor. The village has now come to be called Melatur and ever since its inception, dance-dramas have been performed at the local Varadaraja Perumal temple. The dancers are Bhagvatas, men servants of the gods, and their dance is known as Bhagvata Mela Nataka.

About 160 years ago, Venkatarama Shastri wrote a dozen dance-dramas which became Bhagvata Mela favourites. They are *Usha Parinayam*, *Rukmangada*, *Golla Bhama*, *Rukmini Kalyanam*, *Sita Kalyanam*, *Dhruva Charitram*, *Harishchandra*, *Kamsavadha*, *Shivarathrivaibhavam*, *Bhasmasura Vadham*, *Markandaya* and *Prahlada Charitram*. All of them have Vaishnavite themes and are written in Telugu. They have great literary merit and integrate acting, dancing, music and singing with great success.

Natesa Iyer was the next great Bhagvata. Although he did not write any plays, he was an actor famous for his female roles and, as a teacher, he produced actor-dancers of the calibre of Bharatram Nallur Narayanaswami, K. Subramania Iyer and Kodanda Rama Iyer. Natesa Iyer had no sons but his adopted daughter, Padmasini Bai, learnt from him and became a well-known Harikatha or devotional singer. His house at Melatur is a place of pilgrimage and it has become customary to end every dance-drama by going to it in procession and singing the closing chorus there.

The leading figure today is Balasubramania Shastri. He is its organiser and source of inspiration. His group includes K. Subramania Iyer, P. K. Subbier, R. Nagarajan, N. Venkataraman and G. Swaminathan. Every year in May or June, during the Narasimha Jayanti festival, they present the dance-dramas to the public. A cycle of four is now performed annually, *Prahlada Charitram*, *Harishchandra*, *Markandaya*, and *Usha Parinayam*.

The roles in these dance-dramas are handed down from father to son and are cherished as family inheritances. To be worthy of this great tradition and because of the religious significance of the plays, the dancer-actors prepare themselves by penance, prayer and fasting. The spirit of love and dedication which infuses the players in the Passion plays of Oberammergau bears a striking resemblance to that of the Bhagvatas.

The technique, music, costume, make-up and stagecraft are, in the main, similar to those of Kuchipudi, although there are some significant differences. The main characters introduce themselves with the daru, and the adavus, jatis and varnams are rendered in the Kuchipudi manner. The satiric and comic interludes are in Tamil, the language of the area, whereas the dance-dramas themselves use Telugu. While in Kuchipudi, solo dances are given considerable freedom, an example being the Dasavatara, in Bhagvata Mela solo dances are only permitted if they form a part of the main action of the drama. In the past, lighting was provided by placing earthenware oil lamps, divas, on the trunks of banana trees. Today, electric lights are used. For the stage itself, drop scenes and curtains have recently been adopted. These are rather crude innovations and one wonders whether they add anything to the atmosphere of the art.

The chief play, *Prahlada Charitram*, is always the first to be performed, since it concerns Narasimha, the man-lion incarnation of Vishnu, to whom the temple is dedicated. The legend tells of the destruction brought on by hubris. The demon, Hiranyakasipu, wanted to be immortal. Therefore, in order that he might obtain this gift from Brahma, he undertook to repent of his sins by embarking on penances and fasts. Brahma, benignly and perhaps a trifle naïvely, granted the boon. Hiranyakasipu would henceforth be preserved from death by day and by night, indoors and in the open, in heaven and on earth; he could be killed by neither man nor beast. The demon was delighted, his self-importance knew no bounds. In his foolishness, he challenged the supremacy of Brahma himself. Hiranyakasipu now decided that in future all the people should worship, not Brahma, but himself. They were compelled to recite hymns in his honour and tell their beads to the accompaniment of his name. But there was one who refused to obey. It was Prahlada, his own son. The boy was a devotee of Vishnu and nothing could persuade him to transfer his allegiance. His father argued with him, threatened him and even tried to kill his own son, but the hand of Vishnu protected the boy and no harm came to him. One evening in the palace, Hiranyakasipu was raging at his son. Prahlada maintained that God was omnipotent and omnipresent.

Bhagvata Mela Nataka

His father, beside himself in his wrath, struck a mighty blow with his sword at a nearby pillar, hacking at it as he screamed, 'If he's everywhere, he must be in this too!' 'Yes, he is,' said Prahlada. At that moment, Narasimha, the man-lion Vishnu, sprang out of the pillar and, clawing Hiranyakasipu, dragged him to the doorstep. It was now the time between the end of day and the beginning of night, the precise time when the demon was not immune from death. He lay on the doorstep, neither indoors nor out. His body was neither on the earth nor in heaven. It was thus that Narasimha, who was neither man nor beast, destroyed the demon.

The mask of Narasimha, which lies encased within the sanctum of the Varadaraja Perumal temple, is of mysterious origin and said to be possessed of inexplicable powers. No one knows how it came to Melatur, or for what precise length of time it has been in the temple. When the *Prahlada Charitram* is staged, the mask is taken out and worn by the actor who plays Narasimha. Normally, no masks are worn for either Bhagvata Mela or Kuchipudi, and even in the special case of *Prahlada Charitram*, the man-lion dons it for only one scene in which he has a verbal duel with another character. At the climax of this scene the actor enters a trance-like state and becomes, as it were, Narasimha himself. This condition of complete identity is attributed to the sacred mask and the people of Melatur believe that once every year the god Narasimha manifests himself to them through the body of the Brahmin actor. Immediately the play is over the mask is returned to its place inside the temple.

The inducement of hypnotic states through dancing is by no means uncommon. It exists among the dervishes of the Arab countries, the tribes of Africa and those of African descent in the West Indies and America, to mention only a few. In the West it is clearly seen in the contemporary popular dances so widely prevalent among young people. Unfortunately, these dances and the rhythms which go with them, have been assimilated into the cultures of Europe and North America without regard for their original context and value, so that here they no longer have their intended therapeutic effect. Something of the same pattern has occurred in the opposite direction, especially in the field of music. The avidity with which certain Indian musicians took to the otherwise worthy European harmonium, has created untold havoc with a musical tradition which is, by its very nature, unsuited to such an instrument.

Dasi Attam

During the actual performance of Bhagvata Mela there are two departures from Kuchipudi. The jewelled statue of the Lord Narasimha is placed in the main entrance hall of the temple and the doors are left wide open so that he may see the dance-drama and hallow the proceedings with his presence. The second difference is the entrance of the elephant-headed god, Ganapati or Ganesh, the remover of obstacles. In Bhagvata Mela, an actor representing Ganapati appears after the exit of the musicians who perform the invocatory duties.

Although Bhagvata Mela may be performed only by men, it is becoming increasingly fashionable for some women dancers to present short excerpts from these dance-dramas to form the abhinaya items of their Dasi Attam performances. There is, of course, no harm whatsoever in this, so long as it does not misrepresent the original renderings of the dance-dramas.

Bhagvata Mela Nataka used to be performed in five other villages in the neighbourhood of Melatur. At Theperumanallur and Nallur the tradition died out about forty years ago, and a little later also at Oothkadu. The last dance-drama at the village of Soolamangalam was performed in 1950 through the efforts of E. Krishna Iyer and Rukmini Devi, but in spite of their attempts to resuscitate the art it has died out in this village too. The only village of the five where it is still performed is Saliyamangalam, but even here the performances are sporadic.

7

Kuravanji

The Kuravanji is a folk dance of South India based upon the free use of Dasi Attam techniques. The dancers are usually young women and belong to a hill tribe called the Kuravas. They are well known for their good looks and their cheeks are often tattooed with motifs made up of small dots. These marks may serve three quite different purposes. They may be used purely as beauty spots to enhance the looks of the girls. On the other hand, there is another theory about beauty. Extreme perfection, it is thought, is likely to invite admiration or even jealousy and hence, the evil eye. If, however, some tiny mark is added which mars absolute perfection the cause of the original jealousy is removed and the evil eye is averted. The 'evil eye' is a superstition taken very seriously in India. Whenever complimentary remarks are made, it is a matter of course to indicate that no envy is felt, by adding a short phrase such as 'By the grace of God' or 'May the evil eye be far from you'. There is also another custom, whereby the evil eye is averted from anyone who is likely to be admired, by making a small black mark with kohl behind one ear. A possible third reason for the tattoos on the faces of the Kurava women may be, that by this means they disfigure themselves permanently, and so are unlikely to tempt the gods to take them away from the earth while they are in the prime of their beauty and youth. The gods of India, like the gods of Greece were sometimes susceptible to the attractions of the daughters of men.

The Kuravas are a nomadic gypsy people. The men-folk are snake-charmers, acrobats and tumblers, the women usually fortune-tellers. Their living is necessarily precarious and they have acquired a reputation for petty thieving and pilfering. There are many wandering tribes in India, all of whom are beyond the pale of

Dasi Attam

society and the caste system. They represent the unassimilated elements of the original Dravidians who could not or would not be incorporated into aryanized society. It is possible also that among these tribes a certain number is made up of those who had been expelled from their own castes, and therefore had no place in a settled community. One of the ways in which this could happen was a transgression of the Laws of Manu concerning marriages and sexual misdemeanours. These were tolerated between men of one caste and women of a lower caste but not the other way round. If a woman had any relationship with a man of a lower caste than herself, or was even suspected of this, she, together with the children of such an alliance, was turned out of her home and village with great ignominy. She would then have no alternative but to either become a prostitute or join a group of wandering gypsies.

The very great similarity between Dasi Attam and Kuravanji makes the theory all the more plausible that it was such women who introduced this dance-form to the Kuravas. The Kuravas were, as we have seen, complete outcasts and excluded from all social and religious functions, and so would have no other means of seeing and imitating Dasi Attam. This seems the only possible explanation for the influence of a highly sophisticated dance like Dasi Attam on the primitive folk-art of a nomadic tribe. There is no doubt that Dasi Attam does contain some elements of the pre-Aryan dances, but these do not now stand out as distinct from the whole, and would not account for the resemblance between the two dances.

The Kuravas then, are an example of those non-caste tribes which were forced into coherent units through the will to survive and out of sheer economic necessity. These tribes were ostracized by Hindu society and later the British government exacerbated the situation by classifying them, and stigmatizing them, as 'criminal tribes', the members of which could not enter the municipal limits of cities or towns, and were not allowed to own property or enter government service in any capacity no matter how humble. The only friends these tribes had were the missionaries who did what they could for them by way of medical care and education.

It was only after the Independence of India that these 'criminal tribes' were given constitutional and legal rights. The state and welfare organizations took an interest in the social uplift of these people and it was discovered that they had rich and fascinating folk-lores.

The legends of the Kuravas always revolve around fortune-telling

Kuravanji

and romantic episodes. There is a well-known story among them about Subramanya, the son of Shiva, who fell in love with Valli. This beautiful dancer was the daughter of a hunter. All Subramanya's eloquence and powers of persuasion could not win the heart of this maid of the forests. The rejected lover finally appealed to the wise elephant-headed Ganesh and they decided upon a plan. Ganesh transformed himself into a fully grown elephant. The two then concealed themselves in strategic positions near the path which the girl was in the habit of using. As she approached, Ganesh suddenly appeared. Valli was frightened and started to run but the rogue elephant followed fast. Subramanya, of course, 'rescued' the distraught maiden from the terrifying elephant. After this she could hardly spurn his appeals and she succumbed to his charms.

There are many other stories which tell mostly of a forest girl's love for a prince or a temple deity and how this true love was returned.

The Kurava women dance these themes in the form of a folk-ballet. Six to eight dancers take part in a Kuravanji performance. The Dasi Attam movements become fluid and lively and sometimes passionate in intensity. There is no time limit, the duration of the ballet depending upon the inspiration of the dancers and their audience.

Like Dasi Attam, this dance was often Shaivite in inspiration. One of the earliest known Kuravanjis is the *Thirukutrala Kuravanji*, composed in honour of Shiva as Thirukudanthar. The other well-known ones are the *Chitrambala* and the *Kumbesara*. All of these are performed during Shaivite festivals. There is, however, one Kuravanji, the *Azhagar*, which is danced for the god Vishnu.

Mr M. D. Raghavan, the Madras University anthropologist, states that in recent years the Kuravanji dancers have usually been men made up as women, symbolizing the consorts of Shiva and Vishnu. They dance and sing, each group trying to outdo the other in proclaiming the superior qualities of its own god. This seems to imply that it is only recently that the Kuravas have felt the full impact of Vaishnavism and that the rivalry between this and Shaivism still occupies an important part of their consciousness.

Shanta Rao has often incorporated Kuravanji dances into her programmes with considerable success. In her ballets for the Kalak-shetra troupe, Rukmini Devi also has used Kuravanji, especially the *Thirukutrala*. One hopes that other choreographers will follow this lead and make use of this interesting dance-form.

PART TWO

Kathakali

8

History of Kathakali

Kathakali has a comparatively short history, but as such a complex art cannot, it is obvious, come into being suddenly and out of nothing, it is worth while to examine the conditions which made it possible. The home of Kathakali is Kerala, the second smallest state of the Indian Union. It lies in the extreme south of the peninsula, and occupies a narrow strip of land facing the Arabian Sea stretching right down to Kanya Kumari (Cape Comorin) at the southernmost tip of India. The state is composed of the two erstwhile princely States of Travancore and Cochin. Its smooth white beaches with coconut palms, its quiet backwaters and picturesque paddy fields create an atmosphere of calm beauty.

This is where traders from other countries first came, for the Malabar coast has the longest history in India of contact with other lands. Phoenicians, Greeks, Romans, Arabs and Chinese all came here for spices, hardwood, gold, peacocks, apes and ivory. Jews took refuge here after the second sack of Jerusalem and St Thomas the Apostle brought Christianity. Many settled here and most left some mark of their visit. The large square fishing nets of Cochin and the temple architecture are both the legacy of the Chinese. The Arabs brought slaves and the influence of Islam and seem to have settled quite happily. There is a powerful and wealthy community of Christians here, who take great pride in the ancient origin of their Church and regard the Protestant and even Roman Catholic Churches as more recent offshoots.

Nevertheless, for all this history, geographically this is a comparatively new land, and shouldered its way out of the sea by underwater volcanic action some time before the Aryan incursions into India. This scientific fact has been absorbed into the mythology of the country, with that remarkable aptitude for an explanation of

Kathakali

events, in which the Aryans excelled, especially when such an explanation could be turned to their own advantage. It is said that the Brahmin warrior Bhargava, who was an avatar of Vishnu, had in error committed the terrible sin of matricide. To atone for this hideous offence he undertook many austerities and penances. When he felt sufficiently cleansed from his sin, he flung his axe far out into the sea in an act symbolically renouncing violence. The gods were pleased and the waters receded to the point where the axe had fallen and so this new land was born of the primaeval depths of the ocean. In those days, as often today, it was thought proper to make offerings and gifts to holy and learned sages in order to rid oneself of the stain of sin. Such practices have been encouraged by all religions from time immemorial. Accordingly, Bhargava granted this new kingdom to the Brahmins in a final act of expiation. This legend was doubtless propagated by the Nambudri Brahmins as a justification for their riches and vast land holdings.

How the Nambudri Brahmins actually came to Kerala is not known with any certainty, but what is known is that they came very late in the history of Kerala. One theory is that they were Aryans who had filtered into South India many centuries after their settlement of Northern India, probably about the third century B.C., and after subjugating the local tribes had established their supremacy in matters of both State and religion. The other, and more plausible theory is, that although some may well have come this way, the majority of Nambudri Brahmins came very much later than this; not in fact, until the latter part of the Middle Ages, when Muslim power in the North extended up to the borders of Assam. To escape conversion or subjection, some high-caste Brahmins of Bengal, like the Pilgrim Fathers, set sail from Bengal. Hugging the coastline, they sailed past Ceylon and right round the peninsula, choosing for their settlement, the hospitable shores of Kerala. With them they brought Sanskrit and a rich heritage of learning, their wealth, and that most important of their assets, a power over men's minds. This theory gains added weight from the observations of anthropologists, who have noticed similarities between the cultures of Brahmin Kerala and Brahmin Bengal.

Every legend has its symbolism and inner meaning. An example is the story of Parasurama and the snakes. The name means Rama-of-the-Axe and is another appellation of Bhargava. After he had given Kerala to the Brahmins, they found it difficult to settle there

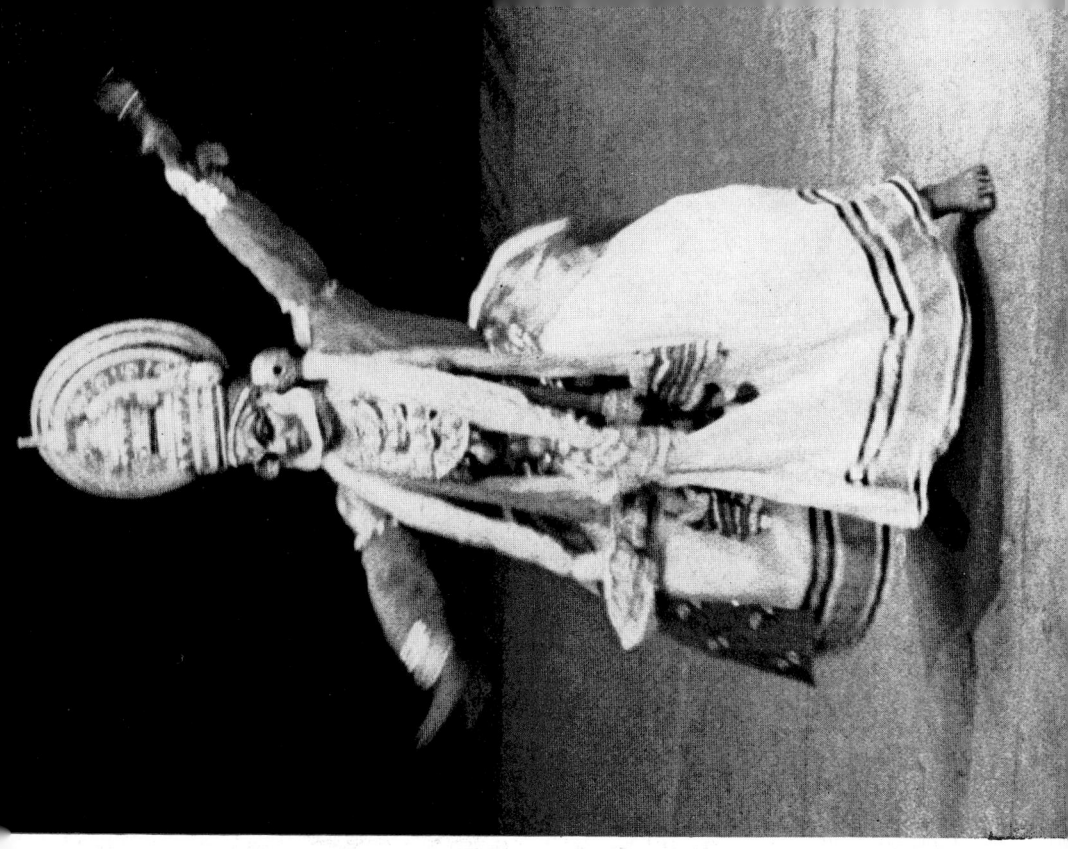

A paccha character
India House, London

Nritta movement
Marc Alexander

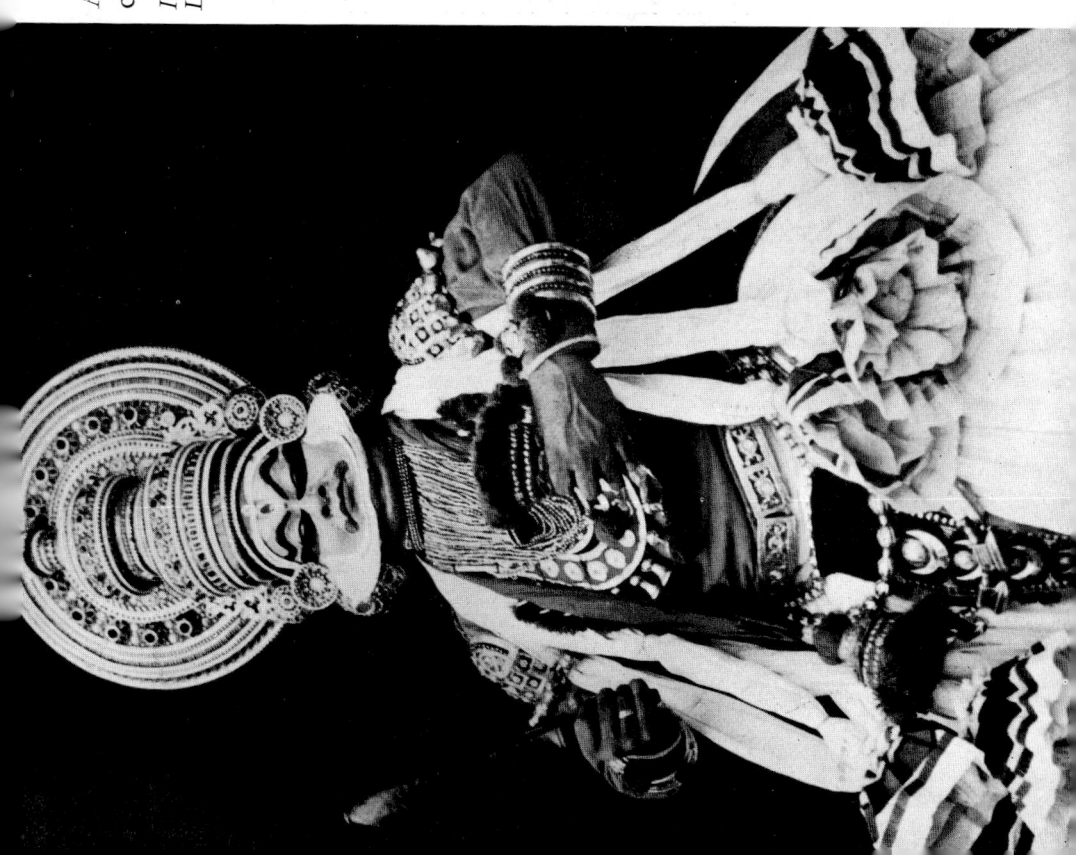

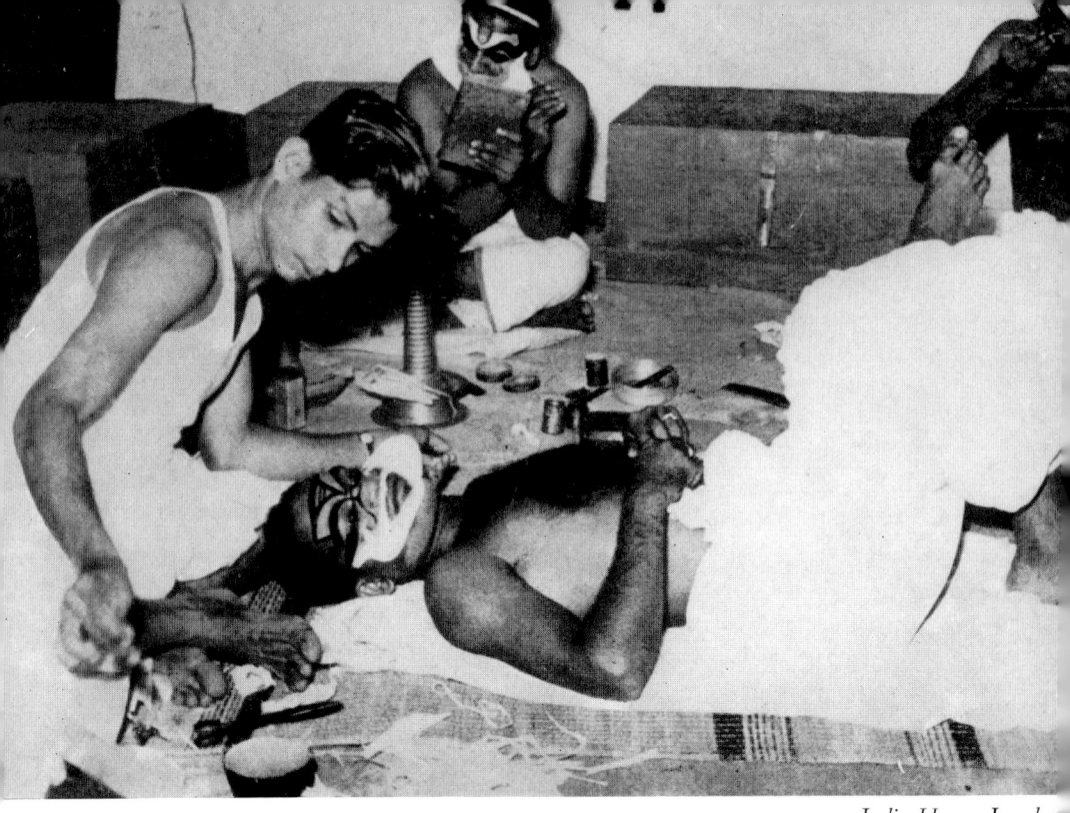

India House, London

Preparation for a performance

A Kathakali performance in its traditional setting

India House, London

History of Kathakali

and abandoned the country. Some time later they came back, determined to colonize it, but found that the snake people, the Nagaloka, had taken possession of it. There was, naturally, a battle between the two, for the Brahmins regarded the land as theirs by right and the Nagaloka as usurpers. The Nagaloka were eventually defeated, but Parasurama, in a rare peace overture, stipulated that although the land was to be parcelled among the Brahmins, they were, nevertheless, to accommodate the Nagaloka by setting apart a small portion of their land for the use of the conquered people. This portion of land, moreover, was on no account to be touched or tamed in any way. Now, this legend clearly indicates how the light-skinned Aryan Brahmins came to be the chief landowners in Kerala, but not being able to exterminate the Dravidians, took them on as junior partners or relegated them to the forests.

The indigenous Dravidians were worshippers of Bhagvati, the Earth-Mother goddess, and it was only natural that they should venerate the snakes who lived in the earth. The legend clearly identifies the dark-skinned Dravidians with the black cobras so common in Kerala. Later, after the Nambudris' supremacy had been established, the custom of each household actually setting apart a small grove in the compound for the habitation of snakes, became universal. These snake groves are common even today and women and children set milk offerings in them for the nagas (snakes) who, far from harming anyone, are said to protect the household.

This veneration of snakes resulted in one of the oldest dance-forms of Kerala — the ceremony of Pampin Tullal, or the dance of the snakes. This is a ceremony performed by members of the Pulluvan caste, in order to propitiate the household snakes. An important centre for the worship of snakes is at Mannarsala, where special snake-dance festivals are held. These dances are of Dravidian origin, as were others such as the ritualistic dances connected with the ceremonies of Bhagvati and the various devil dances. All these were early influences which helped towards creating the climate for the composite art of Kathakali. Many of them involved the use of fantastic costumes, masks or make-up which, although they do not bear a direct resemblance to those of Kathakali, can at least, be regarded as having created the conventions which allowed the representation of super-human beings to be associated with an extravagant appearance.

Kathakali is in fact, the result of a marriage between the pre-Aryan

Dravidian dances and the later ones which were introduced by the Brahmins. It combines the consciousness, the religious practices and the techniques of these two cultural streams in perfect harmony and balance. The Dravidians were a gentle, peaceful people, worshippers of nature and devoted to Bhagvati, the benevolent Mother Goddess of the earth, who provided them with all their needs, spiritual and material. She brought forth the fruits on the trees and the grain in the fields, and protected them from evil demons. It was because of their unwarlike disposition that the Dravidians were swamped by the aggressive Aryan invaders, and driven into the forests and mountains. Some survive still as aboriginal tribes, mainly in the states of Orissa and Bihar. These children of the forest are known as Adivasis or aboriginals, and their way of life, as described by anthropologists such as Verrier Elwin, gives us some clue as to the nature and character of the original inhabitants of India. Dance for them, was truly a part of their life. Their deities were extremely important to them, and through dance they did honour to these deities, propitiated them and celebrated their triumphs. One of these dances, the Bhagvati Pattu, is in honour of the triumph of Bhagvati over Daruka, the king of the demons. It still just about survives, as do Tiya-attam, Mutti-yettu and Tiray-attam. All these dances were accompanied by the *chenda*, a cylindrical drum which is held upright and struck with two slender sticks. This instrument is now an important part of the orchestra which accompanies Kathakali.

The coming of the Brahmins resulted in the inevitable changes which always occur with the influx of alien elements. When two or more peoples live on the same soil, there must needs be a considerable amount of give and take, and social and religious synthesis. The warrior caste, the Nayars, who are the equivalent of the Kshatriyas in other parts of India now came into being. Racially they were half Aryan and half Dravidian, so it was natural that in them should repose the music, the dance and the religious mores of both races. They combined with the culture of the Dravidians, the sophistication of the Aryans, whose approach to everything was analytical and academic and who defined their laws, artistic, social or religious, by meticulous attention to every possible detail. The Brahmins, moreover, encouraged the Nayar caste who protected, by force if necessary, Brahminical rights and privileges. Nowhere else were the Brahmins so much in rapport with the warrior castes.

History of Kathakali

In fact, nowhere else in India is there a caste system quite like that of Kerala. Inter-marriage was permissible with the Nayars, although not for the eldest son. He alone was obliged to marry a Brahmin girl. The others, if they chose, might marry either within the caste or be found a wife among the Nayars.

In time the benevolent goddess Bhagvati, became identified with the mother goddess of the Aryans, who was the terrifying and bloodthirsty Kali. The Nayars adopted Kali as their patron goddess and an image of her is still to be found in every Kalari.

The Nayars were a highly organized military caste and, justifiably, very proud of their prowess in wielding weapons of war. This skill was scientifically taught and careful attention was paid to developing those qualities which would produce the desired results. They began their training while they were still small boys. They were given special massages and exercises which developed their suppleness, agility and strength. Training took place in sunken gymnasia known as Kalaris, beginning at about three o'clock in the morning and ending late at night, with breaks in between. During their long and hard apprenticeship they learnt not only the skills of the art of war, but also how to gain a psychological advantage over their opponents — what we would nowadays call psychological warfare. This was achieved through training in mime, gesture and acting. A Nayar's very deportment and mien were calculated to portray his own superiority and confidence and to arouse fear and uncertainty in his opponent. His miming skill was said to be so great that he could pretend to throw a lance or spear and do it so convincingly that the enemy would actually feel the pain of his body being pierced. A part of the training was given in the form of martial dances and combat exercises. Some of these dances still survive, especially the dagger dance and a dance with a long incredibly flexible, snake-like sword. The sword dance is particularly spectacular and dangerous-looking, since once the sword begins to twist and hiss through the air with lightning speed, the smallest error in judgement or split-second delay in reaction, would almost certainly prove fatal not only to anyone within range but to the man wielding it as well.

Hand to hand combat was highly stylized in ancient times. The rules were strict and respected by both parties and, as with most forms of physical combat, this codification led to aesthetic qualities appearing in the form of the contest. Gradually, as these qualities were realized, it became a pleasure simply to watch the procedure and appreciate the finer points of the skill of the combatants. This happened in Europe, for example, with fencing and the Graeco-Roman style of wrestling, and in Japan with the war dances of the Samurai. All of these evolved into entertainments from being, initially, serious arts of war. Indeed so great was their aesthetic appeal, that even now, when they are otherwise redundant, they survive solely because of their inherent beauty and skill.

Gradually the need for the Nayars to fight diminished, but they preserved their knowledge, kept themselves in practice through dancing and made Kathakali their own preserve. To this they brought all their traditional skill and training techniques. Even today the exponents of Kathakali are mostly Nayars. They retain the name Kalari for their practice place together with most of the exercises and methods of massage they used as warriors. The basic stance of a Kathakali dancer is a logical extension of the natural position adopted for any form of hand to hand combat. The flexed knees help to absorb the shock of landing and the wider apart they are held, the greater the freedom of movement in any direction. The one curious thing is that the weight of the body is taken by the outer edges of the feet. There are said to be two reasons for this, namely, to reduce further the shock to the spinal column and to make dancing for long periods less tiring to the feet.

The Aryan influences on Kathakali come from the vast store of art forms codified and embodied in the Sanskrit shastras of the Brahmins. One way they could propagate and keep alive the wisdom of the gods was in the form of stories and legends. These sacred texts were recited in the temples, which were forbidden to the lower castes. This form of recitation was known as Chakkiyar-kuttu, because the reciter belonged to the Chakkiyar caste. The Chakkiyars claim descent from the Sutas of the *Mahabharata*. This may or may not be true, but they certainly have existed for a very long time, for they are mentioned in the second-century Tamil epic, *Silappadikaram* or the Epic of the Anklet. A platform known as the Kuthambalam existed in most temples for their use. The Chakkiyar would sit or stand on this platform with his accompanists. First he would offer prayers to the temple deity and after this recite a selected Sanskrit verse. He would then go on to expound his text. The language of the exposition was always the vernacular of Kerala, Malayalam, albeit a Sanskritized form of Malayalam. An obvious comparison of his function is with that of a preacher giving a sermon from the pulpit, particularly if that preacher is of the old fire and brimstone type. The Chakkiyar too, brought in topical analogies and situations to illustrate his text and was not above censuring particular members of his 'congregation'. However, unlike the solemn preachers of the past, he held his listeners' attention by trying to make his discourse as amusing and entertaining as possible. This he accomplished through witticisms and frequent use of mime and gesture to bring his story to life. This abhinaya or expressionistic aspect was later absorbed and considerably emphasized by Kathakali.

The Chakkiyar was accompanied on a large copper drum called a *mizhavu*, by a drummer who was always of the Nambiar caste, and also by a woman who played a pair of small brass cymbals. She was of the same caste but was known as a Nangiar. She beat out the time solemnly, for she was expected to remain serious and straight-faced, no matter how amusing the performance of the Chakkiyar. This solo performance had two other names, Prabhand-kuttu and sometimes Kathaprasangam Manthrakam.

At one time the Nangiar herself stopped being a mere accompanist and took over the Chakkiyar's role. This Nangiar-kuttu became quite popular, but for some reason has now died out.

Later on, three or four Chakkiyars performed together and this new form became known as Kudiyattam, which was really the forerunner of the dance-drama which later developed in Kerala, for they had already begun to incorporate excerpts from the plays of Kalidasa, Bhasa and Harsha.

The performers in Kudiyattam, unlike those in Kathakali, were both men and women, which clearly indicates that there must have been a greater element of lasya here than in Kathakali. The plays were long and performed at night. Particular role-types had different costumes and special make-up colours. All these conventions were later to be absorbed into the Kathakali tradition.

Faithful patrons of Kudiyattam were the kings of the Perumal dynasty, especially Kulasekhara who died in 430 A.D., Bhaskara Ravi Varma and Cheraman.

A third type of dance, the Pathakam, was very similar in form. This gave much greater importance to Malayalam, although the subject matter of the plays came from the same Sanskrit sources.

Vaishnavism had in the twelfth century, given birth to Jayadeva's

Kathakali

Gita Govinda, which had come to be recited and danced in most parts of India.

Some time around 1650 or perhaps a little later, the Zamorin of Calicut introduced to Kerala a dance-drama modelled on Jayadeva's work. Like so many important happenings in India, there is a story attached to this event as well. It is said, that the Lord Krishna himself once honoured the Zamorin by appearing before him and giving him a peacock feather. These divine visitations or darshans were accorded to the selected few, and in commemoration of his vision the Zamorin wrote a drama. This play, written in Sanskrit, was performed in a technique already known and used in the plays of that time. The name given to the work was *Krishnapadi*, and when it was staged with actors, music and dance it was called Krishna Attam. To this day the performers of Krishna Attam wear a symbol of the Lord Krishna in the form of a peacock feather. It was a long play and lasted for eight nights. During these nights the life of the Lord Krishna was unfolded in detail — his childish games and encounters with the demons, his escapades with the maidens of Mathura, his going out into the world to fulfil his mission, his darshan to Arjun as his charioteer, and the famous discourse in the form of the Song Divine, the *Bhagavad Gita*, and finally his return to heaven when his task on earth had been accomplished.

With the passage of time Krishna Attam became a religious tradition. Performances acquired a sanctity, and the people who attended them believed that they earned special blessings by doing so. Krishna Attam is still performed at the temple of Guruvayur during the festival of Krishna Jayanti, which celebrates the birth of the god. The technique and manner of presentation have undergone no change over the years. The make-up, costumes and jewellery are very similar to those of Kathakali. However, in Krishna Attam, Brahma, some monkey characters and demons wear painted wooden marks. This is obviously a legacy of the exorcistic rituals of the devil dances and the rites of the Kali cults. Although abhinaya plays an important part, it is not as exhaustive as that of Kathakali and nritta or pure dance is given more emphasis. On the other hand, there are some beautiful movements in Krishna Attam, which no longer survive in Kathakali. The musical instruments of the two dances are the same, except that Krishna Attam does not use the chenda. The convention of using singers to deal exclusively

History of Kathakali

with the text is a significant innovation which Kathakali took from Krishna Attam. This left the dancers free to apply all their energy and concentration to the interpretative dancing for which Kathakali is famous.

With the popularity of the dance-drama as an art form, rivalry developed amongst the rulers of Kerala as to who could maintain the finest troupe. Now, as the fame of the Zamorin's Krishna Attam had spread far and wide, the ruler of Kottarakkara became curious and asked his neighbour to lend him his troupe. But the Zamorin was proud and jealous of the high standard of his dancers. He refused. Not only did he refuse, but added insult to injury by sending a message to the effect that there was no point in sending a troupe to a court where none was learned enough to appreciate the subtleties of Krishna Attam. Naturally, the Raja was mortally offended at such condescension. He determined to prove that he could vie with the best so far as cultural matters were concerned. To this end he wrote a play on the life of Rama.

For the performance he enlisted the help of another ruler, the Raja of Kottayam who was a brilliant actor-dancer. He also got the help of two Nambudri Brahmins. They were of immense help to him because it was the sympathetic attitude of the Brahmins which had resulted in the emergence of drama in the first place. These two priests, learned in the scriptures, were therefore also well versed in the exposition of the sacred texts through dance.

By the end of the seventeenth century, Raman Attam had come into well-defined existence. It used many of the techniques of Krishna Attam, but also introduced some changes.

Raman Attam too was performed over eight nights. The custom of using singers was retained as it now became more than ever impossible for the dancers to do their own singing. This was because the chenda was added to give more volume, vigour and excitement to the drama, which meant that the dancers had to save all their breath and energy for the increased tempo and agility of the dance movements.

Another addition to the Krishna Attam practice was that the text was interpreted much more fully. To do this the abhinaya was extended, particularly that of the face, *mukhabhinaya*, and that of the hands *hasta-abhinaya*. In order to give full expression to mukhabhinaya, masks were done away with altogether and replaced by more elaborate and varied make-up. New costumes were designed for different role-types, traditionally by the Raja of Kottayam who it is said, saw them in a dream. However, he gave the same voluminous skirts to all the chief protagonists, because his dream, sadly for Kathakali, revealed only the top half of the characters. But the greatest innovation of all was in the language of the play. The Raja of Kottarakkara took the daring but astute step of writing his play in Malayalam. Hitherto the language of culture had been Sanskrit and no literature of classical stature had been produced in the vernacular. The Raja thus no doubt laid himself open to further taunts of lack of refinement from his rival at Calicut. Nevertheless, Chaucer-like, his confidence gave a new status to the common tongue. Because the drama could be understood by everyone, there now existed no reason why it should not be performed outside the confines of the temple. The lower castes, being prohibited from entering the temples, had not been able to hear the Chakkiyars or see Krishna Attam. Now they could wonder at the exploits of Rama, see the episodes of his life from his romantic marriage to his exile. They could see the abduction of his lovely wife, Sita, by Ravana the King of Lanka, and Rama's search for her. Finally they could share his triumph over the demon king, and the joy of his reunion with Sita.

Raman Attam gained tremendous popularity and very soon all the episodes of the Ramayana had been dramatized. Plays were written with themes from other sacred works such as the *Mahabharata*, the *Shiva Purana* and the *Bhagavad Purana*. The name Raman Attam now became unsuitable because of this widening thematic range and so the name Kathakali or story-play was substituted in its place.

However, some scholars tend towards the conclusion that this sequence of events is merely legendary, and that in actual fact Krishna Attam did not come into existence first. One estimate of its date places Raman Attam in the fourteenth century. Krishna Attam, according to this theory, originated almost three hundred years later, that is, in the seventeenth century. But the date of Krishna Attam itself is in dispute, although the earliest date given to it is still later than that given to Raman Attam. Some have suggested that the mid-fifteenth century is a more likely date for the *Krishnapadi*, even though the work itself indicates that it was written about 1650.

Nevertheless, the dates of these two dance-dramas do not make

History of Kathakali

any difference to their contribution to Kathakali. Kathakali, as we know it today, is a comparatively recent dance form when considered in the context of the history of dance in India, although its roots reach right back into pre-Aryan times. Its merits are not increased in any way by the attempts of its misguided admirers to give it a greater age than that which it has.

The development and encouragement, if not the survival of art, has always owed much to the aristocracy and the wealthy. Only those who had the means could satisfy their aesthetic drives. Kathakali was no exception. Although it became popular with rich and poor alike, it was the rulers of Kerala who nurtured it with their scholarship, their talent and their wealth. Not only did they support permanent troupes, but many of them took an active part in the performance and even wrote new plays.

The first of these was the Raja of Kottayam whose four plays were all based on the *Mahabharata*. Later, the Maharajas of Travancore played a similar notable part in the history of Kathakali. Karthika Tirunal who was Maharaja at the end of the eighteenth century wrote no less than seven plays; but his interest extended even further and he wrote a treatise on dance called *Balarama Bharatam* under his own name, Balarama Varma. This book remains a classic among its kind. His younger brother who followed him to the throne, although he wrote only one play, encouraged the art greatly. Prince Asvathi, the grand-nephew of Karthika Tirunal, was a famous composer and wrote four plays. Music was the chief passion of another Maharaja, Swathi Rama Varma, who surrounded himself with musicians from many parts of the country and himself composed 75 padams for Kathakali.

Apart from these royal patrons, there is another name which deserves mention. It is that of the poet Irayimman Thampi (1783–1863), who wrote three new plays. He had a daughter Thankachi, who continued the poet's tradition and wrote another three plays.

The eighteenth and nineteenth centuries saw great development and activity in Kathakali. During this time the dance-drama was at the height of its achievement and collected an immense repertoire of plays.

By the mid-nineteenth century, British power, which had been increasing over the years, had become firmly established. In 1857, Victoria was proclaimed Empress of India, and European influences and ideas spread rapidly. The Victorian age was a time of supreme self-confidence for the British nation. The empire builders and the colonial administrators who followed them felt perfectly justified in adopting a policy of aloofness from the peoples they governed. There were some British scholars who took an interest in the culture of the country, but the administration was, for the most part, indifferent.

Naturally enough, those Indians who were educated in the atmosphere of British supremacy came to accept the values which their mentors instilled in them. Yet there were some who still cared about their own heritage. Kathakali might well have faded into oblivion had it not been for the efforts of one such man, the Malayalam poet Vallathol Narayana Menon.

Vallathol's love for Kathakali began at an early age, when his father used to take him to see the dance-dramas. When he grew up, he realized that it would not be long before the art died out. He felt that it was his destiny to preserve Kathakali from the decline that had set in. There still lived many good gurus and musicians, but these had few pupils, as young men found more lucrative occupations elsewhere. Vallathol's plan was to bring these teachers and musicians together in one place and systematically engineer a revival by rousing the conscience of the Malayali people. He experienced great difficulty in raising funds and had to resort to the expedience of a lottery. This was highly successful and he collected seventy-five thousand rupees. With this he was able to establish, in 1930, the centre upon which he had set his heart. To his Kerala Kala Mandalam (The Kerala Institute of Arts) near Shoranur, he brought the greatest masters of Kathakali, Mohini Attam and Ottan Tullal — men like the late Ravunni Menon, Kavalapra Narayana Menon and Kunju Kurup. The Institute attracted the attention of the public and the Government; students were given grants to attend and the great revival of Kathakali was well under way. He took his troupes on tour in India and abroad and with the profits from these tours, the Kerala Kala Mandalam was able to have its own buildings at Cheruthuruthi near Shoranur. These highly successful tours, in addition to providing much needed finances, had created a demand for Kathakali. To the Institute came students from various parts of India. It produced artistes who are today leading Kathakali dancers.

By 1941, the Kerala Kala Mandalam had proved its worth enough for the government to be concerned about its survival and well-being. It was taken over by the state and Vallathol appointed its director.

The Kerala Kala Mandalam now gets a grant from the Sangeet Natak Akademi, India's national academy of music and drama, and the Institute is among the most important in the country. However, the International Centre for Kathakali established recently in Delhi is now also doing excellent work.

Gopinath and his partner Ragini Devi are two names which cannot be omitted from a history of Kathakali. They pruned the length of performance, simplified its techniques and adapted it to modern stage conditions. Uday Shankar made use of Kathakali's vocabulary of mime in the creation of his ballets as did Rukmini Devi and Mrinalini Sarabhai, and Ram Gopal adapted and presented Kathakali in most Western countries. Krishnan Kutty, Madhavan and Ananda Shivaraman are superb dancers who have each contributed to the renaissance of the art. Shanta Rao is an outstanding dancer of Kathakali and has proved that the more intricate and difficult tandav aspect of the dance is not necessarily beyond the capabilities of a woman dancer.

Now that Kathakali has been firmly re-established, it will be interesting to see how choreographers like Rukmini Devi and Mrinalini Sarabhai will face the challenge of presenting Kathakali successfully in the contemporary theatre.

9
Features of Kathakali Technique and Training

In Kathakali the dancer-actor employs the vivid language of gesture and mime, not only to translate the words of the play as they are sung by the musicians standing behind him, but also to create the atmosphere and setting for each scene in the play. Thus by a mere glance and a gesture the dancer transports his audience to a romantic garden where lovers linger by the lotus pool and later into a fearful and bloody battle where the villain is inexorably slain. To the Kathakali dancer this is not difficult, for he has emerged from the Kalari with complete control over his body and all the skills of a consummate actor.

In general the dancer's exercises are divided into four groups, the *mai sadhakam* or body exercises, the *kal sadhakam* or footwork, the *mudra sadhakam* which is a study of gestures and the *mukhabhinaya sadhakam*, the exercises for facial expression.

The mai sadhakam are very rigorous exercises, designed to give flexibility and suppleness to the various parts of the body. It is due to these exercises that Kathakali dancers are able to retain their agility and grace even at the age of sixty-five or more.

Footwork, kal sadhakam, incorporates a detailed study of the intricate rhythms and their variations. The first two groups of exercises form the basis for the nritta element of the dance. Although Kathakali is basically a dance-drama, its action is interspersed with short pieces of pure dance known as *kalasams*. These kalasams punctuate the *khandas* or four-line stanzas which make up the text of the play. Khandas are, of course, interpreted through nritya.

There are five varieties of kalasams, namely, the Ashta kalasam,

Features of Kathakali Technique and Training

the Valia kalasam, the Eduthu kalasam, the Eratti kalasam and the Eda kalasam.

The first two of these, that is the Ashta or 'eight' kalasam and the Valia or 'big' kalasam are the true test of the merit of a Kathakali dancer. The Ashta kalasam, as the name implies, consists of eight separate pieces which are danced one after another to different tals. The Valia kalasam, on the other hand, is performed in the champa tal of ten beats in combination with other tals.

Although Kathakali, with its strong and vigorous movements, is essentially a dance for men, most exercises for the body and especially those for footwork, have lasya counterparts. This is because the dance-dramas also have female characters and since these are played by men, they must learn feminine movements. The lasya dance-syllables for the footwork are distinctly softer and less complex than their tandav counterparts. An example of an exercise in champa tal makes this clear;

Tandav boles	Lasya boles
Tha thintha kitha dhi dhikitathai	Dhikita thaiyam
Dhikita dhikita dhikitathai	Dhikita thaiyam

The tandav and lasya distinctions are also quite clearly seen in the body movements. The tandav movements are angular and imperious and are given an added majesty by the magnificent costumes of the men. The lasya movements, in comparison with these, appear restrained and delicate. They are, naturally, used in portraying female roles but in addition to these, they are employed in the love scenes, where the poetic and romantic text is best conveyed through gentle and lyrical movements.

Mudras are symbolic hand gestures which form the language of Kathakali. While many of the gestures used in dance are stylized versions of those used in everyday life, others are more technical. Together they enrich the vocabulary of the dancer.

According to the *Hasta Lakshana Deepika*, a text on Kathakali mudras, there are twenty-four basic hand gestures. Each of these has a number of different uses, since the significance of a mudra changes according to the position of the hand and whether it is being used as a single-hand or *asamyuta* gesture, or as a *samyuta*, combined-hand, gesture. Thus, the *pataka* mudra in which the hand is held open except for the ring finger, which is bent, has over forty

Kathakali

uses. As a single-hand gesture it may denote 'day', 'tongue', 'mirror', 'forehead', 'voice', 'body', 'messenger', 'sands on the beach', 'young leaves' or 'going', while in a combined-hand gesture it may be used to depict 'sun', 'king', 'elephant', 'crocodile', 'oxen', 'archway', 'creeper', 'flag', 'waves', 'chariot', 'cart', 'the hips', 'the thighs', 'a hunchback', 'servant', 'moon', 'sunset', 'mansion', 'moat', 'pillow', 'seat', 'anthill', 'cloud', 'Peace', 'discus of Vishnu', 'Hell', 'Earth', 'lightning', 'cold', 'vessel', 'enough', and 'walking'.

In mixed or *misra* mudras, each hand is in a different mudra but together they denote a single idea. Thus 'violence' or 'oppression' is shown by the left hand held near the left breast in the *musti* mudra (with the hand closed and the thumb resting on the first finger) facing downwards and the right placed across the left in the pataka mudra. The right hand is then moved and brought under the left.

Misra mudras are best used to denote deities like Shiva, Brahma, and Rama and also other characters such as Ravana and Garuda. Rama is shown by the left hand in musti placed opposite the left breast and the right hand in *kataka*, in which the thumb and first finger are joined and the middle finger is bent so as to touch the base of the thumb.

For proper nouns which have no special mudras the dancer uses the *nama* mudra. For this the *kartarimukha* mudra (little finger straight and the others bent) is held near the mouth and then moved away.

Hand gestures by themselves, however, are not sufficient to convey the true meaning of the text and must be complemented by appropriate facial expressions. So the Kathakali dancer devotes considerable time to mukhabhinaya sadhakam. The chief constituent of this is *nayanabhinaya*, from 'nayan' meaning eyes, and the technique involves the expression of emotion through the eyes. In Kathakali, in spite of the fact that the dancers devote hours to the exercises for the chin, the lips, the cheeks and the nose, the eyes still remain the primary means of expression. Eyes are the mirrors of the soul, hence any emotion truly felt must be reflected through them. This is the governing principle of Kathakali. A great artiste is one who can convey whole sections of the text through nayanabhinaya alone. Indeed, very often, a dancer may portray the theme of a stanza through his eyes, before he expresses it in dance. This is known as *nokki-kanuka*. (An interesting comparison can be drawn between this and the *bhava dikhana* of Kathak.)

Features of Kathakali Technique and Training

There is a story about the effectiveness of nayanabhinaya. Kunju Pillai, the Kathakali dancer, was playing Ravana in *Ravana Vijayam*. The celestial maiden, Rambha, was on this rare occasion being played by a woman. The episode told how Ravana ravished the girl after she had repeatedly rejected his advances. That, at least, was the way in which it should have been played. Rambha resisted all Ravana's appeals and all went well until finally, Kunju Pillai put all his emotions into his eyes. The dancer playing Rambha could resist no longer. Forgetting the spectators, forgetting herself, she saw only the compulsive desire in the actor's eyes and succumbed. Then realizing too late what she had done, she fled from the stage embarrassed and confused.

There are eight 'glances' which form the basis of mukhabhinaya in Kathakali. They are, *sama* — the natural glance, *meelita* — the half-opened eyes, *alokita* — fully-opened eyes, *sanchi* — eyes looking sideways from the centre, *pralokita* — looking both sides, *ullokita* — looking up, *anuvritta* — looking up and down quickly, and *avalokita* — looking downwards.

Each of these 'glances' has a number of uses. For instance, sama is used for depicting gods or at the beginning of a dance, meelita can show a snake, or a captive, or meditation, and alokita is used when showing the moving wheels of a chariot or when looking at a circular object.

The 'glances' are perfected by means of nine movements of the eyeballs and the eyelids. The eyebrows also are brought into play with seven types of movements. Once a dancer has mastered these exercises he is well equipped to interpret almost any line in the text and give it its true flavour.

In keeping with the laws of Sanskrit drama, Kathakali plays offer full scope for ras abhinaya, the expression of sentiments. Each of the nine rasas is developed and evoked with great care and the true artiste is one who, besides acting and miming his lines, can convey the ras to his audience as an emotional experience.

The training of a Kathakali dancer is certainly the most arduous, if not the longest, of any dancer. He must begin while his limbs are still supple enough to become accustomed to the unnatural postures they must adopt automatically and with comfort. So a boy begins to train usually before he is ten or eleven and continues for at least eight or nine years and even up to twelve years.

An indispensable part of the training is the massage, which is painful and unpleasant. Every muscle, nerve and joint is massaged and the student is made conscious of all these, so that he can learn to use each independently. Even his lungs do not escape. There are also special exercises for hands, face and eyes.

The massage of the body as a whole is done not only by the hands, but by the feet as well. There are, naturally, several types of massage devised in order to develop the different kinds of facility required. The younger boys are massaged by the older students under the guidance of the teachers. First the entire body is given an 'oil-bath', that is, oil is rubbed into it. The student then lies on the floor face down and face up in turn, while the masseur, supported by a rope so that his whole weight is not used unless he wishes to use it, massages the whole body using his heels, his toes, the arch of his feet or the entire soles of the feet. It is fascinating to see how he searches out even the tiniest muscles with his toes.

Gradually, over a period of years the student acquires complete control over his body and is able to use any part of it at will, and in isolation from all the other parts. However, the first thing he must be able to do before any dance lessons can begin, is to adopt the correct posture for Kathakali. For this the head is held straight with chin tucked well into the neck. The spine forms an inward curve, into the waist from the back of the neck and out at the base. The arms are extended straight out from the shoulders to the sides and the hands, completely relaxed, hang perpendicularly down from the wrists. The knees are bent and held out at the sides in the same plane as the arms. For this position of the legs there is a special massage routine. The whole body is supported on the outer edges of the soles, the toes being curled, and the feet placed close together.

Once the student has mastered this basic position, he begins to learn to move without destroying the essential relationship of one limb to another. Since the emphasis in Kathakali is on the tandav aspect of the dance, and on bhayanaka, bibhatsa and vir rasas in particular, the dancer must be something of an acrobat as well. During the more vigorous scenes he has to perform tremendous springs, leaps and even do the splits, always landing, of course, on the sides of the feet. This is calculated to reduce the shock to the spinal column.

Kathakali is also, as we have seen, primarily a dance-drama, with the accent on the drama, but at the same time the actors never say a

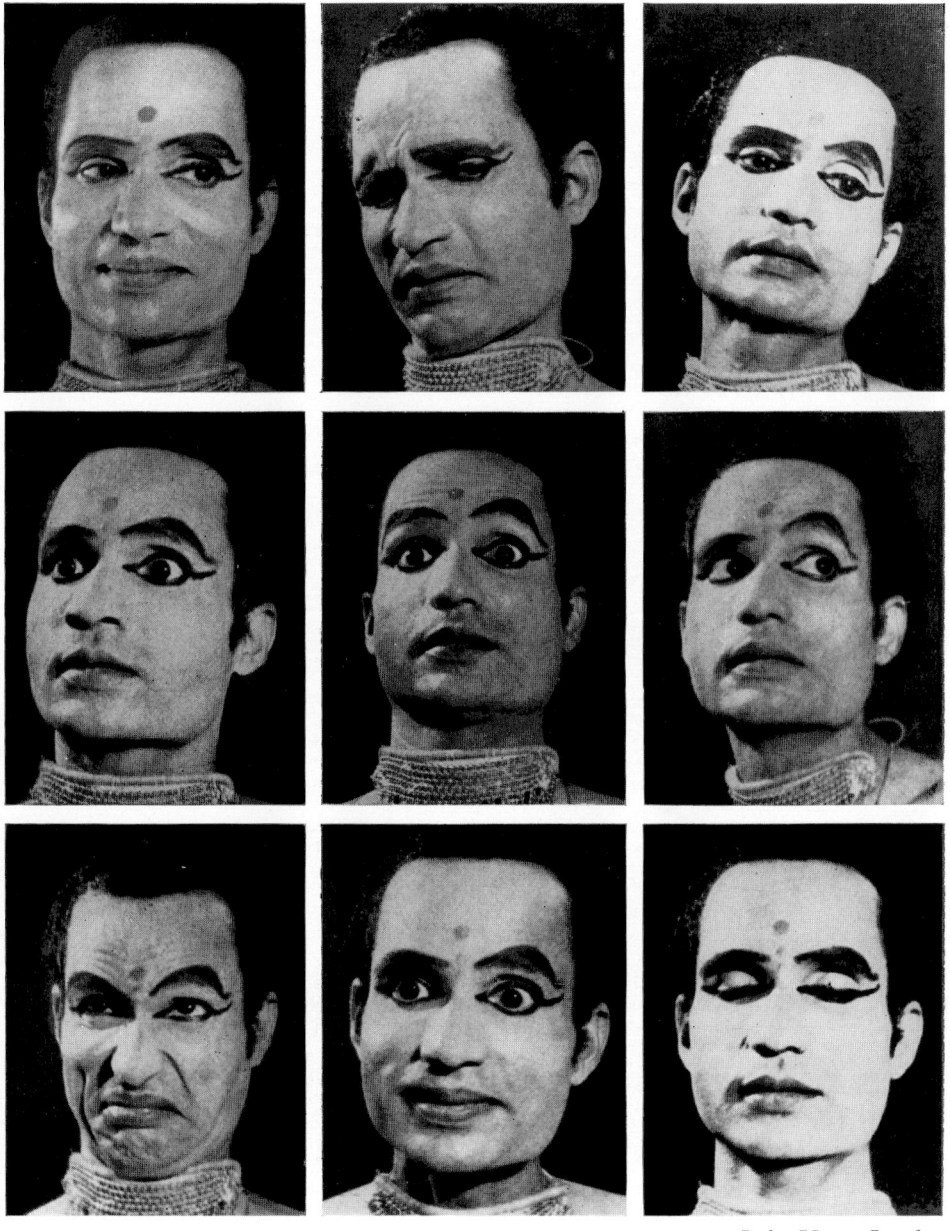

India House, London

Krishnan Kutty demonstrates the Kathakali expressions for the 9 rasas: love, humour, grief, anger, heroism, terror, disgust, wonder and serenity

Marc Alexander

A Mohini Attam pose

Features of Kathakali Technique and Training

word, the demons only being allowed to utter horrifying shrieks. Therefore facial expression and mudras play an extremely important part, and along with his other training, an actor has to learn to convey every conceivable idea through the expression in his eyes. To be able to do this he must spend the first couple of hours in his working day, on eye exercises. These are exhausting and leave the eyes extremely sore until the student has become master of the technique. He must learn to keep his eyes open for incredibly long periods without blinking. The eyelids should be able to reveal up to twice the normal surface of the eyeball. The iris must be able to be completely obscured by the upper lid and the eyeball move up and down, sideways or diagonally while the lids remain wide open. Not only should they move in any direction at will, but they must also be able to move smoothly at any required speed. The very slow movement is particularly difficult, since if anything arrests the sight the movement becomes jerky. So the actor has to try not to see in spite of his fully open eyes. The muscles controlling the lids too must obey the actor involuntarily, so that the upper lids, for example, quiver rapidly to indicate the flight of a bee, or the lower lids do the same to show anger.

A student is made to interpret random passages through the eyes alone, before he is allowed to add other movements, particularly mudras. He is taught to show through his eyes what he 'sees', for instance a lion, or a snake, or a beautiful girl, and he must be able, not only to show what he 'sees', but also show its reaction as well as his own. He must be able to portray the shyness of a girl at seeing him or his own fear on being attacked by a tiger. It is only when a student can interpret a passage exclusively by means of his eyes, that he is allowed to add any gestures.

Among the cardinal gestures of a Kathakali dancer's repertoire are the gestures of the hands, in other words, the mudras. Nowhere in Indian dancing is there a richer variety of mudras than in Kathakali, because it goes far beyond those enumerated in the *Natya Shastra*. The vocabulary includes even such things as adjectives, adverbs and conjunctions. The student then, is given exercises for the hands, fingers and wrists so that each finger is able to move independently of the others, and the wrists and fingers must become so supple that they can be bent back until the fingers touch the top of the forearm.

There are several hundred mudras in Kathakali which are built

Kathakali

up from twenty-four basic mudras; a good dancer must have a vocabulary of about 500.

These then, are the accomplishments which the student must endeavour to acquire. His day begins at 2.30 or 3 in the morning with eye exercises. Ghee, clarified butter, in the eyes makes the muscles supple. This is essential as he has to learn nine movements each of the eyeballs and the eyelids, seven movements of the eyebrows and eight different types of looks, together with their several uses. These exercises last for about two hours. He also gets used to reddening his eyes, and so enhancing their expression, by placing a minute and harmless seed under each lid.

The attention of the student is now turned to the rest of his body and in order to make it nimble and strong he is made to stretch and move his limbs in various directions. When he begins to perspire profusely from this exercise, oil is applied liberally over the whole body. This is basically mustard oil to which certain medicinal herbs have been added. The whole body is then massaged for about half an hour and after this the student goes through a routine rhythmic exercise.

Between 8 and 9 the students have a bath followed by a small breakfast. They then practise technique and actual passages from the dance-dramas until about mid-day, when they have a break for perhaps a bath, then lunch and an hour or so for rest. Their meals are always very simple and frugal consisting usually of rice and a little curry and maybe some pickles and yoghurt. The amount they eat is deliberately small, probably to obviate any danger of excess fat or laziness. The gurus are very conscious of the fact that people tend to eat far more than is strictly necessary or even healthy.

The afternoon and evening are spent in further practice. The students again refresh themselves with a bath and at about 8.30 or 9 follows the final session during which the guru instructs them in the all-important technique of mudras. After mudra practice they sit around the guru as he relates to them the stories and legends from the *Ramayana* and the *Mahabharata*, from which most of their plays are taken. He may sometimes tell them of his own ancestors, or give them an account of histories and traditions connected with the dance.

The day ends with a meal and the exhausted pupils retire gratefully to bed.

10

Make-up, Costume, Head-dress and Jewellery of Kathakali

Unlike the make-up of the other schools of Indian dance, Kathakali make-up is a complex art, the application of which requires between two to four hours. Usually it is the Patukaran or reciter who specializes in this aspect of the drama and because of its importance he is one of the most highly-paid members of the company. The make-up artist begins his work early in the morning. He prepares the paints afresh for each performance and begins by grinding to a fine powder stones of various colours, green, blue, orange, yellow, red and black. He then mixes each, on a smooth surface, with oil. The fine patterns of the make-up are made with a long flexible piece of bamboo with never a tremor to blur the outline.

There are three main types of characters, the Satvik or virtuous beings, such as gods, kings or heroes, the Rajasik, characters with particular vices such as lust, greed or vanity and the Tamasik, or out and out evil characters such as demons.

Kathakali make-up is in no way natural, indeed at first sight, may seem rather terrifying or at least grotesque for it deliberately sets out to alter the normal proportions of the human face. But then nothing about this dance-drama is natural, which seems fair in view of the fact that the characters are for the major part superhuman and those which are mere humans or play only a minor role, have much simpler make-up and costumes. With continual acquaintance, however, the make-up and costumes begin to appear less strange and eventually appropriate and even necessary, for the characters look so different from human beings and behave in a manner which would appear so exaggerated in ordinary people, that it becomes far easier to accept them as supernatural beings.

Kathakali

Moreover, the long preparation, the ritual of applying the new 'face' and putting on the costume, also undoubtedly gives the actors time to discard their own personalities and think themselves into becoming super-beings.

The Satvik characters such as Krishna, Rama, Arjun and Nala wear what is known as the *Paccha* or light-green make-up. The face is first painted green, and the eyebrows and eyes exaggerated and elongated in a stylized form with black. The lips are bright red and look as if smiling and caste marks are painted on the forehead. Finally the chutti or rice paste is applied in rows, to frame the cheeks and chin. It looks like layers of white paper each coming out beyond the one above it. Some actors do in fact use paper but those who are particular about everything being authentic, still insist on rice paste. The chutti is shaped so that it completely alters the normal structure of the face, widening the jaw-line considerably and narrowing again at the chin. It takes a long time to put on, since the shapes must be cut to fit the face and the outline be exactly the same on both sides of the jaw. Once on, it takes over an hour to dry. The Rajasik characters, such as Ravana, the demon king of Lanka, wear the *Katti* or knife make-up. This too has a green base but the green is broken by red patches at the sides of the nose. Above the eyebrows from the bridge of the nose are drawn two broad, flat-ended curves in red and outlined in white. Above these are white lines across the forehead with an inverted capital 'A' between them and the bridge of the nose. Another red and white oval patch is painted on the nose. Above the upper lip is painted a stylized red moustache which curls over the cheeks. This too is outlined in white. The finishing touch is added with two off-white pith knobs, called *chuttipuvvu*, on the tip of the nose and in the middle of the forehead. The more wicked a character is, the larger is the size of these knobs, which are symbolic warts or disfigurations. Fangs are inserted under the upper lip.

The bearded characters are of three kinds and are distinguished by the colour of their beards. The Veluppu Tadi are the white beards and are of good omen. The Karuppu Tadi or black beards are barbaric forest hunters, brigands and robbers. And the Chokanna Tadi are the demonic characters and have red beards.

The Veluppu Tadi make-up is for beings like the monkey-god Hanuman and the monkey character Vivida. For Hanuman for instance, the area around the eyes is painted black, the inner edge

Make-up, Costume, Head-dress and Jewellery of Kathakali

sloping away from the eye along the nose and diagonally down along the cheek, then up to the outer edges of the eyebrows and across them at the top. This black area looks very roughly like two triangles within which the eyes are enclosed, and is edged with a white line which curls over the cheeks on either side. The lower half of the face is of a reddish colour. A red line along the ridge of the nose is outlined in white, and red and white are again used to decorate the chin and forehead. The pattern on the forehead gives the impression of two 'eyes' set very high and close together on the face. The chutti layers are crescent-shaped and may be fixed in scallops down the sides of the face, and in this case, a white decoration is drawn above the upper lip. Sometimes, however, one set of crescents are fixed from above the upper lip and around the mouth to the chin. This has the effect of considerably narrowing the lower half of the face. The mouth is painted thin and black and has ivory fangs inserted into it. The over-all result of this make-up is to give the face a long narrow look like that of a monkey. The white beard he wears is round and flat and is made of wool or cotton thread.

An example of the use of Karuppu Tadi or black beard make-up is the role of Kirata the hunter, a disguise which the god Shiva assumes in order to test the fighting skill of Arjun. The basic colour of the face is black, and patterns in red below the eyes are outlined in white, as are similar curved patterns on the forehead. He too has a white wart-like knob on his nose and wears a thick black beard. But the most demonic and terrible make-up in Kathakali is the red beard or Chokanna Tadi of which Dushasana and Bali are fine examples. For this the top half of the face is painted black and the lower half is reddish. These two areas are divided by two serrated layers of chutti extending from the upper lips to the temples, the total effect being that of a rectangular shape. Designs of red and white are painted on the forehead and nose and two pith knobs are added. Fierce-looking fangs are placed in the mouth and the lips are painted thin and black. A very full red beard completes the make-up.

The wicked female characters are usually ogresses and she-demons such as Surpanakha and Putana. Their basic make-up is called Kari and is black, including the lips, but is relieved on the cheeks and forehead by bright red crescents which are outlined with white dots, as is the whole face. A red and white pattern embellishes the chin and the tip of the nose. These characters too have fangs. She-devils also have large black breasts. The fifth type of make-up is called Minukku. The basic colour of this is natural, that is, a sort of pale beige. All female characters such as heavenly nymphs like Urvishi, queens, goddesses, heroines and even evil ones in disguise, and minor male characters such as holy men, Brahmins, charioteers, messengers and so on, use this make-up. The womens' eyes are outlined in black and eyebrows emphasized with a graceful curve. The lips are given a lovely shape in red, and sometimes the cheeks are adorned with a curved line of white dots which are repeated on the forehead and chin. A dusting of finely powdered mica imparts a soft glow to the skin.

However, in addition to all these there are some characters who have their own particular make-up, for example, Nagaraja the king of the cobras has a make-up which suggests figuratively the head of a snake; Ravana's evil sister, who is a she-demon, has a special black make-up with a large bundle of feathers in her head-dress; Bhima, when he appears in his famous battle of vengeance with Dushasana has the characteristics of Narasimha the man-lion, and accordingly his make-up is lion-like. Narasimha himself too has a special hairy lion-like appearance.

COSTUME

The costume of Kathakali is no less remarkable than its make-up. It is as far removed from the ordinary clothing of the people of Malabar as is its make-up from resemblance to the natural face. Whereas the Malabari dresses in ordinary life with the minimum fuss and ornament, restricting himself to spotless white muslins, in Kathakali he goes to the other extreme. Normally, because of the mild climate, the men find a mundu or sewn loin-cloth with a vest or shirt quite sufficient, and when they go to the temple even this is reduced, for they may not be covered waist upwards. The women wear a sari and in rural areas they often do without a blouse or a petticoat since a sari alone is adequate to cover the body completely. But in Kathakali not only is the body more covered, but covered with a multiplicity of layers. It has been suggested that the costume has been influenced by various foreign elements. This is a plausible explanation since the coastline of Malabar has been an important meeting place of many races since pre-Christian times. The full skirts and the hats of some of the characters bear a striking resemblance to the costume of the early Portuguese who came to Malabar.

The chief male characters all wear up to three or four long-sleeved, high-necked jackets all of which fasten at the back, where there is an opening. This allows the back to be cooled by fanning when the actor becomes too hot from his exertions. The colour of the jackets varies with the type of character. Traditionally, Krishna wears a dark blue jacket, and those who oppose the gods wear red. All demons are in black except the wickedest among them who wear red jackets which have a rough, shaggy surface symbolic of a hirsute body. Hanuman wears a white jacket of fur. The only actors in Kathakali with a bare torso are the male characters who wear the Minukku make-up, the Brahmins and sages among these having the sacred thread over the left shoulder and under the right arm. The female characters too have coloured jackets. All the major characters wear extremely full skirts which have been compared to farthingales. They are indeed similar in general outline, the main difference being that the Kathakali skirts reach just below the knee and are not held out by hoops. The skirts consist of several layers of white cotton cloth draped over a waist-band which is then secured round the waist. The skirt is thus partly held out by the quantity of material gathered into the waist. This is double at the top, because of the tuck-in of material which forms a frill on the inside of each layer. The flare is further assisted by the position held by the dancer, his splayed knees holding it out sideways and the outward curve of the base of his spine causing a bustle-like effect at the back. The length of the 'underskirts' is shorter than the topmost layers, and whereas the others are more or less plain, the top layers have borders of stripes in bright colours as well as gold. They also have sunray pleats although these are not, of course, graduated in width from waist to hem. Over these again are two strips of coloured material, again with rich borders, which are added on either side. The whole skirt is then finally secured at the waist with a sash under another narrower strip of material. The skirts of demonic characters are often black or of a dark colour. All other skirts are generally white.

The Minukku characters, if they are male, wear a simple loin-cloth which is long in some cases, short in others. The females have full-length skirts which have extra fullness in front. These are usually white with borders, but not always, and demonesses generally wear black. The skirt again consists of a long piece of cloth. This is tucked round the waist so that it forms a fan-like frill of pleats in front and the whole is fastened with a golden girdle.

HEAD-DRESS

There are several kinds of head-dress in Kathakali and as with the make-up they go with the types of character, but the two which are most splendid are the Kiritam and Mudi, both of which are made of wood.

The Kiritam is used by the most important role-types. It looks rather like a tiered crown, surmounted by an orb with a point, the whole being backed by a halo. Both the crown and the halo are richly worked in colours of red, green, white, gold and silver. Although occasionally the jewels are real, the majority of companies are too poor to afford such luxuries and the inlaid work is done with imitation jewels of glass, pieces of mirror, beetles' wings which are green when they catch the light, silver beads and gold foil. The patterns on the halo are arranged in concentric circles, making the resemblance to a halo more marked. But, of course, its significance is not quite the same as that of the halo in Christian connotation, because it does not symbolize holiness. Indeed the biggest halo, almost three feet across, is worn by the red-beard characters, an indication that the size of the halo is related to the dimension of character of this role-type and has nothing to do with 'goodness'. The red-beard must inspire fearsome awe and it follows that in order to do this the actor must be as tall as possible. A man of average height or, worse still, a short man would run the inevitable risk of appearing ridiculous. Natural endowments, therefore, are usually more important in casting this role than acting-dancing ability.

The back of the halo is almost always plain, but occasionally it may be decorated. The whole magnificent but nevertheless cumbersome head-dress is firmly secured to the head by means of cloth bands. It is regarded as a very precious item, even revered, for an actor never puts it on without saying a prayer first.

Of the Mudi head-dress there are three main types. One is worn by the Paccha make-up types such as the gods Krishna, Vishnu, Rama and his two sons Lava and Kusa and certain high-minded and noble characters. If its basic form is not made of wood, it is constructed with cane, fibre and cord. This basic frame is covered with red felt which is then decorated with silver bands from which hang rows of sparkling silver droplets. The top of this dome-shaped head-dress is finished off with a crown of peacock feathers trimmed short.

The second kind of Mudi is worn by the Kari role-types as well as the she-demons and Karuppu Tadi characters such as Kirata the hunter. This is tall and cylindrical but gradually widens out towards the top and ends again with a thick edging of peacock feathers still trimmed but a little longer than those of the other Mudi. The basic colour of the head-dress is black but it is decorated top and bottom with bands of white peacock quills. Between these borders, placed side by side, is a row of thin, long silver leaves, which look like the long petals of a daisy which is half open.

The third kind of Mudi, known as the Vatta Mudi is worn by Hanuman and other monkey characters. It looks a little like the hats worn by Italian priests — round crown and a flat, wide brim — except that the crown is surmounted by another smaller dome and a still smaller one which terminates in a point. Hanuman's hat is white and the underbrim is elaborately decorated with peacock quills and tiny silver pendants, which scintillate with the least movement of the head. All those who wear a Kiritam or Mudi, also have long black hair made of grass fastened to the back of the head.

All the other members of the cast wear comparatively simple head-dresses. Those playing female roles wear a cloth which is bound round the forehead and hangs down the back, so covering the whole head and rendering the use of a wig unnecessary. It is fastened by a decorated head band.

Brahmins in ordinary life do not cover their heads, but in Kathakali they wear a piece of plain cloth which is bound round the head and like the women's head covering falls a little way past the waist. This material is somewhat softer and does not look as neat and even as that of the women.

Other male Minukku characters often wear turbans. Sages wear a head-dress which looks like matted hair piled high on top of the head in a bun.

Characters other than the main ones and the Tadi role-types may also wear long beards of dyed hemp.

JEWELLERY

Jewellery and ornament too are extravagant in Kathakali. All those actors who wear jackets have breastplates and necklaces of multiple strands of golden beads. Women have breastplates with the breasts covered with coloured material and necklaces. Unlike the rounded breasts of the ordinary women the breasts of the she-demons are large, black and pointed.

Most of the characters, both male and female, wear large disc-like ear-rings, some concave and some convex, inlaid with bright jewels. These may be worn in single pairs but another smaller pair may be added above the main ones. In addition, a pair of enormous discs are often held by an unseen helper on either side of the face of a rakshasa or demonic character.

Wrists and forearms have bracelets and decorated shoulder pieces are added at the top of the upper arm.

In addition to the many stranded necklaces the principal characters also wear what are known as Uttariyam. These are long white scarves with bordered ends, which are hung round the neck. Each is bound at intervals and ends in a tassel-like shape, so that it looks like a bell on a thick rope. One pair of these 'bells' has mirrors set in it, so that the actor can, if he wishes, check on his make-up. Actors manipulate these stoles to great effect during the performance. The last two items which complete the make-up and costume of the Kathakali dancer are a set of long silver-coloured nails which are worn on the left hand, and bells, which are tied not round the ankles as is usual in Indian dancing but just below the knees.

This description is enough to give a general idea of what the various role-types look like, but of course there are variations from company to company.

Arguments have been put forward for the reform of both make-up and costume in Kathakali with some justification. The make-up, it is said, hides the marvellous movements of the face. But it is an indispensable part of the whole and modifications necessary for a stage performance would have to be carried out so as not to destroy its essential character. Oil-bound paint does not dry very quickly, yet since it is worn for so long there is a danger that it might crack.

Make-up, Costume, Head-dress and Jewellery of Kathakali

The more vulnerable part, however, is the chutti. Some actors already substitute paper for this, but with modern resources there is no reason why a synthetic material should not be used, which would at the same time be more lasting and more flexible. It would be a pity to discard the present form of make-up completely, since it gives a highly imaginative verisimilitude to the characters, for it really only emphasizes the facial characteristics of certain role-types, in an extremely stylized manner. This is not only visually exciting, but was, undoubtedly, positively necessary — because of the very large audience and limited lighting arrangements.

So also with the costume, which certainly lends style and grandeur to the dancing, but at the same time must, by its very nature, be a great burden on the dancers. The use of a single jacket would possibly make the body of a dancer seem too small in comparison with his voluminous skirt and immense head-dress, but a thick lining which is both light and porous would surely overcome this difficulty. The skirt itself too could be made lighter and more comfortable by using modern fabrics.

In view of the present revival and popularity of Kathakali, changes are sure to be made, and it is unlikely that they will be rash, now that so many truly great and dedicated artistes are taking an interest in this dance-form.

11

The Dance-drama and Its Stories

The performance of a Kathakali dance-drama in Kerala normally takes place at night in the open air, usually in a temple courtyard but sometimes even in the compound of someone's home. There is no stage nor even a raised platform, just a small clearing over which is constructed a covering of foliage and flowers. Mats, usually of palm-leaf, are laid on the ground. The only setting is that of the natural surroundings and the stage property consists of a curtain, a stool and a lamp. The curtain, called a *therissila*, is a large piece of silk which is held up by two people at the beginning of the performance and before the entry of important characters. During the performance it is dropped to the ground and then removed. The stool serves many purposes. It may be used as a throne for instance, or the actor may rest on it when he is not dancing. The lamp provides the only light other than that of the moon. It is made of metal and stands about three and a half feet high. Its many thick wicks are fed with coconut oil and held in place by the stump of a banana tree. Throughout the night the lamp is given frequent attention by helpers. The glow around it is soft yet strong enough to illuminate the faces of the dancers.

The orchestra and accompaniment to Kathakali is usually made up of a pair of cymbals, a gong which keeps time, the mridangam-like *maddalam*, the chenda, and two singers. There may however, be as many as twelve musicians, in which case the number is made up with more singers, flutes and drums. The musicians and singers always stand in a semi-circle behind the actors, but during highly emotional passages a singer may go right up to the dancer and sing almost into his ear. The singers and drummers usually work in shifts of about two hours because the work, particularly of the singers, is exhausting. Also, sometimes a special type of voice may

The Dance-drama and Its Stories

be required for the singing. No distinctive costumes are worn by the musicians.

Of all the instruments, the drums play the most important part in Kathakali. They help to create and heighten the atmosphere and almost set the scene. For example, they indicate long journeys, thunder, the gentle patter of rain and are ominous or soft as the scenes require. They may echo the terrible wrath of Bhima or the agony of Putana.

The drumming begins long before the actual performance, for like church-bells, its sound is an announcement as well as an invitation. This drumming is called the *kelikottu* and at the sound of it men, women and children begin to assemble from the farthest limits of its reach. They settle down around the dance area with complete informality, some talking, others sleeping until woken when their favourite piece comes on. The children wander among the crowd and fight and play with their friends.

So far as the actor-dancers are concerned, the preparations for the performance begin hours before it is due to start. At about 8.30 or 9 the drummers begin their exciting prelude and after this the therissila is held up, behind which religious songs are sung. Two students, dressed in their normal clothes, now perform a devotional dance known as the *todayam*. They symbolize *shakti* or primal energy and *maya* or illusion. Their dance is the *lila* or play of cosmic forces and serves as a preface to the drama which is to follow. The todayam is a complicated nritta dance involving all the basic techniques of Kathakali.

At any time during the performance there is nothing to stop members of the audience from walking round the curtain and watching the todayam, and children particularly often do so. This preliminary item is followed by the *manjutara*, songs from the *Gita Govinda*, and another drum interlude in which the drummers show their skill.

The hero of the drama and his partner are now seen for the first time. This is known as the *purappad*. The curtain is lowered half way and the two characters are seen under the canopy of two peacock fans with a pair of fly-whisks held at their sides. Their dance is pure nritta, elegant and beautiful.

The demon or anti-hero is introduced by means of the *tiranokku* or 'curtain look'. He begins by dancing behind the curtain to thunderous drumming. His fingers appear over the top of the curtain which he shakes and pulls at violently as he dances in grand fury. The drumming becomes more frantic and suddenly the demon plunges forward to fan the light in the lamp which flares up revealing his terrifying features. The drumming is so deafening and so evocative of a tremendous evil power, that singing is neither necessary nor possible. The tiranokku is not restricted to the beginning of the play, but may occur more than once during the drama before the entrance of a demon.

The evil characters in Kathakali have a splendour and power which is similar in scale to that of Milton's Lucifer, the idea being that those who would oppose the gods must have a fitting stature for the contest.

Female characters too have an introductory dance called the *kummi*, and as might well be expected, the movements in this case are in a much lower key altogether, slow, smooth and graceful.

It became the convention for plays to begin with a love scene, so very often the first scene of a play is set in a garden where the lovers are conversing. Love scenes however, may occur in any part of the play.

The whole performance is punctuated by means of kalasams. These occur after every verse or dialogue and after a particularly important *charnam* the actor may dance as many as two or three kalasams, and in the last one he may use mudras to emphasize the main points of that charnam.

Kathakali plays last all night. The majority of the stories are well known and set in traditional patterns. This is because Kathakali was enjoyed by the simple villager, as well as by the educated courtly circle.

The plays were written so as to give the actor-dancers the widest possible scope for the exposition of their art. Every word of the play is interpreted through mime and gesture and, since this takes longer to do than the time taken up by the singing, the singer has to fill in by adding musical flourishes, while the actor completes his interpretation. To do this properly the actor-dancer must use not only mime and gesture but convey the bhava and ras as well. In order to show a mountain for example, the dancer will indicate its size by tracing its outline with his eyes and the gestures of his body, such as tilting up his head as his eyes measure the height of the mountain. He also expresses its majesty by means of his own reaction to it, one of wonder and awe. The final effect, incredible as

The Dance-drama and Its Stories

it may seem, is that by evoking the ras he has all but produced the mountain. This evocation of ras is the key to his success, for in this way he not only feels the presence of the mountain himself, but carries the mind of those watching with him and makes them feel it too. It is not surprising then, that a play takes all night to perform. All the stories presented, whether concerning gods, demons or mortals cover between them almost every human situation and emotion.

An example of a story which deals with love is that of Krishna and Rukmini. The lovely princess has to hide her feelings for Krishna because of her brother's hatred of him. Her marriage is arranged with one Sisupala and she can do nothing about it. At last she manages to send word to her lord through a trusted Brahmin. The day of the marriage arrives and the helpless princess is being taken to the temple, escorted by a great company, when suddenly Krishna appears and carries her off. The audacity of this action stuns the guests and before they can recover the lovers have fled.

In another romance the leading characters are humans, Nala and Damayanti. Both fall in love with each other even before they have met. They are helped by a golden swan, are married, parted, and after many adventures finally reunited.

A story which has some element of humour is that in which the busybody Brahmin, Narada, through his clever manoeuvres contrives to bring about the humiliation of the boastful Ravana. He talks the braggart into tweaking the tail of Bali the monkey-chief just to prove that he, Ravana, is the bravest of beings. Ravana, really believing that Bali has spoken of him in derogatory terms, goes up behind Bali to teach him a lesson. Unfortunately for him, the moment he grasps the tail he gets stuck to it. The more he struggles the thicker and longer it becomes and the more he is entangled in it. Thus he is humbled for a long while. There is of course, no actual tail when this episode is danced and Ravana has to convey all by his acting.

Krishna is the hero of yet another story, which concerns Sudama the poor Brahmin, his childhood friend and devotee. Sudama's piety and devotion are such that he neglects even his wife and children who are hungry and in rags. His wife persuades him to seek out his friend Krishna and ask his help. In spite of his misgivings, Sudama goes to Krishna. Poor and ragged as the Brahmin is, Krishna, the

Kathakali

prince, embraces him warmly and helps him out of his difficulties. The story illustrates the belief that God will look after those who are truly devoted to Him and in no circumstances will He let them down.

Women in Kathakali usually have passive roles but evil female characters can be quite violent. Putana the ogress is one such. When Krishna was a baby, Putana was sent to poison him. She appears at the house in the form of a beautiful maiden and makes sure that she can be alone with the infant. At first she amuses him and plays with him to gain his confidence. She then picks him up and suckles him at her poisoned breast. Soon, she thinks, the child will be dead, but it is her life which is gradually drained from her. As Putana realizes what is happening she changes back to her real hideous form. She tries to tear the babe away from her breast. Nothing she can do will detach him. Helpless she writhes in excruciating agony until finally she gasps out her last breath.

Normally, the actor does not need to make any changes in his make-up to indicate the transformation of Putana, for his acting is vividly eloquent. Sometimes however, while still on the stage, he may turn his head away momentarily and cleverly insert fangs into his mouth and add ugly patches on the cheeks.

Perhaps the most violent and terrifying of all the episodes in Kathakali is the combat between Bhima and Dushasana. Bhima has vowed to avenge the insult to his wife Draupadi of Panchal who had been dragged by the hair into the court of the Kauravs and there outraged by Dushasana. Bhima has to wait thirteen years before he is able to challenge Dushasana to do battle with him. The fight is long and furious. Dushasana falls and Bhima assuming the form of Rudra Bhima and the characteristics of Narasimha the man-lion, disembowels his enemy. He revels madly in Dushasana's blood, devours his entrails and smearing himself with the remains dances victoriously. He then fulfils his vow and binds up his wife's hair with his gory hands. They recall the incident which led to the dreadful vow. Calmer now, Bhima goes to Krishna, tells him of the whole episode and asks for absolution. The god blesses Bhima whose avenging fury has now completely left him. With justice done, the balance restored, for both actors and audience, the drama ends in '... calm of mind, all passion spent'.

As if this gruesome scene were not horrifying enough it is usually given even greater realism by the use of red wool for entrails and

The Dance-drama and Its Stories

red liquid for blood. Although the *Natya Shastra* speaks of death on the stage, this type of violence contradicts the spirit of its law. Kathakali however, is a law unto itself in more ways than one. Bharata defined the limits of the stage and the auditorium, but Kathakali knows no barrier between its 'stage' and 'auditorium'. Just as the spectators spill on to the acting area and even behind it, so the actors too may encroach upon the 'auditorium'. Sometimes the demons crash about among the spectators and in the story of Draupadi, Dushasana drags her through the audience towards the 'stage'. This turns the spectators into extras for a crowd scene and they become actual participants in the play.

The general rule in Kathakali performances is that they begin quietly and gradually work up to a crescendo towards dawn when the most violent scenes are enacted. Some plays end with a marriage or a reunion, but the last scene is always one of benediction. The blessing is given by an actor dressed as a god. This god may or may not have been a character in the play performed during the night.

For some few hours the people have experienced the essence of the primal passions in an unreal and unearthly atmosphere. With the rising of the sun they go home cleansed and uplifted, having walked with the gods.

12

Mohini Attam

Mohini Attam is named after the seductress supreme of Hindu mythology who appears in several stories. But the original, far from being a mortal woman, was in fact the god Vishnu who had assumed feminine form.

The gods and asuras, it is said, once churned the oceans, in order to extract Amrita, the elixir of life. All went well until the elixir had been extracted, but then there arose a dispute as to who was to have it, the gods or the demons? Since the gods considered that the demons were being unfair, Vishnu decided to take the matter into his own hands. Accordingly, he assumed the form of the most beautiful woman imaginable. This Mohini had the graceful curves of a vine, her limbs shone with the full golden bloom of youth, her face enchanted all who looked upon it. As soon as the asuras saw Mohini they desired her. She fled and they followed. In this way the asuras were enticed away from the Amrita and the gods carried it off.

This legend was danced by Menaka in her ballet called *Deva Vijaya Nritya* (Victory Dance of the Gods). There is also a sequel to the story.

When the god Shiva was told of Vishnu's stratagem, he wanted to see Mohini; so Vishnu obliged. Immediately, Shiva too conceived a passion for Mohini. The result of this passion was that Shiva produced Shasta his son from his own thigh. It is this Shasta who is so beloved of the people of Malabar and there are many shrines to him in the countryside of that region, particularly in forests and at crossroads.

There is yet another story about Mohini, which is often danced in the Kathakali dramas. This concerns a king of Ayodhya, one Rugmangada. During one of his hunting expeditions into the forest, the king encountered a beautiful enchantress who was really a

Mohini Attam

wicked ogress in Mohini's form. He fell so passionately in love with her that he completely lost all sense of proportion and was prepared to do anything to attain her. So much so that it did not strike him as odd that so lovely a creature should ask him to kill his only son for her sake. Although reluctant, he was just on the point of performing this terrible sacrifice when suddenly Vishnu appeared and stopped him.

From stories such as these, the name Mohini came to be synonymous with the essence of femine beauty and allurement, and Mohini Attam is a dance which displays just such qualities. It is a solo dance, reserved exclusively for women.

Its history is not very certain. What is known is that it was patronized a little over a century ago by a prince of Travancore, and became very popular. In technique it lies somewhere between Dasi Attam and the lasya aspect of Kathakali. Because of its inherent qualities, Mohini Attam was eminently suitable for use by loose women, and was frequently used by them to attract would-be clients. This led to its unpopularity and eventual decline at the beginning of this century. Nonetheless, when the Kerala Kala Mandalam was founded, Vallathol managed to find Kalyani Amma, a fine exponent of it, and engaged her on his staff. She began teaching it there, and then later at Tagore's Santiniketan. The demand for Mohini Attam grew, but the Malabaris had not forgotten its insalubrious associations. They finally managed to persuade the Maharaja of Cochin to ban it, and this ban was not finally lifted until 1950. The dance has since regained favour and Shanta Rao, Mrinalini Sarabhai and Roshan Vajifdar are among its best exponents today.

Mohini Attam is for the most part nritta although abhinaya is by no means absent. Its allarippu is similar to that of Dasi Attam, but is known as *solukattu*, and like Dasi Attam it has swarajatis, varnams and tillanas. Although their technique differs somewhat its movements are more graceful and alluring than those of Dasi Attam. It is always soft and gentle with no sudden jerks or heavy emphasis on tal with the feet.

Its music is Karnatic and the language of its songs is Malayalam. The nritya has many points in common with Dasi Attam, but the influence of Kathakali is much more marked here, especially in the use of mudras. Stories, such as those from the *Gita Govinda*, are danced in Mohini Attam, but most of its songs deal with the various situations connected with love. All these are exquisitely conveyed through gestures of the eyes and hands, expressions of the face, and voluptuous poses of the body.

In Dasi Attam the dancer is not obliged to sing all the time, but here she should really do so even if it is only with the singer among the musicians who accompany her.

There have never been any restrictions as to where or when Mohini Attam ought to be performed. As dancing is almost certainly a part of any celebration in India, Mohini Attam was often danced at private festivities such as births, anniversaries and the like. In this sense it adapts more easily to the stage. It does not, like Dasi Attam, have to create an atmosphere of devotion. It is not handicapped on the stage by subtleties such as those in Kathak, and it does not have the staging problems of Kathakali.

Indeed, it requires nothing but to be danced. The costume is uncomplicated. A white sari with a traditional border is worn with a plain choli, which is a fitted blouse. The hair is gathered into a large smooth chignon on top of the head but to one side. This is decorated either with a circlet of jasmine or a traditional hair ornament. Jewellery of the traditional kind worn in Malabar adorns the ears, neck, wrists and fingers. A girdle of gold emphasizes the waist. The make-up is natural but highlights the eyes and lips. Ankle-bells are, of course, indispensable. Some dancers of Mohini Attam use the costume worn by the female characters in Kathakali.

Mohini Attam does, of course, require training, just as any other dance, but it is a dance which is learnt comparatively easily, since there is nothing in its technique which might cause extraordinary difficulties. This, together with its obvious charm and beauty, is attracting more and more girls to it, although a good artiste will always give to it the aesthetic quality often missing in the performance of amateurs.

13

Ottan Tullal

Literally Ottan Tullal means 'running and jumping'. It is a dance created by the poet Kunjan Nambiar who lived in the mid-eighteenth century. He can best be described as a people's poet. Such was his influence on the literature of Kerala, that he marks a milestone in its development, and a whole period of writing is named after him.

The Nambiars were a caste somewhat lower than the Chakkiyars and one of their functions was to play the *mizhavu* or drum during Chakkiyar-kuttu. There are two stories about Kunjan Nambiar, both of which relate how he came to devise Ottan Tullal. According to one, he was a member of a troupe maintained by the Raja of Ambalapuzha. For one particular performance he was, it seems, overlooked for a part which he felt was in accordance with his talent and experience. However, he satisfied his ego by taking an artist's revenge. On the day of the performance he stationed himself opposite the palace and began to sing at the top of his voice as he danced to the accompaniment of loud drumming. The content of his song was satirical in its criticism of the establishment. He attracted crowds, and Ottan Tullal was born.

In the second account, Kunjan Nambiar is said to have been playing the drum for a performance of Chakkiyar-kuttu and at one point made a mistake. The irritated Chakkiyar immediately showed his annoyance by making slighting remarks about the Nambiar. Embarrassed at this public rebuke, Kunjan resolved to prove his worth and redeem his good name.

The next day the Chakkiyar was performing as usual in his corner of the temple, with an attentive and admiring audience around him, but this time he had competition. In another part of the temple stood Kunjan Nambiar. He was dressed in an entirely new kind of costume, his singing and dancing too were quite different from anything the people had ever seen. At first they turned to him from sheer curiosity but gradually, as they listened, they became absorbed in this novel exposition until finally the Chakkiyar was left with hardly anyone to pay attention to him.

This perhaps was the very first performance of Ottan Tullal, and the pattern of the temple was repeated over and over, and its popularity proved phenomenal.

Ottan Tullal had many advantages over Chakkiyar-kuttu. The Nambiar had greatly simplified the Sanskritized Malayalam of the Chakkiyar. He used a language which was closer to the average man and understood by him without difficulty. Kunjan Nambiar also made the music more interesting. He 'borrowed' the Chakkiyar's immunity, and like him, made critical, witty and outspoken remarks about people and their foibles, social conditions, and anything else which appeared to need correcting. At the same time he was careful never to offend and always to preserve good humour. It was perhaps this which really protected him most of all, for unlike Chakkiyar-kuttu, which was confined within the temple walls and so had sacred protection, Ottan Tullal could be performed anywhere, in the temple, at a private house, for a festival or just in any convenient open space. Neither was it restricted to any particular time, although the afternoon is now most popular.

Encouraged by the success of the first tullal, Kunjan Nambiar composed about fifty more, all based on the sacred epics and puranas but all, nevertheless, made relevant to contemporary conditions.

Ottan Tullal has now come to be known as 'the poor man's Kathakali'. This is because, in comparison with that dance-drama, it is cheap to put on. There is only one performer, who plays all the parts in turn. The musical accompaniment is also simple, for it requires only one drummer, who plays on an elongated drum called the maddalam, one cymbal player who keeps the tal on his little cymbals, and sometimes a singer. This singer assists and occasionally takes over the singing from the dancer, who normally does at least some of the singing himself. The technique of the dance too is very similar to that of Kathakali but is not quite so formal and inflexible. There are neither settings nor props, not even a curtain. The make-up of the dancer is not very intricate and though the costume is colourful, it is not as elaborate as that of

Ottan Tullal

Kathakali.

A strong white line is drawn on the face, following the contours of the cheek-bones and the beard line of the chin. All the area within this is painted green. The eyes and eyebrows are emphasized with black. The lips are painted red, and around the caste-marks on the forehead is made a pattern in black and white. The eyeballs too, as in Kathakali, are made to look red. The head-dress is a crown with a large semi-circular frame and two huge discs like ear-rings. It is decorated with gold, silver and multi-coloured glass. The bare torso of the dancer is also richly adorned with multiple necklaces and a small breastplate. At the top of the upper-arm and cupping over the shoulders, he wears decorated wooden epaulettes, and on his wrists, two bracelets. The most interesting part of his costume, however, is his skirt. This is made up of strips of white and red cloth which are looped, so that they make a kind of skirt reaching to the knees. This 'ribbon-skirt' is bunched at the back and sides, while in front hangs a bright red cloth.

As in Kathakali the bells used by the dancer are tied, not round the ankles, but just below the knees.

A performance of Ottan Tullal usually lasts a manageable two hours. It is always preceded by an invocation to the lord Ganesh and Saraswati the goddess of learning and the fine arts. The dancer usually sings a verse first and then interprets it with mime and gesture, using his hands, face, eyes and body. He may, if he wishes, leave most of the singing to his musicians. The interpretative passages are interspersed with pure dance which, as the name implies, is energetic and full of life. If at any time the dancer wishes to get his breath back, he simply turns away from the audience and has a rest, while the musicians continue to play. The dance is quite informal and sometimes the dancer actually goes in among his audience and addresses members of it individually.

There are two other varieties of tullal, Seetankan Tullal and Parayan Tullal but neither of them are as common as Ottan Tullal.

They differ from it in the cadence and metre of the songs and in their costumes which are much simpler.

There are not many dancers of Ottan Tullal today, since there is little monetary reward for the hard work involved in the acting, dancing and singing which together make up this dance. Its greatest exponent today is Malabar Raman Nair of Quilon.

Kathakali

This dance lies somewhere between a folk-dance and a classical dance. Its roots are certainly the same as those of Kathakali and, broadly speaking, it follows the same principles. At the same time it has a very close link with the people. It has played a large part in their relaxation and entertainment for it deliberately sets out to be non-academic. The common people themselves were particularly partial to it because it often championed causes near to their hearts, but its future now seems very uncertain. Even if it does survive Ottan Tullal will probably never regain quite the same old popularity.

14
Yakshagana

The best-known form of dance-drama in Mysore State is Yakshagana. For its subject-matter it has about fifty plays based on the stories of the *Ramayana* and the *Mahabharata*. Most of the dramas present the dilemmas and conflicts of war and the dancing itself is always vigorous and masculine.

As with Kathakali the whole plot unfolds through dance, song and abhinaya. However, the abhinaya content is not as developed as in Kathakali and the dancers, who are always men, sing the verses and dialogues themselves. Also, since it is a rural dance, the dancing and make-up are somewhat simpler than those of Kathakali. The character-types which Yakshagana portrays are grouped under two categories only, the *sumya* or gentle, and the *rudra* or fierce.

There is a considerable comic element in which the spectators delight. This is introduced by a clown who appears on the scene with the other dancers. He mimes their singing, tries to dance even better than them, and makes stray impromptu comments about the characters. The dance is generally performed after the harvest has been collected, so the village audiences are in the mood for light-hearted buffoonery and merrymaking.

Yakshagana is enacted in the village square or common. It has no stage, is an open air performance and in the local dialect is often referred to as Bayalata, from 'bayal' meaning field.

PART THREE

Kathak

15
History of Kathak

Historically, Kathak dates back to Vedic times, when the epics of the *Rig-Veda*, the *Mahabharata* and the *Ramayana* were composed. The word Kathak, story teller, derives from 'katha' which means story. Communities of Kathaks wandered around the countryside conveying the stories of these great epics and myths to the people by means of poetry, music and dance, all three of which were closely linked. The chief aim of the Kathaks was to instruct the indigenous population of the subcontinent in the knowledge of the gods and mythology of the Aryans. This means of instruction has a parallel with the early Greek theatre and with the beginnings of English drama. Indeed, the link is more than superficial, for all Indo-European languages, myths, legends, rituals, superstitions and sex symbols can be traced back to the common Aryan source.

India's earliest contacts with the outside world were initially established through trade. There were regular routes along which caravans moved from China and Central Asia, through the Indus valley to Turkey, Iran and Egypt. These commercial links must surely have resulted, in some degree, in the interchange of cultural ideas.

In the fifth century B.C. there arose in North India a new religion which was, to begin with, very different from the Vedic religion then prevalent. It was founded by Prince Siddharta of the Sakya tribe who, forsaking riches and power, preached equality among all men and by his own example showed the path to self-realization. He came to be known as Buddha or the Enlightened One and his teaching spread in due course, especially under the saintly king, Ashoka, to most of the countries of Asia. Buddhism was a spartan religion in comparison with the Vedic rituals of the Brahmins. It called for the simple life because according to it, the

Kathak

greater the detachment from the world and its temptations, the nearer was the source of enlightenment. This new religion involved no gods and no elaborate worship of them. Therefore, it did not need to employ the arts, all of which had hitherto been connected with religion. Buddhism was propagated through monks and nuns who had taken vows of poverty and chastity and who devoted their lives to social service with an almost Christian dedication. Religious dancing like that of the Kathaks was irrelevant to its needs. Nevertheless, Buddhism tried neither to stamp out Hinduism nor campaigned actively against the Kathaks, who continued to practise their art. It was not until much later, when Buddhism became a sect of Hinduism and the Buddha himself was enthroned in the Hindu pantheon as an avatar of Vishnu, that it used the arts of painting, sculpture, music and dancing.

After Alexander's incursion into India in 326 B.C., the northern part of the subcontinent was subjected to the invasions of the Scythians, the Kushans, the White Huns and the Gurjaras, all of whom came through the mountain passes in the North-West. Each of these peoples left the imprint of their racial and cultural characteristics on the population of Northern India. This constant influx was bound to weaken the structure of the caste system carefully laid down by Manu for the consolidation of Brahminism. The increasing struggle for dynastic power led to an emphasis on temporal and military matters, and for this reason the Brahmins did not exercise the same control over society as they were able to in the South. The patronage of the arts must also, to some extent, have passed from religious leaders into the hands of kings and princes, although the themes would undoubtedly still have found their inspiration in the scriptures of the Hindus.

The population of the Indo-Gangetic plain had by this time undergone considerable racial change and it is fair to assume that the classical dance of this area too must have been modified and enlarged according to the new characteristics of its ethos.

From the eighth century the new dynamic force of Islam appeared in the subcontinent. It was brought first by the Arabs and then, in a more permanent form, by the Turks. For over a millennium, in spite of the many invasions which had taken place during that time, Indian society had not been called upon to adjust itself to so radically new a situation. Here was the complete antithesis of the caste system. Islam preached that all men were brothers under One

History of Kathak

God, that there was only one path to heaven which lay through the teachings of the Prophet, and that it was morally dangerous to make representations of living things. This attitude was seriously to affect Kathak dancing, which was not only concerned with many gods and goddesses but also portrayed them in human form. This made the dance doubly sacrilegious to the Muslims and therefore it was vehemently condemned. The Kathaks had to find Hindu patrons, often Rajput princes of Central India, or disperse into the countryside where they could safely continue to dance in their traditional manner. With the passage of time, under less severe rulers, these Kathaks were to be permitted once more to dance with impunity.

Muslim society was based largely on merit and even slaves could aspire to kingship, but the caste system of Hinduism had at this time become stratified and effete. It had no equipment to counteract this new element of fluidity which was so rapidly forcing itself into society from without. The temper of the times had however, long been conducive to new movements, both in the Hindu and Muslim religions. In Islam it took the form of Sufism and later, in Hinduism, of Bhagti. Both were mystical in intent, preached toleration, and practised devotion to God and service to humanity. The best minds in Islam were attracted to Sufism. It was as the indirect result of the tremendous influence of the teachings and poetry of the Sufis, that later Muslim monarchs became tolerant of, and even encouraged and fostered the Hindu arts. The Bhagti movement, on the other hand, which matured into fullness later than Sufism, strove to mitigate the inequalities of the caste system by stressing the brotherhood of man and of God's love for all human beings irrespective of religion, caste or social background. It was this great synthesis of the quintessential best in both Hinduism and Islam, that produced Bhagats like Kabir (1440–1518), who was born a poor Muslim weaver in Varanasi and who became the generative source of great poetry and music.

The Kathak dancers used much of the Bhagti-inspired poetry for the nritya parts of their performances. This poetry was intensely emotional and declared the poet's love for God in personal terms.

The rise of the Vaishnavite cult which came before the Bhagti movement, had an important bearing on the development of Kathak. This embodied the worship of Vishnu, the god of preservation in the Hindu pantheon. In his incarnation as Krishna he was the chief subject of music and dance. There are understandable reasons for the Lord Krishna's long-sustained popularity with the common man throughout India. His romantic love for Radha symbolized the love of God for Man in terms which were simple and immediate. He was, moreover, always depicted as an engaging young man of dark complexion, and as such represented a major concession by the fair-skinned Aryans to the original dark-skinned inhabitants of the Indian subcontinent. Krishna, therefore, represented the synthesis of the Aryan and Dravidian cultures. His warm human qualities made it possible for people to identify themselves with him without feelings of blasphemy or sacrilege. His mischievous audacity evoked delight not fear, love not awe, and so lent itself admirably to presentation in dance form.

The art of mediaeval India was dominated by the Krishna theme and legends about him became a permanent feature of the Kathak repertoire. As a child, Krishna was both playful and precocious. He constantly played tricks on his foster-mother Yasoda. He was particularly fond of milk and butter, and the story goes that as a child he would organize raiding parties of young friends. Together, they would steal into the house where the butter had been hung from the ceiling out of reach and carry it off in triumph. Once, when he was very small his mother thought he was eating mud. She made him open his mouth, and saw not mud, but all the world and its profound mysteries. This brought home to her that her son was no ordinary mortal. As he grew older, Krishna's interest turned from milk to milkmaids! Many are the stories of his dalliances with them in the glades of Vrindaban and by the banks of the sacred river Yamuna. In his role of Murli Manohar or Govinda (flute-playing cowherd) he would charm the gopees (milkmaids) from their mundane tasks with the ethereal music of his magical flute. Once when they were bathing in the river, he hid their clothes, and then watched their confusion from a tree-top. The chief target of his attentions however, was the beautiful Radha, and he would seek every opportunity of waylaying her. One of her daily household chores was to fetch water from the banks of the Yamuna and he delighted in teasing her, upsetting her pitchers and embarrassing her with his amorous advances.

The Krishna stories also have a serious aspect. In the *Mahabharata*, Krishna appears to Arjun as his charioteer and discourses with him on his duties as a warrior, as a statesman and as a man seeking the

Rina Singha
in a thumri pose

Rina Singha
in *Mughal Miniatures*

Uma Sharma reaches the *sum*, at the climax of a movement

Marc Alexander

History of Kathak

truth. Krishna's main teaching was that duty, however unpleasant, must come before all else and man must endeavour without hope of reward.

All these episodes were excellent subjects for poetry, music and dance, which, in Vaishnavism, were important means of worship. There are, therefore, many famous poets, musicians and dancers connected with this cult. It reached its culminating point in the twelfth century with the poet Jayadeva, author of the *Gita Govinda*, who composed numerous keertans or devotional songs, and whose wife expressed them through dance. Later the poet-musicians Chandidas, Tulsidas, Mira, Vidyapati and Surdas carried on this tradition. Much of their poetry incorporates actual dance-syllables known as *boles*. This clearly indicates that dance was an essential of such hymns and neither was complete without the other.

The Muslim religion, as we have seen, excludes such arts as sculpture, painting, music and dance as forms of worship and these arts have no place in Islamic religious ritual. So when the Muslim influence established itself in India, this attitude had a profound effect on the hitherto Vaishnav-dominated Kathak. Because of its religious connections the early Muslim rulers, regarded this indigenous form of dance as unsuitable for their patronage, but they were by no means insensitive to the pleasures of music and dancing when divorced from religion. The result was that they sent for musicians and dancers from Persia and Central Asia. These dancing girls were known as domnis, hansinis, lolonis and hourkinis. Each of them had their own distinctive style of dancing.

Now as we have already seen, this was not the first cultural contact between India and the lands lying to the north-west. There had been rapport between them for many centuries. Musical modes from Persia such as Yamani and Kafi were incorporated into the Indian raga system at the time of Amir Khusro, who lived from the mid-thirteenth to the early fourteenth century. His genius touched not only music, but literature as well and so contributed towards the synthesis. Consequently the dancers and musicians were easily able to absorb those features of the Indian arts which they considered would be acceptable to their patrons. The few Hindu dancers who found their way to the courts were, in their turn, influenced by the new styles. This apparent secularization was to have a significant extension in the later Mughal period of Indian history.

The Mughals brought political unity, economic stability and

social justice. They took an intensive interest in, and fostered the Indian arts. The flower which resulted from the Islamic seed sown in the rich soil of Hindustan, displayed the colour of both cultures. The lotus had met with the rose.

Akbar the Great had married a Rajput princess, with the result that Hindu dancers and musicians at long last performed in the royal presence and came under the Emperor's direct patronage.

Kathak now entered its golden era. Dancers, musicians and poets flocked to the imperial court in Akbar's splendid new capital, Fatehpur Sikri, and to the provincial courts of the Rajas and Nawabs.

With the growing stability in government came a new affluence which was reflected in every aspect of life. Dress at court was of course, modelled on Persian styles and the court dancers too adopted the costumes of the day. In the last few years of Akbar's reign there is evidence that dancers, both men and women, wore an interesting new costume. The men wore a jacket, and the women a choli, a fitted blouse with short sleeves which leaves the midriff bare. Both had tight trousers called a 'chust pajama'. Over these they wore plissé skirts made of stiff material in three tiers the longest of which reached several inches above the knee. These skirts bear a remarkable resemblance to the tutu of Western ballet which was not invented until very much later. They also wore, over their shoulders, a transparent scarf of silk or muslin, known as an 'orhni' or 'dupatta'. The head-dress consisted of a muslin turban.

In the time of Akbar's son Jehangir, the dancers adopted the dress which was popular in the early part of his reign. The popularity did not last long at court, but whereas the fashions of the nobility changed, the dancers retained this costume and it has been in use ever since. It consisted of the 'chust pajama' in a bright colour over which was worn a high-necked diaphanous dress called the 'angarkha'. The soft, flowing, bell-shaped skirt was of full length and, like the sleeves, was left unlined. For women, an embroidered waistcoat of rich satin emphasized the body line. Men wore a double-breasted 'angarkha' which fastened on the left, with their 'chust pajama'. The women also wore a gossamer 'orhni'. The palms of their hands and bare feet were dyed with henna. Numerous miniatures of the seventeenth and eighteenth centuries show dancers in this costume. Its advantages, so far as the Kathak dancers were concerned, were that the full skirt fanned out at every fast movement, accentuating the fluidity of the dance, and yet was transparent enough to reveal the outline of the figure and perfection of the pose when the dancer was still.

The themes of the dances were now no longer confined to the myths and legends of Hinduism. The wider repertoire included imperial, social and contemporary themes. In fact, under rulers less tolerant than Akbar, Kathak developed along purely secular lines. The dancers concentrated on brilliant variations of rhythm, the beauty of which was heightened by tantalizing pauses and lightning pirouettes.

The Dhrupad style of music is essentially religious and had been connected with Kathak since the late fifteenth century. It came to its peak with the genius of Tansen during the reign of Akbar. This mode is dignified and majestic and has no room for frivolous ornamentation. The poetry is chaste and uplifting, using similes of sixteen selected flowers, fruits, birds and animals, four of each. As these similes adorn the music, so in Kathak, they serve to embellish the bhava, which is the language of gesture for the expression of various moods. With the emphasis on nritta, however, and the absence of religious themes, this music was used less and less in later times, until it became the convention to use just a single phrase of music, called the *lehra*. The lehra was convenient because, as it was repeated over and over, it did not distract attention from the rhythmic variations of the dancer and drummer.

The decline of the Mughal Empire and the rise of European power saw the gradual decadence of Kathak. Most of the petty princes and warlords had little appreciation of the fine arts and so Kathak degenerated into voluptuous and sensual styles. Although there was an attempt to retain the basic graces of Kathak, the tendency was increasingly towards lasciviousness, and the performers became notorious as women of easy virtue. It was this debased form of Kathak which the European adventurers called 'nautch', which was a corruption of the Indian word 'naach' meaning dance.

This infamy touched even the temple dancers, and certainly did much to discourage girls from respectable families from adopting professional dancing as a career.

The true spirit of Kathak, however, survived in spite of these social stigmas. High caste Hindu girls, especially in Rajasthan and Bengal, had to be accomplished in the arts in order to make a good marriage. They were therefore tutored at home, often to very high standard, but their attainments were reserved exclusively for the pleasure of the family.

The first dancer of genius to break this embargo was Menaka. Her achievements were truly outstanding — trained under the best gurus, she revived Kathak as an entertainment worthy of public support and what is more, she gave to it the imprimatur of social acceptability in its homeland, and also introduced it to other countries.

Menaka first formed a residential school of dancing at Khandala in 1938, and gathered together some of the best teachers in each style. Her main interest was in exploiting the possibilities of Kathak in productions of ballets. In this she was helped by Dr Raghavan, Karl Khandalawala, Maneshi De, Ram Narain Misra, Vishnu Shirodkar and Ram Chandra Gangooly. She produced three ballets in which she employed pure Kathak techniques, discarding the lehra and using classical music skilfully blended to complement the ballet themes. *Deva Vijaya Nritya* is about Vishnu's transformation into the beautiful Mohini in order to rescue the Amrita or elixir from the demons. The second part of this ballet tells of how Shiva fell in love with Mohini and how he went into tapasya, meditation, so that he might regain his self-control. *Krishna Lila* deals with the life of Krishna in Vrindaban and how Radha fell in love with him. The third ballet, *Menaka Lasyam*, is the story of the sage Visvamitra's attempt to gain immortality through tapasya, and of how the god Indra sent an enchanting apsara, Menaka, to tempt him and so interrupt his meditation. Menaka's fourth and most important ballet was Kalidasa's *Malavikagnimitram*. In this she employed for the first time, Kathak and Manipuri as well as Kathakali techniques. Her friendship with Pavlova was a constant source of inspiration to Menaka, and of great help to her in staging these ballets.

Today, there are two main branches of Kathak, named after the cities in which they took shape and flourished. These are the Jaipur and Lucknow schools. These schools or *gharanas* have their own distinct personality which was imparted to them by different gurus. Very often the traditions of the gharanas were sustained by succeeding generations of the same family. This gharana system also prevails in music, both vocal and instrumental.

The Jaipur style developed under the patronage of the Rajput rulers of Rajasthan and has a very strong religious flavour. One of the founders of this school was Bhanuji, a devotee of Shiva, who is said to have been taught by a saint. The greatest contribution to this style was made jointly by the brothers Hari Prasad and Hanuman Prasad, descendants of Bhanuji. Hanuman Prasad was a very religious man and it is said of him, that once at the festival of Holi he arrived late at the temple and the doors had been shut for the night. Nevertheless, his devotion was such, that he danced in the courtyard outside. At the climax of his dance, the temple bells within came miraculously to life and the doors burst open of their own accord. Even if this story is apocryphal, it is an indication of the power of this guru's dancing.

A more recent name is Jai Lal, another descendant of Bhanuji. Jai Lal started dancing at an early age and was highly accomplished in the two percussion instruments, the *pakhawaj* and the *tabla*. It was due to this, that his dancing was famous for its rhythmic quality. He included long *parans*, which are pure dance pieces set to subtly varying syllabic beats of the pakhawaj. His partiality for pure dance is evident to this day in the dancing of the exponents of the Jaipur gharana.

Sunder Prasad, the younger brother of Jai Lal, is the present guru of this school and teaches at the Bharatiya Kala Kendra in Delhi.

There is a minor off-shoot of Kathak not widely known, which appears to have been connected at one time to the Jaipur gharana. It was founded by Janki Prasad of Jaipur, but its adherents settled in Varanasi and Lahore. The main differences between this branch of Kathak and the two major gharanas are that it stresses clarity of line and execution even if this means sacrificing speed, and whereas, for footwork, the Lucknow and Jaipur gharanas allow the use of percussion instruments, here the dance syllables only are permitted. Its exponents at present are the brothers Sohan and Mohan Lal, Nawal Kishore and Kundan Lal.

The Lucknow gharana matured into a distinct and individual style in the time of Wajid Ali Shah, 'Akhtar', the last Nawab of Avadh.

By the end of the eighteenth century, the Mughal Empire had declined to such an extent that the Governors and tributary Nawabs and Rajas were independent in all but name. Delhi had been the centre of culture. All the arts had had full scope and flourished in rich profusion. With its decline, its poets, musicians and artists gradually began to leave. In Avadh the Nawabs now saw an opportunity to transfer its glories to their own capital, Lucknow. The migrants from Delhi were welcomed and given pensions and grants, and a new centre evolved. Lucknow became synonymous with elegance and aesthetic appreciation. When Wajid Ali Shah ascended the throne in 1847 at the age of twenty, the court circle already included artistic protégés of all kinds. He was by nature inclined towards the arts and resolved to outshine all his predecessors. The young Nawab devoted himself to this end with an energy which now seems suicidal. He spent twenty million rupees on building the famous Qaisar Bagh palace, the Imperial Garden palace. He established a centre for the training of dancers known as 'Pariyon ka Khana' or 'House of Fairies', because all the girls were selected for their beauty. He surrounded himself with famous poets of the day who wrote in Urdu as well as Persian, and was himself a prolific writer of verse, a competent musician and a dancer. His dance guru was Thakur Prasad whom he respected so much that he elevated him to the highest seat in the court.

Wajid Ali Shah's palace always echoed to the sounds of music and dancing, and he himself organized many productions of Rahas which were based on Indian themes of the Ras Lila but were set in a Persian background. The scenarios set down precisely and in minute detail, all stage directions and instructions as to how each role was to be played. These productions were lavish and reserved only for the court circle. The Rahas had most of the elements of ballet but were similar to pageants in that they were not produced on a stage. They were extravagant entertainments for a highly sophisticated audience, and were at a remove from the realities of life. The music was provided by his court musicians Sikandar Piya, Kadar Piya, Lallan Piya and Akhtar Piya whose fortes were *dadra*, *thumri* and *ghazal*, which are particular types of poetry set to music.

One of the important poets at the Nawab's court, Sayed Agha Hassan Amanat, wrote a dance-drama in Urdu verse entitled *Inder Sabha* or The Court of Indra. This is a significant work because it is the first drama written in Urdu and takes Hindu legend and clothes it in the rich poetic sensibility of Persia. The apsaras of India become the purrees (peris) of the Caucasus. Indra and his court are seen in Mughal dress and the whole atmosphere conjures up a dream world of every kind of beauty and luxury that the Persian poets associated with the pleasures of Paradise.

Inder Sabha, which resembles the Sanskrit classic *Vikramorvasia*

History of Kathak

returned, perhaps unconsciously, to the original concept of Hindu drama, where poetry, dance, music and costume were equal members of the same body. The play also brought back to Kathak after many centuries, its element of natya and led to a wide extension of bhava.

Wajid Ali Shah's passion for these arts was carried to a point where he neglected his state duties. This lack of interest in political affairs made it possible for the English to annex his kingdom and he was sent into exile.

Thakur Prasad's two sons Binda Din and Kalka Prasad succeeded him at the court of Wajid Ali Shah. The Lucknow branch of Kathak as it exists today is a direct result of the contribution made by these two brothers. Kalka Prasad's forte was a mastery of rhythm. Binda Din enriched the lyrical content with his own compositions of thumris, dadras and ghazals. Between them the brothers evolved a style which had lyrical grace as well as technical precision.

So, as we have seen, the Lucknow gharana at this point had all the elements of Kathak which are now extant, the last additions being thumris, dadras and ghazals. In fact, the thumri in both music and dance was invented by the Nawab himself.

The last outstanding patron of Kathak was Raja Chakradhar Singh of Raigarh. He too was a dancer and musician and his patronage extended to all dancers irrespective of their gharana. Jai Lal of Jaipur and Achhan Maharaj, the eldest son of Kalka Prasad of Lucknow, both served him for many years. He encouraged and nurtured young talent wherever he found it.

The Raja's fate was almost identical with that of Wajid Ali Shah, and for the same reasons. He was forced to abdicate in favour of his son and deprived of the means to indulge his interests, died a broken man about twenty years ago.

At present there are three gurus of the Lucknow gharana, Lachhu Maharaj, and Shambu Maharaj, sons of Kalka Prasad, and Brijju Maharaj, the son of their eldest brother Achhan Maharaj, who died some years ago.

Lachhu Maharaj teaches Kathak in Bombay and has choreographed many ballets, the most important being *Malati Madhav*, which the Bharatiya Kala Kendra invited him to choreograph and produce. It was first presented at the Sangeet Natak Akademi Dance Seminar in 1958. He is an outstanding choreographer and has experimented with adopting Kathak for Indian films. At present he is producing Kathak ballets in conjunction with the Dagar brothers, Moinuddin and Aminuddin, who are the leading exponents of the Dhrupad style of music today.

Shambu Maharaj and Brijju Maharaj teach at the Bharatiya Kala Kendra in Delhi, where many of their pupils are Government of India scholarship holders. This school was a result of the efforts of Nirmala Joshi, whose great dream it was to form an institution where the best teachers of Kathak and Hindustani music could train suitable pupils and, at the same time, experiment in ballet productions. She finally succeeded in 1952 when the Bharatiya Kala Kendra came into existence.

Shambu Maharaj is a great exponent of bhava and has revived many thumris and bhajans. He has the distinction of holding two of the highest awards in Indian art. Hundreds of dancers have been trained by him, among the best known of whom are Bharati Gupta, Damayanti Joshi, Gopi Krishan, Kumudini Lakhia, Maya Rao and Sitara.

Brijju Maharaj's efforts are directed towards adapting Kathak ballet for the modern stage. This presents an interesting challenge, for the theatres today contain a very much larger audience than was ever possible in either the temple courtyard or the intimate atmosphere of the Mehfil, the select company of connoisseurs. The choreographer must communicate delicate nuances and at the same time provide movement on the stage. The music for his highly successful ballets *Kumara Sambhava*, *Shan-é-Avadh* and *Dalia* was provided by the two Dagar brothers.

The stage settings and costumes were especially designed as these were period pieces. For ballets set in the early Hindu period the women wore a sarong-like skirt which was a little above ankle length. This allowed full freedom of movement and at the same time made it possible for the footwork to be seen to advantage.

Kathak dancers today have considerable freedom in their choice of costume, as a wide variety of permissible styles are in use. Broadly speaking these are either Hindu or Muslim inspired.

Among the Hindu costumes the oldest and that which is most generally used is the 'ghaagra and orhni'. The ghaagra is a long, very full, gathered skirt with a broad gold or silver border. Narrow silver or gold bands radiate all the way from waist to hem. The rich coloured silks used for the ghaagra must not be so heavy as to hinder the dancer during fast dance movements. The choli, worn with the ghaagra, is usually of a contrasting colour and has embroidered sleeve-bands. The light, transparent orhni is interwoven with gold patterns and draped over the head and left shoulder. The jewellery worn with this costume is rich and varied. Bracelets, armlets and necklaces are of gold. The heavy ear-rings, also of gold, are set with precious or semi-precious stones. Their weight is taken off the ear-lobes by fine gold chains or, more usually, ropes of tiny seed-pearls which hook into the hair. A jewelled 'tika' is suspended in the middle of the forehead.

Another costume which is becoming increasingly popular is the sari. The heavy silk sari has a wide gold border and pallav. This is the part which in normal wear hangs over the left shoulder, but for dancing is taken round the waist and allowed to hang down from it on the left side so as to show off its full beauty. An orhni is worn over the choli and draped over the left shoulder. The jewellery worn with the sari is much the same as that which goes with the 'ghaagra and orhni', the only addition being an ornate girdle or belt which emphasizes the slim line of the whole ensemble.

The Hindu costume for men consists of a silk dhoti with a brocade border. This is draped round the waist and between the legs to give a loose trouser-effect. A silk scarf is tied round the waist. The upper part of the body is left bare except for the sacred thread which is always worn, though sometimes a loose fitting jacket with short sleeves may also be worn. The jewellery is elaborate and consists of a wide gilt necklace with stones and a variety of smaller necklaces. Small pieces of gilt jewellery in a traditional pattern are mounted on cloth. These are tied round the wrists and arms.

The Muslim costume, as we have seen, was added much later, but has become so popular and so closely associated with Kathak that many people really believe that this is a Muslim dance brought from Persia by the Mughals. The costume is still essentially the same as it was in Jehangir's time, except that the skirt of the angarkha is now shortened to calf length. The jewellery worn with it is necessarily delicate and light, so as to be in keeping with the gossamer effect of the angarkha. The earrings are plain gold rings, each with a drop pearl and two smaller stones on either side. Two rows of pearls may be worn round the neck. Armbands and bracelets are of gold or silver filigree decorated with coloured stones. Sometimes an unusual hand ornament is worn. This is basically a circular jewelled ornament for the back of the hand and is kept in place by delicate jewelled links attached on one side, to a bracelet round the wrist, and on the other, to five rings worn one on each finger and the thumb.

A Jhumar or Chapka is an ornament for the head which may also be worn. This is a fan-shaped piece of jewellery which rests flat on the hair. The apex of the triangle lies near the parting and the delicate jewelled 'ribs' of the fan shape radiate forwards to rest flat on one side of the head.

There is no invariable rule about the details of a Kathak costume and dancers make adjustments to suit personal needs and preferences. For instance, there are many types of dhotis. The angarkha and waistcoat vary a great deal in style and cut. While some dancers wear a tight fitting bodice in the same colour as the angarkha and 'chust pajama', others prefer a contrasting colour. In the 'Kathak' dances of Indian films, the neckline of the waistcoat is cut below the bust to give a more alluring line.

Indian films have used dances which were supposed to be Kathak, but are best described as having drawn some inspiration from Kathak. The discrepancy arose not necessarily because the dancers did not know Kathak, for some such as Sitara certainly did, but because directors had to take into account the tastes of the 'groundlings' who are not interested in subtleties. Apart from a few exceptions Kathak has generally suffered at the hands of film makers.

A medium which should prove excellent for Kathak as a solo dance, is television. It is ideal for conveying to the audience the delicate bhava and abhinaya of the artiste. Skilful direction and camera work with close-ups of the eyes, the facial expressions, the hands and the feet could, possibly, add a new dimension to Kathak. Moreover, television functions in an intimate atmosphere and the dancer could easily produce the feeling among viewers that the performance was directed to each one individually.

As far as the theatre is concerned, on the other hand, it would seem that the future of Kathak lies in ballet, where its rich and varied repertoire of nritta, nritya and natya can be fully exploited.

16

The Technique of Kathak

The most striking thing about Kathak in comparison with the other dance styles is the impression it creates of extreme subtlety. It retains the qualities of grace and courtliness together with an emphasis on speed and close attention to footwork. This is achieved by a contrast of sudden stillness with swift flowing motion. Indeed, sometimes, it might seem that Kathak is devoted entirely to the nritta aspect of dance to the exclusion of both nritya and natya. This is far from true, for although pure dance plays an important part in Kathak, nritya and natya are by no means neglected and the expression of mood and sentiment forms an essential element of it.

Being originally a religious dance, Kathak was first performed to Vedic *chhands* and chants, and later to religious songs in the *prabhand* style. *Keertans* and *Dhrupads* were added in the fifteenth century. All of these were interpreted through gesture and mime.

The music for a Kathak recital is usually provided by a singer and two musicians. One musician gives the rhythm, the other the melody. The percussion instrument is either a long drum called the *pakhawaj* which is struck by the hands at both ends, or a pair of smaller upright drums struck also by the hands, known as the *tabla*. This name has come to be applied to both the drums, although tabla is the name for the right-hand drum only and the left-hand drum is called the *banya*. The pakhawaj is the older instrument and at some time during its history it is thought to have been 'cut' to form the two smaller drums. The *sarangi* which provides the melody is a stringed instrument played with a bow. The singer accompanies only certain items in the programme, for in some items there is no singing and in others the dancer is singer as well.

Normally, a musical phrase within a given time scale is repeated continuously. This refrain or *lehra* came into general use in the

Kathak

Mughal courts and serves a very useful purpose. It provides the dancer and the percussionist with an ever-present and constant time measure. There are slight variations in the phrasing of the lehra but these are apt to pass unnoticed by the unaccustomed ear. The percussionist sets the rhythm or *tal* by playing within a selected time measure such as *trital*, a measure of sixteen beats, *ektal*, twelve beats or *dadra*, six beats. These beats are known as *matras*. There are many time measures to choose from but trital is the most popular. The tal is played in a *laya* which may vary according to the mood of the music.

Broadly speaking laya has three categories; *vilambith* (slow), *madhya* (medium) and *druth* (fast). More precisely these are known as *tha* (slow), *doon* (twice the speed of tha) and *chaugun* (four times the speed of tha). Sometimes even *athgun* (eight times the speed of tha) is used. In addition to these there are more complex patterns of laya which involve fractions of tha.

Kathak has a highly developed and complex technique of footwork which is unique to this style. It follows then, that footwork and tal are closely related and interwoven. The skill of the dancer and percussionist is judged by the accuracy with which, after complicated variations, they arrive simultaneously at the *sum*. The sum is the first beat of the time measure. A variation is usually spread over several bars and the excitement reaches a climax, not with the last beat of the time measure but with the first beat of the next cycle. It is impossible to miss the sum, for it is always pointed with a sense of achievement and satisfaction. And when the sum is accurately executed after difficult and exciting variations, the audience bursts into spontaneous applause.

Footwork in Kathak is known as *tatkar*. It displays the technical virtuosity of the dancer and, as such, comes within the nritta aspect of dance. A student's dance training begins with tatkar and he has to spend many hours each day practising it. When Shambu Maharaj himself started Kathak, he would do his tatkar to a beat of eight for up to four hours at a stretch — a tremendous feat of endurance! His mother would, from time to time, bring him a glass of milk to keep up his energy. The average student however practises footwork for not more than an hour or an hour and a half at a time. At the Bharatiya Kala Kendra, where Shambu Maharaj is the Kathak guru, the students' day begins at five with at least an hour's footwork. Each practises separately without the help of tabla or sarangi

The Technique of Kathak

holding the lehra in his or her mind, but they do wear *ghungurus*. These are small, round ankle-bells made of brass which are strung together on a cord. They are held in place by a knot and have the space of a finger-width, *ungli*, between them. Girls usually wear 101 and men 151 on each ankle. The cord with bells on it is bound round the ankle so that each bell lies flat and evenly. Great care is taken over this so that the bells, which are tuned to produce a pleasant tone, sound simultaneously and not in a blurred jangle. Since no protection is allowed under them the constant friction of the brass causes bruises on the ankle until the dancer gets used to them. Tatkar is also hard on the shins and the calf muscles, which ache and burn with exertion. Apart from learning the actual technique of tatkar, the student must master the many tals and learn innumerable metrical patterns. This is done by memorizing the *boles* or rhythmic syllables with the help of a system of clapping. An example of the first set of tabla and corresponding dances boles in trital is:

STRESSES	+ 1				2				0				3			
TABLA BOLES	dha 1	dhin 2	dhin 3	dha 4	dha 5	dhin 6	dhin 7	dha 8	dha 9	thin 10	thin 11	tha 12	tha 13	dhin 14	dhin 15	dhat 16
DANCE BOLES	+ tha a 1		thei ee 2		thé ee 3		tha th 4		aa a 5		thé ee 6		thé ee 7		tha th 8	

These are the eight dance syllables or boles which correspond to the sixteen boles of the tabla. The diagram makes it clear that, for every two tabla beats there is just one dance beat. In both cases three beats are stressed. For the tabla boles these are the first (marked +) which is the sum, the fifth, and the thirteenth. The corresponding stressed dance beats are, the first, again the sum, the third, and the seventh. The fifth dance beat, and in the case of the tabla the ninth beat, is known as the *khali* meaning empty (marked o).

The student recites these dance syllables and at the same time claps the accented syllables with the fingers of the right hand and the palm of the left. The khali is indicated by turning the right hand away, palm upwards.

The tal explained above is called trital because it has three (tri) claps (talis). As another word for three is *teen* the tal may also be called teental.

The footwork of a Kathak dancer is similar to that used in the jati of Dasi Attam but is more complex and varied. The Jaipur gharana is especially noted for the brilliance of its tatkar.

Another important constituent of the nritta is the *tukra*, literally piece or fragment. Tukras are usually short items lasting for about six or seven bars of the basic time scale. At the end of a tukra the dancer assumes one of the typical Kathak positions and holds it for one bar.

A Kathak performance always progresses from a very slow speed at the beginning to a very fast one at the end, and so there are various types of tukras which are danced at slow, medium, and fast speeds. Examples of the slow tukras are *amad* and *salaami*, of the medium ones, *tatkar*, *natwari*, and *sangeet*, and the fastest are the *paramelus* and *parans*. When a tukra is danced three times successively at the same speed it is called a *chakkardhar tukra*. This tukra offers the opportunity of displaying *layakari*, which is the dancer's mastery of the play of rhythm within the tal.

In the Jaipur gharana of Kathak, there is a type of tukra which is also danced three times, but in this case the speed is doubled with each repetition. The proviso here is, that each rendering of the tukra should be an exact reproduction of the first in all but speed. Since this tukra must, of its very nature, start slowly, it normally comes in the early part of a performance.

An essential part of a tukra is the *chakkar* or pirouette. The point to watch here is, that the chakkar should be executed with great speed and yet without in any way spoiling the beauty of the line, abbreviating the movement of the arms, or straying from the spot where it was started. Some expert dancers can execute up to a hundred lightning pirouettes at a time and at the Allahabad Music Conference in 1937, a dancer apparently pirouetted at such speed that she appeared to have two heads. But of course, no one who depends solely on sheer spectacle and a series of tours de force can expect to be taken seriously by connoisseurs, any more than a ballet dancer who performs fast pirouettes can expect to be regarded as a prima ballerina on this basis alone. Nevertheless, chakkars are another aspect of technique which take up a large part of the student's time. They can be executed to various numbers of beats such as eight, three or one and are always practised several at a time to ensure that the dancer does not become giddy during a performance. It was common at one time for this to be done within a small square bounded by bricks. If the student moved too much the feet suffered. Hard but effective! The gurus today are kinder and do not insist on such painful teaching-aids.

The Technique of Kathak

Very similar to the tukra is the *torah*. Sometimes the dancer recites the boles of a tukra or torah which is about to be danced. This is especially effective with an audience which is familiar with the finer points of rhythmic patterns. The dancer first recites the boles finishing triumphantly on the sum. There is a pause of one bar or one *avardhi*, and then from the next sum the boles are rendered in dance. In this way the audience can hear the boles reproduced by the ghungurus. A torah is usually danced very fast.

Every school of Indian dancing has its expressionistic or nritya element. The mode of expression is somewhat different in each style, although, because of geographical proximity, there is a similarity in this respect between Dasi Attam, or Bharata Natyam, and Kathakali. The methods employed by these two styles to depict events and convey emotions are bold in relief and clear in definition. Kathak on the other hand, uses subtlety and understatement to evoke the same emotional responses. Kathak dancers do delineate stories, as for instance in *gaths*, but their main concern is in weaving into being the atmosphere inherent in the story. A song is not interpreted word for word except in some special cases. As a general rule each situation is sketched in brief outline so that it can be danced quickly to create the over-all effect. Like a Japanese painting, Kathak is executed swiftly and with economy of line.

The very connotation of the word Kathak means that nritya was of prime importance to the earliest dancers, since to accomplish their aim they had to interpret their stories in a lucid and agreeable manner. It continued to be important even when the emphasis of their function shifted from that of teachers to that of entertainers. For it was only because the Kathak dancers already had a wide vocabulary that they were able, with no great difficulty, to adapt their dances from religious to secular subjects. They already knew how to express actions and emotions. Love was love, whether between Radha and Krishna or between a prince and his beloved. All that was needed was an indication of the character's identity.

Such an indication of a particular god or mortal occurs in the first kind of gath to be presented, the *gath nikas*, which only sketches in the story to follow. The dancer comes forward to four beats arriving at the beat before the *khali*. A dramatic pause of four beats follows while the dancer holds a characteristic pose. From the sum which follows she begins a *chaal* or gait. The sound of the ghungurus after the short silence adds to the interest of the chaal.

Kathak

These chaals or *gatis* are of great significance as they give a clue to the character of the person being depicted and suggest the type or class of the *nayika* (heroine) and *nayaka* (hero). By means of chaals the dancer also portrays various moods, birds and animals. Examples are the peacock gait, the deer gait and the swan gait.

By the free use of mime and gesture, the dancer concentrates on bringing out the mood or emotional state of the hero or heroine. This technique is called *nayika bheda*. Examples of these are *vasakasajja*, which shows the nayika dressed and richly adorned awaiting the arrival of her lord, and *kalahantarita* which shows her desolate after he has left her.

Mudras or *hastas* as they are called in Kathak, are of course used, but the function of these hand gestures is not isolated: they are seen as an integral part of a dance movement. For this reason the Kathak student does not learn the hastas separately. They do not, for her purposes, constitute an end in themselves. Singly or in combinations they are used to amplify and elaborate the gaths. Although the hastas in Kathak conform to the canons of the ancient texts, they are used in conjunction with the other parts of the body, and all of these together form a composite unit of dance, that is, the gath. Hastas are also used in certain tukras like the *rang manj ki puja* and the salaami and in *kavita torahs*. Kathak also employs certain hastas in pure dance items. These are known as *nritta hastas* and are used in *thaats*, *paramelus* and *parans*. Of the two main schools the Jaipur gharana uses a richer variety of nritta hastas.

In Kathak the whole body, rather than any particular part of it, is used to convey the image. This is logical and natural since Kathak is a dance of liquid movement, so that if the dancer wishes to represent the moon not only will her hands show the corresponding hasta but she will at the same time, curve her body to suggest the crescent moon. The simple *ghungat gath* may use as many as ten varieties of hastas, each hasta giving a different idea of the nayika performing the action. The pain of unrequited love is pictured as the lonely chikore flying towards the moon. This the dancer will suggest by the yearning restlessness of the fingers in the appropriate hasta, and the eyebrows rising alternately, symbolic of the flapping of wings. Four books written in the last century give detailed accounts of gaths. *Madan-ul-Musiqui* describes twenty-one, fourteen of which are also described in *Ghuncha-e-raag*. *Saut-ul-Mubarak* by

Radha waits for Krishna but ... a sakhi tells her ... he is dancing with another

The dancer in the role of the kalahantarita nayika—the woman grieving for her departed lover

Partap Pawar and Tirath Ajmani in a Kathak duet

The Technique of Kathak

Nawab Wajid Ali Shah and *Naghmat-ul-Hind* are the other two which give descriptions of gaths. The last mentions in addition, that 360 gaths were detailed in a book by Prakashji of the Lucknow gharana but unfortunately this work seems to have been lost.

After a brief introduction in the gath nikas, the story unfolds more elaborately in the *gath bhava*. Since a single dancer has to portray more than one character it is essential to have some means of separating them and demarcating the several actions. This punctuation is achieved by a pure dance figure called the *palta*. In this the dancer moves from a half-turned position in one direction, through a complete revolution of the body, to a half-turned position in the opposite direction.

The subject matter of gaths falls into three sections, namely, those which deal with simple actions, those pertaining to Krishna, and those which are based on mythological characters and episodes. For example, the simple action of drawing the veil over the face is called the *ghungat gath*. In *gath bhava* the dancer would show the emotional state of the girl when she performed this action, for instance, whether she was genuinely shy or simply being coy. A Krishna gath such as the *Kaliya Mardana* would tell the story of how the giant serpent Kaliya was subdued by Krishna who then danced triumphantly on its hood. The *Sita Harana gath* is based on an episode from the *Ramayana* and tells of Sita's abduction. Rama and his faithful wife Sita have been exiled from their kingdom. Destitute, they wander through the forest. One day when Rama is away hunting, Sita is carried off by the demon king Ravana. Rama scours the country in search of his wife and finally rescues her with the help of the clever monkey-god Hanuman.

The choreography of this gath as taught by Shambu Maharaj is very simple, yet it communicates vividly the ras and outline of the whole story.

In a gath nikas the prince, Rama, is first identified by his *jatta*, the coil of hair he wore on the crown of his head. Then follow his other identifications, the sacred thread worn over one shoulder and diagonally across the chest, his mighty bow, and the quiver of arrows at his back.

Now follows the gath bhava. The golden deer episode in this is called the *Marich gath*. The dancer's hands make the hasta which shows a deer prancing, and the eyes complement the movement.

There is a palta. The dancer now becomes Sita by drawing aside her veil. Entranced by the deer, Sita's eyes follow it. She then draws the veil further over the right shoulder as if looking at Rama and asks him to bring her the deer. This is done with great economy of movement. The dancer just extends her right hand as if placing it on Rama's shoulder and points to the deer with her left. The eyes do the rest.

The palta again shifts the action from Sita to Rama, followed by movements almost identical with those of the nikas. Here Rama is shown preparing for the hunt. He secures his long hair by making a jatta, shows his sacred thread, the bow, and the quiver. Then, with an appropriate gati, he moves to stage front, and shoots an arrow at the precise moment which coincides with the khali of the tal. Having shot the deer, he returns in a wide arc towards his first position, as if going back to his forest hut. Half way there a worried look begins to steal over his face. The bow falls from his hand. When he gets there he cannot find Sita anywhere. He sits down and his attitude expresses deep despair.

It can be seen from this description that the bhava of the story is allusive and it is not mimed in detail. Just enough is told to enable the audience to fill in the rest for themselves. Ravana is not shown abducting Sita in the guise of a hermit. Instead this is left to the imagination and Rama's vain search for his beloved and his distressed condition provide the clue.

It is usual for other nritya items to be named after the styles of singing in which the words are rendered; so that there are *dhrupads*, *keertans*, *horis*, *dadras* and *ghazals*. When performing any of these the dancer is normally expected to do the singing as well. This means that a dancer who concentrates on bhava — the expression of emotions and feelings — must be a competent singer as well.

In Kathak, however, it is possible to dance a story, theme, or episode and yet dispense with the assistance of words altogether. Still another aspect of nritya in this dance, is the manner in which a thumri may be rendered. Here the rendering of the poem is of prime importance and the accompanying bhava is so delicate that footwork would be a distracting element. It is, therefore, excluded. The dancer sits with a shawl draped over the legs and feet. The bhava is expressed mainly by the face, the eyes in particular. The hands and body play a secondary role. The performer repeatedly sings a line of the poem, interpreting it differently each time with corresponding changes in bhava and so exploits every shade of meaning. The greater the performer the more variations he presents. Maharaj Binda Din interpreted a single line from a theme about the Lord Krishna from dusk to dawn without ever duplicating a variation or a nuance. A rendering in this manner is known as *thumri andaaz*.

One of the finest artistes of thumri andaaz today is Shambu Maharaj. He has a wide repertoire; one of his favourite thumris is 'Bata do guniyan, kaun galiṅ gayo Shyam?' which means 'Do tell me, dear friend, which way has Shyam gone?'

'Galiṅ' means 'lane', and 'Shyam' is another epithet of Krishna as the Dark One.

Shambu Maharaj sings this line several times, underlining a particular word or syllable in each rendering. His face and eyes display the bhavas, and hastas assist in their expression. The acting brings to life metaphors, images, similes and metaphysical conceits which are not explicit in the poem. For example, he shows Radha applying *surma* or kohl to the lower eyelid as an eye-liner. The movement of her finger is the lane and the black surma symbolic of Krishna the Dark One. In another sense this could mean 'Shyam has entered my soul as the surma enters my eye'.

The line is repeated. Radha is preparing to meet Krishna; she combs her hair and as the dark tresses are loosened she associates them with the Dark One. As she plaits her hair the plait itself becomes suggestive of the lane.

With the next repetition Radha applies *sindhoor*, a red powder, in the parting of her hair and Krishna is represented as entering her heart as the sindhoor enters the parting.

In yet another instance she is searching for Krishna and the dark clouds gathering overhead, heavy with monsoon passion, fill her with desire for her dark lover.

Varying the image again, Radha opens a phial of *attar*. She dabs some on the back of her hand and inhales the perfume. Just as the sweet scent gratifies her senses, so Krishna enters and uplifts her soul.

His renderings show that Shambu Maharaj has the sensibility of a poet and it is this which enables him to interpret and express the sentiments implicit in the poem. He extends the significance of each one by adding to it from his own creative imagination.

Like the Indian musician who has to be an impromptu composer as well, a performer of thumri andaaz too must be an inspired poet of gestures that suggest and explore different levels of meaning.

Several thumris danced today are the compositions of Maharaj Binda Din who was a devotee of Krishna. Both thumris and bhajans were very often addressed to Krishna in terms of human love. This convention is sometimes followed in ghazals as well, which are poems in the Urdu language, and since these are in the Islamic tradition they are addressed to God. The idea is not unique and there are numerous examples of it in Donne and some of his contemporaries. For instance, here is a stanza from Francis Quarles the seventeenth-century English metaphysical poet:

> 'Why dost thou shade thy lovely face? O why
> Does that ecclipsing hand, so long, deny
> The sunshine of thy soul-enliv'ning eye?'

This might almost be a translation of a bhajan addressed to Krishna by the poetess Mira and exactly the kind of song that made excellent nritya material.

There is one constituent of Kathak which deserves special attention, because although it combines nritta and nritya this is not immediately apparent. The *kavita torah* is performed to the recitation of a poem the accented syllables of which are emphasized, and which includes boles or dance syllables. Since a poem in Sanskrit is called 'kavita', and as pure dance to boles is known as a 'torah', a dance accompanied by the recitation of such a poem is called a 'kavita torah'. This dance is always performed at great speed and so the nritya element is not easily discernible. The ghungurus echo the words of the kavita just as they would reproduce the syllables of any other tukra.

17

A Kathak Performance

A Kathak recital usually begins with the Ganesh Vandana. This is a salutation to the elephant-headed god Ganesh, who represents good luck and symbolizes the dispelling of misfortunes. There is a certain legend about him that explains these associations.

It is said that Parvati the consort of the Lord Shiva, took a great deal of time over her toilette. She would spend hours bathing, dressing and adorning herself. This meant that Shiva was kept waiting — something which went much against his dignity. His remedy was to burst in upon her unannounced and catch her in a state of unreadiness, whereupon he would proceed to tease her. Now Parvati was not to be outwitted so easily, and hit upon the idea of setting their son Ganesh on guard. Whenever Shiva was approaching, Ganesh would warn his mother. One day Shiva was so frustrated by the child's action that he cut off his head. Parvati, utterly distracted at her loss, completely withdrew herself from her lord. Shiva now realized that the only way to win back his wife's favours was to restore the child to her — but the head was lost. He therefore resolved to use the first available head he could find. This happened to be that of a baby elephant. Accordingly, he joined the elephant's head to the child's body. The situation was saved. The boy not only regained his life, but now had the added advantage of the elephant's wisdom and, not least important, Parvati was reunited with Shiva. From that time, Ganesh became the symbol of good arising from adversity and thence an averter of evil.

All religious ceremonies begin with slokas honouring Ganesh. Both the *Abhinaya Darpanam* and the *Sangeet Sara* lay down that all dance performances must be prefaced by this invocatory gesture.

In the Ganesh Vandana, the praises of Lord Ganesh have dance syllables blended in with the words. Although this invocation used

Kathak

to be the first item actually danced, the normal practice now is for it to be only played on the pakhawaj before the dancer enters.

The first item to be danced may be one of two pieces, the *rang manj ki puja* which is the offering to the stage, or the Muslim salutation called the *salaami*. In the rang manj ki puja the hands are cupped together above the head and the fingers open out like a flower in the *pushpanjali hasta*, as the hands come down towards the chest. They are then tilted forwards as if offering flowers to the stage. Then follows the water offering and obeisance to the presiding deity. This torah ends with a namashkar which is the Hindu salutation.

Before Kathak went to the Muslim courts this was, of course, the only opening item. Now, *puja* is a form of Hindu worship, so even though rang manj ki puja is purely nritta, its symbolic religious associations made it unacceptable to Muslim patrons. Consequently this was re-choreographed to embody the Muslim salutation or salaam and called the salaami. Nowadays either opening is permissible. In the salaami the right hand only is used and the left is kept at the side. The fingers are held together and very slightly bent. The thumb rests across the palm. The hand is then raised to touch the forehead while the head is bowed as a mark of respect.

The opening item is followed by the *amad*, which is the Persian word for 'entry' or 'coming'. The amad corresponds somewhat to the *alap* in Indian music, in that it establishes the atmosphere. It is always danced to a very slow tempo. The dancer is first seen in one of the characteristic Kathak poses. For example, the pose might be one where the left arm is extended horizontally with the elbow slightly bent and the palm of the hand facing downwards. The right hand is held above the head with the elbow again slightly bent and the palm facing the audience. In both hands the forefinger is bent at the second joint so that the thumb touches it. The left foot is crossed behind the right and rests on the ball of the foot, and the knees are slightly bent. The body from the waist upwards is then turned to face the audience. This produces the tribhanga, or three bends, in the body. The eyes exhibit shringar ras. The attitude is one of composed self-possession.

Very often the amad blends imperceptibly into the thaat, which is the next movement and means generally a decorative or graceful attitude. The neck glides subtly from side to side in time with the tal, and the tremulous fingers, wrists, and eyebrows heighten the

A Kathak Performance

beauty of the thaat. In the Lucknow gharana the thaat is performed on one spot, the only concession to movement being, that the upper half of the body may be swayed very slowly from side to side. The disadvantage here is that the delicate subtlety of the movements can only be appreciated by those sitting fairly near the dancer. Originally, of course, the audience was very limited in number and so this type of thaat was quite possible, but in the comparatively vast auditoriums of today, it tends to be lost to most of the audience. The thaat of the Jaipur gharana is different, in that the dancer glides gracefully first to one side and then the other. The sum is beautifully marked by a sharp turn of the head.

The thaat heralds the gaths. The tempo of the music is increased and the sarangi plays a faster lehra, but the dance itself is still performed at a slow speed. Gaths introduce nritya for the first time and the dancer takes up one theme after another. These need not be connected in any way or presented in any particular sequence. They are easily recognizable as each begins and ends with a palta. The first gaths to be danced take the form of gath nikas. These give only a thumbnail sketch of the story to be represented. After a palta the dancer takes a few steps forward and stops in one of the basic positions, the only movement a barely discernible undulation of the fingers and wrists, giving a hint of the energy held in check. There is a tantalizing pause and then she starts one of the beautiful gaits or gatis for which Kathak is noted. The gati clearly suggests the type and condition of the character portrayed. For example, to show a gopee fetching water from the well, the dancer may take four steps forward, bending to one side in the action of picking up a pitcher and putting it on her head. The gait which follows, together with the expression on her face, would show that a girl is moving slowly with a heavy pitcher on her head.

After gath nikas the programme continues with gath bhava. Even here the story is suggested in an allusive manner, for it is assumed that the audience is familiar enough with the legends to be able to follow them from brief references. In India, of course, this is perfectly justified as the people do know the stories, but outside India it is not so. This should not, however, deter Western audiences, for the stories to be danced are either in the programme or are explained before they are danced. Also, very often the dancers first show how each of the characters are identified. The Lord Krishna for instance, is shown by the hands in the attitude of holding his flute, or by the appropriate gesture for the peacock feathers he wears in his headdress. Shiva is characterized by the snake round his neck or the crescent moon on his head, and Radha by drawing the veil, the ghungat, over her face. The use of mime is very apparent here, and Kathak perhaps uses the technique of mime without the help of words, to a greater extent than any of the other styles. There are numerous stories which might be danced as gath bhavas. One of the most popular is called the *Panghat Gath*. Radha is seen going to fetch water from the well. Krishna is following her. She fills her pitcher and starts on her way back. Krishna meanwhile is bent on mischief and shatters the pitcher by throwing a stone at it. Radha is drenched. She pretends to be angry with him, although perhaps secretly pleased to see him. Brushing him aside with mock indifference, she walks off, wringing her skirt as she goes. All this is shown by the one dancer, who changes from Radha to Krishna, Krishna to Radha, marking each change with a palta.

Up to this point the tempo of the dance has been fairly slow, therefore nritya items like bhajans, ashtapadis, dadras, and thumris may be introduced at any point in the performance so far. It is not usual to add them later than this. The reason is that in Kathak the tempo of the dancing increases gradually as the performance progresses. Reduction in laya is regarded as a fault. All these are poems, so the dances accompanying them are, naturally, interpretative and bhava plays a very important part in them. It would be impossible to do justice to them later for two reasons; the laya would have to be reduced and the dancer's bhava would be impaired for lack of breath after the faster pieces. The nritta items which are to be danced are inserted at any time of the performance according to their laya.

The gaths over, the dance progresses into passages of pure dance in various complex rhythms. These take the form of tukras. Although at first sight all tukras appear to be similar, this is not in fact the case. The *natwari* type of tukras are usually danced first. Natwar is one of the epithets of Krishna the dancer, and the boles of these tukras are said to reproduce the sounds created when Krishna danced on the serpent Kaliya's hood. All boles with *ta-thei thut* and *tigda-digdig-digta* and their variations are classified as natwari.

The pace of the dance is now faster, and in the parans the nritta is danced to compositions played on the pakhawaj. The dancer has

A Kathak Performance

to reproduce the sounds of the boles with her ghungurus. The movements are vigorous and represent the tandav aspect of the dance. The dancer recites a phrase of boles and then dances it as the accompanist repeats it on the pakhawaj. The dancer then recites a longer and more complex phrase and dances this, and so on. Occasionally it is the other way round, and it is the pakhawaj player who calls the phrases. This may result in a friendly competition between them of 'going it better and faster than you'. Such a thing occurs more often between vocalists or instrumentalists during a recital of Indian music. In the days of the princely courts this competition was not infrequently vicious, each trying to prove his superiority over the other. The patrons encouraged this by giving costly gifts or titles to the one who should outdo the other. The defeated one, who had lost face, would either beg permission to leave the court and seek his fortune elsewhere, or would sulk for months, avoiding the company of his fellows. In the meantime, of course, he would be practising furiously, hoping to stage a comeback and regain lost favour. Indian history is full of stories of such rivalries between artistes, wits, theologians, chess-players and even gods and goddesses.

The next part of the recital is usually the paramelu, which is a little faster. The word is from 'para' meaning different and 'mela' meaning union, and in the paramelu the sound syllables of various percussion instruments such as the nakara, the pakhawaj and the tabla, are blended together with the Natwari boles. Paramelus are danced at great speed and come to a climax with the pure footwork of the tatkar.

The tatkar ends the recital. The rhythmic patterns are all-important. The dancer's body is held quite still and the arms are usually folded. Only the feet move, seeming to tread air. There may be an accompanying melody at the beginning but as the tatkar reaches a climax, no sound is heard except that of the drum and the ghungurus. There should be no stomping unless it is required to provide clear punctuation of the rhythmic pattern. The dancer begins with a simple rendering of a tal and goes on to progressively more complicated variations. Sometimes these match the drum beats and at other times they counterpoint them. Just as in a jati, so in a tatkar, the dancer must know within a beat what the drummer is going to play. As some sequences extend over a hundred beats or even more, and boles are not generally recited, the task of the dancer becomes exceedingly difficult. Nevertheless, the essential rapport and unity between dancer and drummer must be maintained without a single lapse. The pleasure lies in the pure aesthetic enjoyment of the rhythm. Tremendous excitement is generated by the sheer precision and clarity of the variations, for no matter how fast the tempo, every fraction of the beat is sounded separately and clearly on the ghungurus.

The suspense, built up with each successive variation, is released in an ecstatic catharsis with the perfect arrival at the final sum.

18

Kathak Training

The caste system does seem to have resulted in some benefits to the social and cultural life of India. Various arts, handicrafts, branches of learning and even scientific disciplines were jealously guarded by the particular sub-caste specializing in each. This strict system of guilds operated a stringent closed-door policy when it came to admitting non-members. The result was that many of the professions became, as it were, secret societies; but on the other hand, they preserved an unbroken tradition by passing the skills and experience of hundreds of years, from father to son. For the son of a dancer it was only natural, and to be expected, that he would follow his father's profession. It would not even occur to him, for example, to take up soldiering or to acquire a formal and academic education in order to work in commerce or the civil service. It was possible, in very rare instances, for a non-caste member to be apprenticed to the guru, but he had to prove his worthiness over many years. He began when very young by performing, more often than not, the menial tasks of the household, and only when the master was convinced that the pupil's *lagan* or call to the vocation was strong enough, would the actual training begin. Meanwhile by simply being in almost constant attendance upon the guru he was able to absorb the atmosphere of the art to which he aspired. This attitude of near servility on the part of the pupils is called *chilmen bharna* and refers to one of the chief duties of the new pupil. He was responsible for preparing the master's hookah. The red clay tobacco container, *chilm*, needed periodic cleaning and replenishment with tobacco and live charcoal. The water through which the smoke passed also had to be changed, and its container freed of nicotine. The pupils were responsible for keeping the hookah in smoking order at all times, and if for some reason it was not ready or prepared exactly the way the master liked it, the offending youth was punished in all manner of ways. Even when he was a trained artiste, it was not below his dignity to see to his guru's or ustad's comforts by pressing and massaging his teacher's feet. This was done, not necessarily because the master's feet were aching, but because it was regarded as a way of acknowledging his superiority, and showing him the respect due to someone who embodied a particular tradition of art and culture.

A word commonly used in the art history of northern India is gharana. The word literally means household, but in its wider context, it means a particular style or method, or more simply, school. The gharanas of music and dancing take their names from the cities in which they flourished or the musician or dancer-saints who founded these schools. The most important school of Hindustani music, for example, was founded by the saint-musician Mian Tansen at the end of the sixteenth century, and those who are descended from him, or have a family tradition of training in his Dhrupad style, no matter how great in their own right, always show their respect for him by touching their ear-lobes whenever they mention his name. In Kathak also, whenever a dancer mentions the name of her guru, she pays her symbolic respect in the same manner.

The gharana system still operates in North Indian music and dance, but now it is possible for more pupils from varying backgrounds to study under the gurus. Two main factors are responsible for this; there has been some breakdown in the caste system, and the princely patrons have been replaced by the State and by academies of art. Any young person nowadays, who has talent and the will to work hard, can win a scholarship to be trained under a recognized teacher. This does not imply a complete alteration in the system of training, as the children of dancers and musicians still follow their family profession. Some gurus and ustads have been employed by the state but have not been, indeed cannot be, reduced to the status of civil servants.

The leading centre for Kathak today is the Kathak Kendra (centre), a department of the Bharatiya Kala Kendra in New Delhi. It has on its teaching staff gurus of both Kathak gharanas, the Lucknow and the Jaipur. The Lucknow gharana is represented by Shambu Maharaj and Brijju Maharaj and the representative of the Jaipur gharana is Guru Sunder Prasad.

Kathak Training

At the moment the centre is functioning in temporary premises, but the Bharatiya Kala Kendra has plans for a new building which should be ready quite soon and which is specially designed to cater for its needs. Until recently it was housed in some old barracks built during the war for the British army and it is on this site that the new centre will stand. These barracks once the epitome of pukka British army tradition, for many years echoed all day to the sounds and rhythms of Indian music. Ordered military uniformity was replaced by an assortment of individual personalities and the seemingly random comings and goings of streams of artistes, dancers and musicians. The barracks consisted of rows of huge rooms, each with a square pillar in the middle to support the roof. As in earlier times there were four occupants to every room. Each girl had a fairly large corner with a bed and very often a stove, since they cooked their own meals. Adjoining this 'hostel' part of the barracks were some smaller rooms which needed no pillars and were probably officers' quarters. These comprised the 'college' section of the Kendra, as it was called for short, where classes were held in vocal and instrumental classical music as well as dancing.

A day at the Kendra begins early. The students start practising at about five in the morning. There are several rooms and in some the singers and musicians go through their scales while in others the dancers practise their tatkar. There is no musical accompaniment for this basic practice and the students have to carry the rhythm in their heads, listening carefully all the time for any flaws in the sound of the ghungurus. The beats must be regular and clearly heard. The aim of every student is to increase the speed of her basic footwork, yet at the same time to sustain the even rhythmic quality in the sound of the ghungurus. Chakkars also form a part of this early morning routine. Here again, the perfection of the chakkars in terms of rhythm and line, must be maintained as the speed of their execution is increased.

This practice session lasts for about an hour. It is then time for a leisurely breakfast and comparing notes. After breakfast there is plenty of time for a shower and a change before lessons begin with Shambu Maharaj. In general they are even able to practise the previous day's lesson before he arrives. There is no special practice costume, as Maharajji prefers the girls to wear their usual saris.

Shambu Maharaj usually comes at about ten o'clock and as they wait for him, the students wonder in what sort of mood he will be that day. Will he ask them to go through the amad or a gath or a difficult tukra? He is a tall, well-built man with an imposing personality. He has a loud voice and a hearty laugh, and it is the laugh that the students are waiting to hear as he greets people on his way to the classroom, for they can then be sure that he is in a good mood. If he is grave or serious, they know they must literally watch their step.

He enters, and each student greets him by touching his feet as a mark of respect. He places his hand on each head to bless them in return. A chair is set for him at one end of the room and he also uses a footstool to rest his leg because of a recent knee injury. On one side of him sit the *tabla navaz* (expert tabla player) and the sarangi player. Shambu Maharaj has a very acute ear and can detect any student, from among the ten or so, who is not in tal — even when they are all doing complicated layakari together.

During the class he sits for most of the time, although when he teaches a new movement or composition, he demonstrates it first, usually without ghungurus. On rare occasions, he asks a student to tie ghungurus round his ankles and, forgetting his injured knee, dances the tatkar with consummate ease, as if floating on air.

He insists that students learn to dance in a very slow tempo initially. There are about four seconds between each beat, and the student has to concentrate on the boles with great attention, lest she should go *bétal* (lose the tal). His theory is, that once a student can be accurate at this painfully slow pace, she will have no difficulty in being precise at the very fast speeds which are used in Kathak. This is really a way of developing sensitivity to time. By doing movements in slow motion, a dancer can also be aware of how correctly she is performing them. She becomes conscious of the feel of correct and incorrect movements.

The dance training begins with *kharé rehné ké tariqué*, which means 'standing positions which have to be held', and the rang manj ki puja. Students quickly learn that there are only small, but nevertheless crucial differences between the passable and the perfect. When a new student first assumes a position, Shambu Maharaj makes a few slight changes. A small adjustment of the arms, a little turn of the body, a tilt of the head, instructions on where to look, and in a few moments she is a perfect statue, balanced and graceful. It is not until she tries, vainly at first, to reproduce the effect on her own, that she realizes just how elusive and important those small and apparently easy changes were. The *nigah* or look of the eyes is another difficulty. Glances in Kathak are subtle and expressive, and those with large eyes are sometimes at a disadvantage, since they tend to look wide-eyed. It takes time, but at last one day the look of approval on Maharajji's face shows that both posture and glance are correct.

Since the tempo during the initial training is so slow, the student has to hold each position for some seconds. Consequently, she learns the various kharé rehné ké tariqué in their natural context, and they become second nature to her when she is dancing. It is essential that she should be able to assume these poses instinctively, because they often come at the end of a fast passage of dance, as in a gath nikas or at the end of a tukra, and have to be held for one bar. If, after swift chakkars, she freezes on the sum in an incorrect pose, not only would her consequent correction be patently obvious to the audience, but her previous virtuosity too would be cancelled out. As a matter of fact, although speed in the execution of chakkars is important, the perfection of line is of even greater importance. It is for this reason that Shambu Maharaj never encourages his students to increase their speed until they have acquired grace of movement at the slower pace.

The rang manj ki puja consists of slow and graceful gestures symbolic of a puja or offering of prayers. The students perform about four different rang manj ki pujas, all with the same boles but with slightly different hand movements or variations in rhythm.

Amads are learnt next, still at a very slow pace. Here again, as far as boles are concerned they learn only two amads, but these are repeated again and again, a little differently each time. In this way the students learn each basic movement without losing interest, because with every repetition they concentrate on a new variable. Some amads contain bhava, which here expresses different moods. This is rendered through facial expression as well as the body as a whole. In this way the students are gradually introduced to bhava in the early part of their training. There are no elaborate eye exercises as in Kathakali, for bhava in Kathak is natural and not so highly stylized. The right glances are achieved by trying to feel the mood being expressed.

Difficult off-beat rhythms too form a part of the early training. Again, if students can execute these rhythms perfectly at a slow speed they will have no trouble with them when the speed is increased. After about six months, when the students have satisfied Shambu Maharaj by their grasp of the basic postures and tals, the training begins to incorporate a greater variety of dance items. First are the gaths. Gath nikas includes many of the typical Kathak poses. The various gaits are also a feature of gaths, and these too are now learnt. Shambu Maharaj is famous for the beauty of his gaths, and these are always an exciting part of Kathak training. His demands as to the line and form of the movements are so exacting that he can spot the smallest mistake immediately. At times he is so intrigued by an error that it inspires him to create an entirely new gath. The family of gaths is thus increasing all the time. Gaths are very short and may take as little as two minutes to perform, but whereas some are learnt quickly others can take days or even weeks to perfect.

Tukras are learnt in the order in which they are danced, starting with tatkar ké tukré, which use the boles ta-thei-thut. With tukras, are always learnt their appropriate boles and in class these are recited before any tukra is danced, so that when they dance them the students can hear the boles being correctly reproduced by the ghungurus. Gradually whole ranges of tukras which belong to each family of tukras are introduced until at last all the varieties are covered. It is only when a student has cultivated a sense of rhythm and what is permissible in each tal, that she can take it upon herself to improvise variations on it.

At about 1 o'clock the morning session ends. If the Guru is happy with the class then, while they are taking off their ghungurus and relaxing after their exertions, he stays on to tell them stories and anecdotes about his great forbears or his own experiences as a dancer.

There now follows a quick shower and lunch. The students then rest for it is too hot for any activity. The heat-haze rises from the roofs and the roads, not a leaf stirs and even the birds are still. Sleep at this time comes easily.

At about four the institute begins to wake once more. Brijju Maharaj now comes to conduct the ballet rehearsals. He is the best male Kathak dancer of the younger generation, enthusiastic, a great experimenter and choreographer. Kathak has always been a solo dance restricted to a small space. The audience sat very near the dancer and she often had only a few square feet in which to perform. An intimate atmosphere existed between artiste and audience, her

Kathak Training

slightest suggestion and subtlest nuance being easily appreciated. In this ambience of the Mehfil there was no need to underline or exaggerate any movement or action. The audience itself consisted of connoisseurs, men of culture, taste and breeding. Today the dancer has to perform on a big stage before large numbers of people. This results in many problems of choreography. Brijju Maharaj has, first of all, to face the difficulty of creating some means of movement within the laws of Kathak. He must also harmonize the actions of several dancers moving at the same time. In spite of such obstacles Brijju Maharaj has produced interesting experimental work.

Before the music directors and the orchestra arrive, the ballet group practises footwork, movements, and such tukras as Brijju Maharaj has composed especially for the ballets. Then, while the orchestra assembles and tunes up, the dancers have a short break. A wide variety of instruments is used to accompany these ballets. The sitar, the sarode, the flute, the violin and the jal-tarang provide the melodies, while the tabla and the pakhawaj are the two percussion instruments used. In addition there are about four singers. Most of the members of the orchestra and the singers are senior students at the Kendra.

Ballet rehearsals go on until 8.30, when the students again have a bath and a meal. Some put in another hour or more of practice before finishing for the day.

During the winter months the Bharatiya Kala Kendra ballet goes on tour to the other important cities and art centres of India.

When the ballet first went on tour in 1958–59, there were not many cities with modern theatres. Most of the time the company had to make do with temporary structures. For instance in Ujjain, the birth-place of the poet Kalidasa, where the troupe performed one of his plays as a dance-drama, the auditorium was a school playground. The stage was erected on one side of it at the end of one of the main corridors, and the classrooms served as greenrooms. But in spite of these makeshift arrangements the whole area was packed with a highly responsive audience. On the other hand, some of the larger cities of India like Delhi, Ahmedabad and Hyderabad have excellent theatres, with every kind of modern equipment and thoughtfully planned greenrooms. There are, however, hazards on some of the older stages, particularly for Indian dancers, since they dance bare-foot. Apart from nails left by stagehands, it is easy to trip up in one of the many crevices of the concrete slabs that form the floors of these stages. But fortunately, many of the new ones are now floored with a hard wood or smooth concrete. The other difficulty is that in order to give the audience a better view, some stages slope down a little towards the front. This means that a dancer can easily lose her balance during fast tukras, and the chaals lose much of their effect. In duets known as *savaal-javaab*, literally 'question-answer', the dancers try to outdo each other in rhythmic variations of tukras, stepping forward for each new one. These, performed even on the slightest incline, can end almost on top of the footlights.

Lack of trained lighting men can also lead to an uncomfortable time for the performers, more so if special lighting effects are needed. This happened once in a duet called *War and Peace*. War was dressed in a fiery red costume and was supposed to dance her fast tukras on a fully-lit stage with red or orange spots. In contrast, Peace was in white; her dance was in a softer style with sangeet tukras. The lighting planned for her was very much more subdued, with just one spot to follow her round. The amateur who was responsible for it, got the whole lighting scheme mixed up, but remembered that Peace was to have a spot. Peace got the spot — straight on to her face, and no matter what she did, he kept it there. The bright light shining directly into her eyes, completely blinded her, so that she was unable to judge even whether she was facing in the right direction. There might well have been an accident, but luckily she managed to get through the performance without mishap.

Fortunately, there are some excellent technicians who work on a freelance basis. One of them is Tapas Sen who has done the lighting for many important ballets such as *Kumara Sambhava* and whose work is always highly professional.

The ballet troupe was also fortunate in having, at that time, Rani Ripjit Singh as its administrator. Ninadi, as she was called, accompanied the troupe on all its tours and was manager when it visited America. Hers was the responsibility of creating all costumes for the ballets. These were made to suit each individual, yet at the same time the general effect was always one of harmony in colour as well as design. She never made false economies in the matter of materials, with the result that in the long run, money was saved. Although Ninadi is no longer with the Kendra, she is still associated with it and will always be remembered by the dancers who gained so much

Kathak Training

from her understanding and sense of humour.

In India those who wish to specialize in stage management, lighting or theatre design, have to join a large company and start as stagehands. At the Kendra they were also dancers, taking part in crowd scenes and folk dances. They worked hard and were extremely efficient; after each show they would have the stage cleared and everything packed and ready in an incredibly short time. One of them, Raj Kumar, was also a talented artist and a great asset to the company since he could both design and make the sets.

When on tour the company was faced with the problem of boarding and lodging a group of forty or fifty artistes. Hotels were considered unsuitable for young ladies, chaperoned though they might be! Consequently, the sponsors who had invited the company had to rent a large house and hire cooks.

In Calcutta the troupe's visit once coincided with a general strike. The rented house in which the dancers were staying was only a block away from the main trouble spot. For three days no one was allowed to go out, so they whiled away much of their time on the roof, watching police vans and ambulances rushing to and fro.

Rampur was quite different. Members of the ruling family there have been great patrons of the arts; the Nawab Sahib, who died recently, on this occasion allowed the troupe to stay at one of his old palaces. Set on a square platform in the middle of a garden, this palace still has a Mughal atmosphere. After dusk, its marble floors, its wide pillared halls and its latticed doors evoked once more the colour and the pageantry, the romance and the splendour of a bygone age.

Touring in India is a stimulating experience. In a country which is so vast there is naturally, every kind of climate and scenery, there are many languages and many different customs and food habits. Food particularly varies quite considerably from region to region. To the members of the Kendra company, most of whom were used to North Indian food and were non-vegetarians, Gujerati cuisine tasted rather sweet and South Indian cooking was quite foreign. They also missed meat, because in many of the towns they went to, the people were almost exclusively vegetarians.

Yet all these minor inconveniences were more than compensated for by the fact that the company's efforts were applauded all over

Kathak

the country, and its dancing appreciated by audiences normally used to other styles of classical dance. The dancers felt that through their art they had been able to communicate where otherwise they might not have done so at all. Regional differences of language and custom had been surmounted by sharing an aesthetic experience. This was the most inspiring part of the tours because the performers, as well as those who saw them, realized that they were integral parts of the same cultural tradition.

Even for a touring company all is not work and the members are often able to go sight-seeing. They may be lucky and arrive at a town during a festival or during one of the many traditional fairs. One year the Kendra ballet group was at Ujjain during the festival of Kartik Purnamashi. It is believed that during this time, if anyone makes a wish and then bathes in the river before the first rays of sunlight appear, then that wish will come true. (It would be as well however, for the visitor to ascertain the distance to the river before setting out, as people can be rather vague about such things. Ten miles can seem more like five to pilgrims who are familiar with the route, and the most determined visitor can still be many miles from the river when the first rays of sunlight appear!)

In spite of a certain amount of prejudice against the performing arts, people are on the whole very kind. No effort is too great for an Indian host. A guest, even if he is a mortal enemy, is regarded as almost sacred.

The ballet troupe has twice been abroad. It toured Russia with *Kumara Sambhava* in 1961 and the United States with a number of short ballets in 1962.

There are four other important centres for Kathak training, Bombay, Baroda, Poona and Lucknow. Lachhu Maharaj has for some time taught in Bombay, and has recently been joined by the two Dagar brothers who compose and direct the music for his ballets. The Baroda University has a very active department of music, dance and fine arts. The Kathak teachers there are Kundan Lal and Sunder Lal, both of the Jaipur gharana. Rohini Bhate has a school in Poona and at Lucknow there is the Bhatkhande Sangeet Vidyapeeth where Mohanrao Kalyanpurkar is head of the dance department.

19

The Ras Lila of Braj

The *Natya Shastra* describes 'ras' and 'rasak' as secondary forms of drama, but today the meaning is more specific and refers to the Ras which Krishna danced with the gopees of Vrindaban.

Krishna as a young man was so attractive that all the gopees were in love with him and longed for him constantly. Krishna, seeing that their love was sincere, promised each one that he would fulfil her desire by dancing with her by moonlight.

One night, when the moon was full, the silvery notes of Krishna's flute echoed through the forest. Each gopee left her home for the banks of the Yamuna, drawn by the irresistible call of the flute. Here Krishna awaited them. He projected himself in such a way that each gopee had a Krishna as a partner. They formed a big circle and the dance began. So enchanting was the dance, that even the gods and goddesses were envious and wished they too could join in. The dance lasted for six months, yet when the gopees returned home they found that their husbands and families did not even know they had been away.

There are five chapters in the *Bhagavad Purana* devoted to a description of the Ras.

The Ras Lila is found as a folk-drama in many parts of India, but the Ras Lila of Braj deserves special mention. It was here in the home of the Krishna legends, that it was first enacted in its present form and has been danced in an unbroken tradition since the sixteenth century.

The stage techniques employed in Ras Lila are very simple. The stage, on the same level as the audience, is quite bare except for a small square platform on which there are two seats, for Radha and Krishna. The only curtain used is held up by two men when a special dramatic effect is required, such as before the *jhankis* or tableaux or sometimes before the introduction of a character. Jhankis punctuate the whole dance-drama and are an important feature of it. They have retained their authenticity and look like sixteenth-century miniatures brought to life.

The Ras Lila may be divided into three distinct parts, the prologue or *nitya ras*, the *sangeet* or didactic piece, and finally the *lila* or play proper.

The dance-drama has a traditional opening with Radha and Krishna seen seated. First the chorus sets the mood by singing devotional songs. The gopees then offer a puja and invite Radha and Krishna to join the dance in the *ras mandal* which is the actual dance area. They form a circle and the Ras begins.

The nitya ras introduces the chief characters but its main interest lies in its dance content. It is the only part of the dance-drama where stylized dance movements and interesting rhythmic pieces called *parmuls*, are used. These have a strong affinity with the Kathak style of the story-tellers of the North Indian temples. There are special parmuls for the introduction of each character. This function of the parmuls can be compared with that of the Pravesar Nritya of Sattra Ras, which has similar dance pieces with distinctive boles for Radha, Krishna and the gopees. Parmuls are danced at speed and have fast pirouettes.

The nitya ras also contains short dance pieces rather like the gaths of Kathak, and even incorporate graceful chaals and eyebrow movements. The interesting choreography of the nitya ras makes a colourful and exciting opening to the Ras Lila.

The sangeet which comes next contains a sermon and devotional songs and poems sung by the chorus. Since, for Vaishnavites, the arts were a means of devotion and were used by them to teach people the traditions and practices of their religion, it was not unusual to find direct instruction such as sermons and expositions, sandwiched between acts in dance-dramas. The sangeet also served to remind people of the religious aspects of the Radha-Krishna legends.

The third and last part of the dance-drama is the lila or main play. For this, one story is chosen from the great wealth of Vaishnavite mythology. The selected story is then danced from beginning to end in one long sequence, without breaks or divisions into acts.

This part of the Ras Lila is entirely in the folk tradition. The gestures and abhinaya are a part of everyday language, used and known instinctively by the villagers. There is no single pattern of presentation. The characters may recite or sing their lines, and the chorus may repeat them. Sometimes the lines are explained in prose as they are being recited. The recitations are punctuated by short dances which include gaths, and by jhankis. Although the dancers appear to vary their styles a great deal they do, nevertheless, follow the chosen, carefully-planned pattern of presentation.

Much of the tradition of sixteenth-century Vaishnavism has been preserved in the Ras Lila. The numerous Radha-Krishna miniatures show the same structure of presentation and the same costumes as are worn today, namely ghaagra, choli and dupatta for women and dhoti for men. Even the language has a sixteenth-century flavour, and the similes used give an insight into the social conditions of those times.

There is much speculation as to whether the Ras Lila, which is a folk art, has borrowed from the classical style of North India. Certainly there are many points of similarity between the two, but these may have arisen because both deal with the same Vaishnavite themes, although Kathak is by no means restricted to these. Bhava in the mime of the Ras Lila, like that of Kathak, is natural although not as developed. Again this resemblance may exist simply because both grew in roughly the same geographical area. They share much Vaishnavite poetry which incorporates dance boles, and was intended to be expressed through singing as well as dancing. The kavita torah in Kathak and the kavita with dance boles in Ras Lila are examples of this. Now, while it is difficult to state categorically that the Ras Lila borrowed from Kathak, it is quite possible, since both dances were at their peak at the same time, that certain elements from Kathak, mainly the gaths, permeated into the Ras Lila through the influence of the professional Kathak dancers, so numerous and popular at that time.

Until comparatively recently, the Ras Lila was performed mostly in temple courtyards, and this sustained its religious character. The dance itself is far from the austere solemnity associated with religion in Western thinking. People enjoyed the Ras Lila. Through music, poetry and dance they brought the happiness of their own lives to their worship, but the religious experience was, nonetheless, profound. The dance is no longer confined to the temples, but has not in any way lost its religious significance.

During the festivals of Vasant, Holi and Janamashtami, the fairs of Vrindaban and Mathura resound to the rhythms of the mridang and the streets are crowded with pilgrims and visitors. The temples, decorated with buntings and marigolds, are filled with the heavy perfume of incense and the rhythmic chanting of Sanskrit hymns. The intermittent call of the conch shell penetrates the noise and bustle to remind the happy crowd that this is essentially a religious festival.

These festivals would not be complete without performances of Ras Lila in the *ras mandals*, dance enclosures, and the open spaces around the town. Meanwhile, the quiet glades and mango groves, so favoured for love trysts, pulsate with the fullness of life and the voice of the koel echoes to the throb of the distant drums.

PART FOUR

Manipuri Dance

20

Manipuri Dance

In the secluded north-eastern corner of India, where the majestic Himalayas loop southwards towards the sea, lies the picturesque valley of Manipur, the Jewelled City. This is the home of the Meities, a people of slight build with slanting eyes. The Meities are a deeply sensitive and artistic race that, by their very isolation from the rest of India, have evolved a unique pattern of life. Here, both the expression and the appreciation of art — and mainly of dance and music — seem to be the focal point in the everyday life of the people. The Meities love to dance. All their joys and sorrows, hopes and aspirations, are interpreted through the dance. Their graceful, rhythmic yet carefully-disciplined movements create their own vivid imagery, whether interpreting life or legend.

It was against this background that Manipuri dance, known as Jagoi in the Meitie language, first took shape. In order to fully comprehend it in its modern setting it is well to know the influences, religious, environmental and historical, that have fashioned the cultural ethos of Manipur; for any art that is so inextricably woven into the daily lives of a community, must surely be a reflection of them.

The Meities were originally followers of the Bratya religion, which was a Tantric cult with an admixture of primitive concepts of cosmology and a worship of Shiva and the Mother Goddess. The early history of the Meities and their religion is obscure, but as the Meities strongly adhere to tradition, many legends have been handed down through the generations and help to unravel some of the mystery surrounding them. Most of these legends relate to Shiva who, according to some authorities, was actually a pre-Vedic deity worshipped in many parts of India long before the advent of the Aryans. All these legends emphasize the Meities' inherent love

Manipuri Dance

for dancing, while some go as far as to attribute the very creation of Manipur to a dance. The story goes that once, while Shiva was seeking a beautiful but secluded spot for dancing the Ras with his consort Parvati, he came upon a lake surrounded by green hills. Seeing that the exquisite beauty of the scene provided an ideal setting for the dance, Shiva drained the lake. The enchanting valley that emerged was now the stage for a Ras that lasted seven days and nights. The hills echoed the strains of the celestial music played by the Gandharvas, heavenly musicians, while the whole valley was lit by the Serpent-god, Nagadeva, with the brilliant reflection from the Mani (Jewel) which he carried in the centre of his hood. The valley thus came to be known as Mani-Pur or the Jewelled City.

The people of Manipur also believe that they are descendants of the Gandharvas and refer to Manipur as 'Gandharvadesa' or the land of the Gandharvas (desa means country or home-land). They substantiate their claim by quoting various passages and episodes from the Hindu scriptures. For instance, Somara is a mountain peak on the eastern border of Manipur, lying directly on the Tropic of Cancer. Here, according to Manipuri tradition, is a gate set by the gods, and known as Mongpokhong. The people who guard the gate and live on this hill are the Tangkhus. Tangkhu is the Meitie name for Tandu, the disciple of Shiva who taught dancing to the sage Bharata. The Tangkhus therefore, regard themselves as the descendants of Tandu. The *Ramayana* does in fact describe such a peak on the eastern border of India, where the sun starts its 'Dakshinayana' or its southward movement. There is also mention in the *Mahabharata* of a gate which stands on this peak.

Another passage in the *Ramayana* describes this same peak as the place where Usha, the goddess of the dawn, first made her appearance with the rising sun. It was Usha who taught the dance of Parvati to the women of India. The women of Manipur, therefore, regard themselves as disciples of Usha, and the black and red stripes which adorn their costume represent the dark night and the rays of the dawn. The Chingkheirol, one of the oldest of Manipuri dances, is a representation of Usha's dance.

These and similar legends are very much a part of Manipuri tradition and have guided and inspired the people through the centuries.

There are virtually no reliable records of the history of Manipur before A.D. 1714. Whatever little is known about the early period, therefore, has been pieced together from references to major events in contemporary literary works and archaeological discoveries. One of the earliest records is found on a copper plate inscription which gives King Khowai Tampak the credit for the introduction of the drum and cymbals into Manipuri dancing. It also describes him as a great patron of the arts. This is very much in accordance with an ancient tradition whereby the kings of Manipur were not only the patrons of the arts but were actually heads of the various art guilds. These guilds were called loisangs, and the guild for the dancers was the Palaloisang. Before gaining any recognized status as a dancer an artiste had to be accepted into his particular loisang. The kings, on the other hand, being the heads of all the loisangs, were the repositories of all art and were often accomplished artistes themselves. The loisangs continue to this day. All the leading present-day gurus are members of the Palaloisang, and it is one of their important duties to constructively criticize and approve all new dance compositions.

The next recorded event — one that found mention in several literary works of the eleventh and twelfth centuries — was the tender love story of Taibi and Khamba. The *Moirang Parba*, a Manipuri epic, is based on this semi-historical legend. Taibi and Khamba were both from a Moirang village just south of Imphal, but while Taibi was a wealthy princess from a high caste, Khamba was of humble birth. He won Taibi's heart by his many valiant deeds, once saving the Manipuris by killing a man-eating tiger single-handed with his spear. But the path of their love was never smooth. Taibi's family of course disapproved of Khamba and went to great lengths to dissuade her from marrying him. Finally, after overcoming several difficulties, the lovers were united, but their happiness was shortlived. One day Khamba, in a teasing mood, tried to frighten Taibi by driving his lance into her tent. Without thinking of the consequences, Taibi took the lance and hurled it back. It pierced Khamba through the heart and killed him instantly. Taibi was overcome with grief and decided to join her beloved. She took up the lance, drove it into her own body and fell dead beside her husband.

Khamba and Taibi are especially remembered for their dancing of the 'Lai Haroba', translated as the 'Merrymaking of the Gods', which is perhaps the best known of all Manipuri dances. They were such exquisite dancers that the Meities came to regard them as

Manipuri Dance

incarnations of Shiva and Parvati, known in Manipur as Nongpokningthou and Panthoibi.

The story of the two ill-fated lovers is related in detail in the *Moirang Parba* and has been incorporated into the main theme of the Lai Haroba of the Moirang School.

The history of Manipur between the twelfth and late seventeenth centuries is obscure, except for references at various stages to cultural exchanges between Manipur and its neighbouring kingdoms, Burma and China. It is said that dancers and musicians from the court of King Kyamba were sent in 1467 to the court of King Pong of Burma, who returned the gesture by sending some of his best musicians to Manipur.

The dawn of the eighteenth century was the beginning of an entirely new era. Vaishnavite missionaries from Bengal found their way into Manipur and propagated a form of Hinduism which regarded Vishnu, the Preserver, as supreme among the Hindu deities. They propagated the attainment of salvation through bhagti. The word bhagti is derived from the root 'bhaj' which means 'to adore'. Bhagti was thus adoration of, or devotion to God. This devotion demanded complete self-surrender, resulting in a union of the soul with the supreme spirit. Vishnu was worshipped chiefly as Krishna, the Blue God, whose love for the gopees of Vrindaban was symbolic of the love that united God with the soul.

The Vaishnavites recognized nine forms of bhagti. These included 'shravna', or listening to the praises of God, and 'keertana' or singing of hymns. Literature, music and art, thus received a great stimulus through Vaishnavism.

King Pamheiba, then ruler of Manipur, was greatly moved by the teachings of the poet-sages of this new faith and readily accepted Vaishnavism. He also tried to convert his subjects to the new religion, and even used force where necessary. Thus he ordered all earlier State records or any literature which referred to the Bratya religion to be burnt. The earlier Meitie images were also destroyed and the use of the Meitie language, in song and worship, was forbidden. Several superstitions were evolved to force the people to give up their earlier beliefs. For instance, it was said that anyone who sang Meitie songs would be turned into an owl if he died at night and into a crow if he died during the day.

This sudden breaking away from earlier traditions proved to be very detrimental to the Meitie Jagoi (Manipuri dance) and Guru

Manipuri Dance

Amubi Singh and Guru Atombapu Sharma, two of the leading gurus of the present day, in a paper on Manipuri dance in 1958, cited this as one of the main causes of the decline of Jagoi in the nineteenth century.

Nevertheless, Vaishnavism had taken root in Manipur and by 1764, when Pamheiba's grandson, Bhagyachandra, became the ruler, it had been firmly established as the religion of Manipur.

Bhagyachandra was himself an ardent devotee of Krishna. It is said that he once had a vision in which Krishna asked him to carve his image from the wood of a certain jack-fruit tree. The king gave orders for the image to be made and then built the famous temple of Govindji at Imphal.

In yet another vision the Ras dance of Krishna was revealed to Bhagyachandra. Inspired by the vision, Bhagyachandra composed the Ras Lila of Manipur, which was first performed at Imphal in the Govindji Temple. He is responsible for three of the six main varieties of Ras in Manipur, the Maha Ras, the Vasanta Ras and the Kunj Ras.

The Ras dances were performed mainly to help the people to understand clearly the divine nature of Krishna who, despite the fact that he lived and loved among the cowherds of Vrindaban, was really an incarnation of Vishnu. In the Maha Ras, Krishna dances with the gopees who, not realizing who he is, become very proud. Radha, when she gets tired, even asks him to carry her. In order to humble their pride Krishna vanishes. Radha and the gopees are extremely distressed. They search everywhere for him and are disconsolate. Krishna finally relents and returns to them; and when they dance again in the moonlight, Krishna appears beside each one. The love of Krishna in this story symbolizes God's love for man, and the search for him is the intense longing of the soul for union with God. The climax, with Krishna making each gopee feel that her fervent prayers have been answered and that she alone, above all others, has been favoured, depicts God's equal love for man, and His revelation to those who truly seek Him.

Dancing thus served an important purpose in Vaishnavite worship. It helped the common man to comprehend the true nature of God. Realizing this, Bhagyachandra erected ras mandals or halls as annexes to temples.

It is also said that Krishna revealed to Bhagyachandra, the true nature of Manipuri dance. This resulted in the composition of the

Achouba Bhangi Pareng, 'Bhangi' meaning dance poses and 'Pareng' a series. This is a dance which incorporates the fundamental body movements of Manipuri dance, and their variations.

The elaborate costume of the Manipuri Ras, known as Kumil, was also a result of Bhagyachandra's genius. The Kumil consists of a long skirt stiffened at the bottom, with a much shorter gathered overskirt of a very fine material. Both are beautifully embroidered with mirrors, silver sequins and silver and gold thread. A close-fitting blouse, usually of dark green velvet and decorated with fine embroidery at the neck and sleevebands, is also worn. At the waist a rectangular strip of material, which is also heavily embroidered in gold and silver, hangs above the shorter overskirt in front. A belt of similar material accentuates the narrow waistline.

Ornaments are profusely worn. There are a variety of necklaces, bracelets, armlets, rings, anklets and ear-rings. The head-dress is particularly beautiful, with a very fine veil covering the face and secured in position on the head by many silver ornaments.

Because it is stiffened at the bottom the long skirt or Kumin hides the movements of the legs, and gives the appearance of gliding when the dancer moves. According to an ancient custom in Manipur, it was improper for a female dancer to reveal the movements of the lower part of her body. The faces, which are half-hidden under the veils, also add to the elusiveness of the picture. This costume is ideally suited to the liquid grace of the Manipuri dance movements, for the overall effect it creates is one in which the dancers appear to float on to the stage, as if from another world.

The Kumil, which is today the main costume for the Ras, has never entirely replaced the earlier costume, Phanek, which is still widely used in some of the Meitie dances, especially the Lai Haroba. In the Phanek, the upper part of the body is covered by a tight fitting blouse. The skirt is a sarong-like garment which has black and red stripes with a border decorated in the traditional pattern of the lotus and the bee. The design of the lotus and the bee on the border of the Phanek is an ancient one, and even decorates some of the earthen pots excavated at Mohenjo Daro in the Indus valley.

Both the Kumil and the Phanek observe the rule of the Trikasta, or the tying of three knots at three places on the waist, as decreed by the shastras. There is one knot at the centre of the waist in front and one at the back, while the third knot is tied on the left side. The

Nyron Sharma

Radha and Krishna in Vrindaban, interpreted by Manipuri dancers
Thambal Yaima and Bihari Sharma

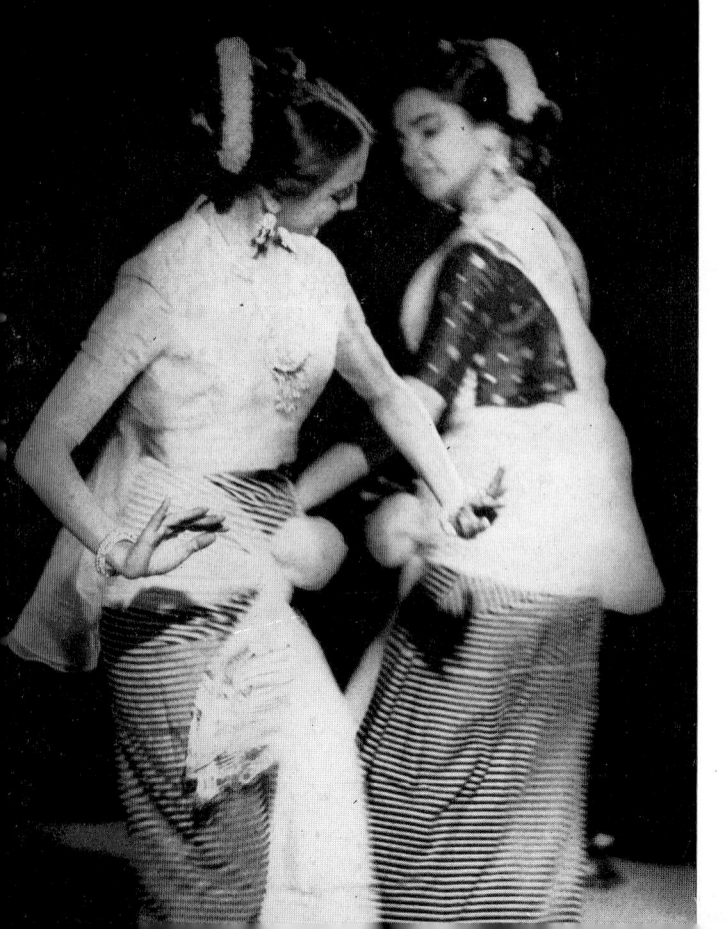

The Pung Cholom
Nyron Sharma

Ranjana and Darshana Jhaveri dance a Manipuri nritta movement
Marc Alexander

Manipuri Dance

Trikasta was also observed by the Kshatriyas, the princely caste, during war.

Bhagyachandra's greatest contribution to the art, however, lies in his efforts to codify systematically all the rules and fundamental principles underlying the technique of Manipuri dance. Dance gurus, from all parts of Manipur, were summoned to his court to help in this work. The *Govindasangeet Lila Vilasa*, attributed to Bhagyachandra himself, is an important text detailing the fundamentals of the Ras and other dances.

Bhagyachandra died in 1789. His reign had seen some of the most significant changes in the history of Manipur. Vaishnavism had been established as the state religion, and with it music and dancing had received a great stimulus. In the field of classical dancing, Bhagyachandra, who was himself regarded as a guru, had composed several new dances, codified the classical dance movements and also fashioned an entirely new costume for the Ras. The kings who immediately succeeded Bhagyachandra carried on this tradition for a few generations and added considerably to the traditional repertoire.

Maharaja Gambhir Singh, who ruled from 1825-1834, was thus responsible for two parengs of the tandav variety, the Goshta Bhangi Pareng and the Goshta Vrindaban Pareng. In 1850 Chandra Kriti Singh ascended the throne of Manipur. He was a gifted drummer and he composed at least sixty-four Pung or drum dances. He also composed two more parengs, both of the lasya variety, namely the Vrindaban Pareng and the Khrumba Pareng. The Nartana Ras is also attributed to him. The death of Chandra Kriti Singh in 1886 brought to an end the golden age of Manipuri dance, which had begun with Bhagyachandra.

A period of decline and gloom now set in. In 1891, Manipur was annexed by the British. As in other parts of India, Indian traditions and customs came to be regarded as old-fashioned and a link with the ignorant past. Dancing, in particular, was frowned upon and regarded as immoral. The true tradition of dance in Manipur was able to survive in only a few temples, such as the sacred temple of Govindji at Imphal. This state of affairs continued into the early part of this century, when Rabindranath Tagore recognizing its potential, included it in his programme of study at his cultural centre, Santiniketan. The revival of Manipuri dance is almost entirely due to his untiring efforts.

Dancing was first tried out as part of the physical education

Manipuri Dance

course for the boys. Later, classes were started for the girls, mainly for the Ras. Naba Kumar, a celebrated teacher from Manipur joined the staff of Santiniketan expressly for teaching the Ras Lila to the women students. Several dance-dramas by Tagore were choreographed by him and based on Manipuri techniques. The phenomenal success of this experiment resulted in a new interest in Manipuri dance among the educated classes of Bengal. Other leading gurus like Senarik Singh, Rajkumar and Nileswar Mukherji were also invited to teach at Santiniketan.

In general the dance style that evolved at Santiniketan was based on Manipuri and Kathakali, but its formulating force was the impelling creative genius of the poet himself. His songs and plays related to modern India and the dance style had to adapt ancient techniques to suit contemporary ideas. However, when Guru Atomba Singh came to Santiniketan as head of the Dance Department, Manipuri dance, naturally, underlined most of the new dance compositions.

It was due to Tagore's interest in it that this dance was first seen outside Manipur. This interest soon spread to other parts of the country. In 1928 Naba Kumar was invited to teach his art in Ahmedabad, and Bipin Singh of Assam popularized it in Bombay and other cultural centres. Among Bipin Singh's most famous pupils are the Jhaveri sisters who are well known to Western audiences. The other successful dancers, who are not Manipuris by birth, Ritha Devi, Savita Mehta and her sister Nirmala, and Thambal Yaima, have had to spend considerable time in Manipur in order to imbibe some of the true spirit that characterizes this dance style.

The chief centre of Manipuri today is the Dance College at Imphal which has three of the greatest living exponents on its staff, Guru Amubi Singh, the principal, Guru Amudon Sharma and Guru Atomba Singh. All three are expert dancers and drum players, but each is a specialist in a particular aspect of the dance. Guru Amubi Singh is renowned for the unique grace he imparts to all his dances. Guru Atomba Singh is known for his tandav compositions, especially the Goshta Lila which has won wide acclaim. Guru Amudon Sharma's great understanding of the technicalities of the dance is astounding. All movements in the Ras, abstract or otherwise convey, according to him, a symbolic truth from Vaishnavism.

This dance college is unique because it upholds the Meitie

Manipuri Dance

traditions and provides for considerable research into ancient songs and dances; at the same time it is a policy of the college to encourage the students' creative talents, and their compositions are tested, often by a very critical audience, in the college theatre.

The Sri Govindji Nartanalaya is another important college where dance-dramas are produced every year. Guru Bipin Singh is the head of this institution. He is also the chief guru of the Manipur Dance Academy of Bombay, which is organized by Nayana Jhaveri. Those wishing to specialize in the Lai Haroba dances of the Maibi (priestesses), can do so at Ibetombi Devi's dance centre in Manipur.

This ancient art has received a great impetus in recent years. While much is being done in Manipur itself to recruit fresh talent, some interesting work is also being carried out in Calcutta, Bombay and Delhi.

21

Manipuri Technique and Music

The Manipuri dance style is distinguished by its overall stress on the expression of moods and sentiments through graceful movements of the body. This quality of lyrical grace and fluidity has been developed to a degree not found in any of the other classical dances of India. The head, the hands, and the feet move together in perfect harmony and the mood is created by the entire body, without undue emphasis on any one part.

This natural grace is acquired after years of strenuous and arduous practice on the part of the dancers, whose training follows a traditional pattern and adheres strictly to the rules laid down in several ancient texts, such as the *Laithak Leikha Jagoi*, the *Govindasangeet Lila Vilasa* and the *Krishna Rasasangeeta*. Of these the *Govindasangeet Lila Vilasa* was compiled during the reign of Bhagyachandra and contains a systematic codification of the hastas. It also describes in detail the costume and performance of the Ras Lila, as well as other features of the technique of Manipuri dance.

When the whole of the body is the medium of expression, a clear distinction naturally arises between the soft, flowing movements and the strong virile ones. The former represent the lasya and the latter, the tandav aspects of the dance. Although this classification of dance movements is encountered in all the classical dances of India, the distinction is nowhere as precise and well defined as in Manipuri dance where strict rules govern the movements of the body in both cases.

The men's dancing is swift and vigorous, characterized by leaps, and sitting positions with the knees bent slightly outwards. The women's dancing on the other hand, is distinguished by smooth, gliding movements. The women never jump boldly, except in some of the ancient cosmic Maibi dances which represent both the

Manipuri Technique and Music

male and female energies, and in a few tribal dances. Generally speaking, the lasya movements must be soft, natural and rounded. To achieve this the limbs are never stretched to their utmost limit. The hands are never raised above the head or lowered below the knee; the feet are kept very close together, while the knees are slightly bent. The hands usually move diagonally while the body and head move and bend correspondingly. The result is a continuous flow of graceful movements.

When the dance in the lasya style is slow, with restrained movements, it is called Smitangam, but when the tempo is increased and the movements are more free, it becomes Sfuritangam. The latter involves great variations of rhythm.

Tandav dancing, being masculine, requires strong and virile movements. There are, in fact, three types of tandav movements. In the *gunthanam*, which resembles the lasya, the feet are kept close together but the movements are, on the whole, stronger than in the lasya. The *chalanam* consists of three distinct vertical movements involving the raising of the feet up to the calf, the knee and the thigh. The *choloms*, which are dances performed by male dancers as part of the Sankeertan, an important feature of Vaishnavite worship in Manipur, are examples of chalanams. *Parasaranam*, the last of the tandav varieties, requires a stretching of the limbs to the utmost.

Although the *angik abhinaya* in Manipuri involves an interpretation of bhava through the entire body, gestures and movements of the individual parts are nonetheless significant, and have, therefore, been codified in considerable detail. The *Govindasangeet Lila Vilasa* mentions at least twenty-five gestures of the single hand and fourteen gestures using both hands, and gives their uses. These gestures resemble closely the hastas of the *Natya Shastra* and must originally have been derived from it.

The movements of the hands, or *bahubhedas*, are also classified. The angle of the hand and the extent of each movement is carefully explained. The *shirbhedas*, or movements of the head, are closely linked with the bahubhedas as the eyes must always follow the hands.

There are also movements for the neck, shoulder, thighs, knees, and feet.

The movements of the feet and the accompanying foot positions are known as *chari*. These may be of four types; *bhaumichari* are movements on the ground (bhaumi means the earth), *utpluti* are movements used while jumping, and *upavishta* are movements and positions of the feet in a sitting posture. *Bharmari* are positions during turns or in spiral movements and are generally classed as tandav.

In addition, there are several traditional poses and attitudes. These again may be of many kinds. Standing poses are called *sthankas*, while sitting poses are called *upavishta sthankas*. Here again the position of the hands and head in relation to the rest of the body follows strict rules.

It must be remembered however, that the dance in Manipur is mainly an expression of the creative instincts of an artistic and sensitive people. As such it requires more than the careful physical disciplining of the body to master it. The Manipuri dancer must possess an instinctive understanding of human nature. Although the representation of the sentiments and the emotional states is not through elaborate and stylized facial expressions as in Kathakali, their expression is a major aspect of the dance. Thus while the face remains serenely immobile or uses only the gentlest of expressions, the body establishes the mood through the beautiful flowing movements.

In Manipuri dance the predominant mood is love or shringar. This is best seen in the dances which were composed after the conversion of the Meities to Vaishnavism, when the stories of the love of Radha and the gopees for Krishna became the dominant theme. Two aspects of the shringar ras stand out clearly. They are *viyog* or separation and *sambhoga* or union. These are symbolic of the soul's search for, and ultimate union with, the Supreme Spirit. These two moods and their variations, sixty-four in all, are explained in detail in Rupa Goswami's *Ujjavalanilamani*, which serves as the main authoritative work on abhinaya for the Manipuri dance-dramas.

Abhinaya involves the 'carrying towards', or conveying of an emotional experience to the audience. In Manipur this is specially important, for here the dancers and the spectators are directly involved in the performance. In certain dances like the Thabalchong, the onlookers may only attend a performance if they themselves adopt a dance pose. During the dancing of the Bhangi Pareng, on the other hand, the audience is required to remain quite still and meditate.

The artistes are not bound always to interpret the words of the song exactly, especially in Holikakrida (dance depicting the festival of Holi) and Kanduka Khel (dance of Krishna and the cowherds playing with a ball). There are other dances in which the movements of the body may only suggest the meaning of the songs while not interpreting them word for word.

MUSIC

The music is provided by four kinds of instruments including percussion instruments like the Pung (the Manipuri drum) and other varieties of drums, and wind instruments like the flute, conch shells and a trumpet-like horn. There are the stringed instruments such as the israj, tamboura, and pena which give the main melody and the metallic instruments like the cymbals (known as kartal) which provide an additional rhythmic effect.

Unlike the music of the rest of India, Manipuri music has developed mainly as an accompaniment for the dance. It is, therefore, bound by the technicalities of the dance. Short musical compositions like the *swarmala* (a combination and arrangement of swaras or musical notes), the *chaturang*, and the *keertiprabhand* (a song incorporating rhythmic sounds) form an important part of the dancer's repertoire.

A wide variety of tals is used and these may have from four to fifty-four beats in each bar. The tals most commonly used are the tanchep, of four beats or matras, the menkup, of six matras, and the rajniel, of seven matras.

Some dance compositions, the *pung cholom* and the *kartal cholom* for instance, are based entirely on variations of rhythmic patterns.

A tal prabhand may be composed of two or more different tals while certain dances have rhythmic patterns woven round the recitation of slokas, or verses. Another popular dance composition is the Sheigonnabi in which poems are either sung or recited with the drum following the rhythm of the words or syllables.

22

Lai Haroba and Ras Lila

Manipur has a large variety of traditional dances. The best known of these are the Lai Haroba and the Ras Lila; both are dance-dramas that use the Manipuri technique of projecting bhava through body movements.

LAI HAROBA

This dance-drama dates back to the early Meitie culture and mirrors the synthesis of Tantric and early Hindu cultures. The word 'Lai' means God, and Lai Haroba is best described as 'The Festival of the Gods'. It is danced each year in the villages of Manipur, during the month of Chaitra. The performances last several days and nights. Although most of the villagers participate in the dances, the principal roles are danced by highly-trained professional male and female dancers, who are known as Amaibas and Amaibis in the Meitie language and also sometimes as Maibas and Maibis. The Amaibis are dancers who have dedicated their lives to the service of the temple and may be compared to the Devadasis of the South Indian temples. There are differences, however, for among the Meities these temple-dancers belong to both sexes. The institution is not generally a hereditary one and the Amaibis are allowed to get married and lead normal family lives.

The dancers have to undergo a long apprenticeship, after which their lives are spent in the service of God through the dance, which as we have already seen, is an important mode of worship.

There is a striking similarity between the term 'amaiba' as used by the Meities and its equivalent 'ameebah' in the *Rig-Veda*, a fact strongly suggestive of the antiquity of the Meitie dance or Jagoi. Another interesting point about this dance is that the Amaibas, who

Lai Haroba and Ras Lila

are the male dancers, dress and regard themselves as the female attendants of Shiva and Parvati.

The dancers have a distinctive white costume, unadorned apart from the colourful striped border of the overskirt. The arms are completely covered by the long-sleeved blouses. The ornaments are less elaborate than those used with the kumil. Often a flower is worn behind one ear.

The Lai Haroba is a dance-drama based on the primitive Meitie concepts of cosmology, the belief being that the earth was brought down from heaven by nine gods and seven goddesses. The whole drama is danced in stages.

The first stage consists of seven dances in which the Amaibis summon the deities by placing flowers on the waters of a nearby stream. These flowers are then brought back to the village in procession and the Amaibis enact the *Laihunba* or the scattering of the flowers, symbolic of the infusing of life into the gods and goddesses. An Amaibi now prepares a seat by placing a cloth on a plantain leaf in the centre of the stage. She then worships Indra and moves anti-clockwise to the four corners of the stage, offering prayers to the deities that watch over the stage and the artistes. One can detect here the influence of the *Natya Shastra* which stipulates that every performance must commence with a puja in order to prevent any accidents that may be caused by the forces of evil. The Meitie word for dance, 'jagoi', means moving in a circle, and they claim that the tradition of moving anti-clockwise in the dance is taken from the *Rig-Veda*, which states that dancers must move in accordance with the movements of the planets.

The second part of the dance is the Lai Pou which begins with the chanting of the words 'Hoirou' and 'Hoya', seven times in seven different notes. The Lai Pou is concerned with the birth or incarnation of a god, the building of a temple to house him, and finally the making of fine garments for him. The miming is astonishingly detailed. Using the appropriate mudras, the dancer describes the development of the child inside the womb, and then its birth. In the building of the temple, we see the gathering of the sticks, the laying of the foundation and the thatching of the roof. After this the temple is blessed and dedicated to the god. The next part shows the growing of cotton from a seed to when it is ready for picking. The cotton is picked, and carefully woven into beautiful garments worthy of the deity.

We now come to the love duets which are performed by dancers enacting the parts of Nongpokningthou and Panthoibi, who are believed to be the incarnations of Shiva and Parvati. Meitie tradition has it that Panthoibi was not the wife of Nongpokningthou, just as Radha was not the wife of Krishna. The enchanting movements of these duets are restrained yet powerfully eloquent, and the imposing rhythms have an almost primitive appeal.

The last stage of the festival consists of several dances performed for the pleasure of the gods. In these the dancers depict various sports, fishing and hunting. After many days of dancing the Lai Haroba comes to an end, and the villagers bid farewell to the deities by placing them in boats and sending them downstream on their journey into the unknown.

Today there are three types of Lai Haroba. These are the Chakpa, the Konglei, and the Moirang, each slightly different and particular to its own region.

The Moirang Lai Haroba gives prominent place to the story of Khamba and Taibi, the legendary lovers and dancers. The Khamba-Taibi duet is a dance of fulfilment in which the lovers celebrate their marriage. It is set to an ancient and famous love song. This dance beautifully contrasts the forceful and virile movements of the warrior Khamba with the sweet and gentle ones of the princess Taibi. She wears a phanek with red, pink and black stripes and a flowered border at the bottom. Her emerald-green velvet blouse is embroidered in gold and silver. The hair is worn loose to the waist and the head circled with a red band with delicate gold fillets. Khamba wears a purple and gold dhoti and a green velvet jacket with gold trimmings. His head-dress consists of a handsome white turban decorated with red and gold embroidery and with a majestic peacock plume stemming from its white cloud-like centre. The white stands for truth and peace and the red for courage and sacrifice. The curve of the upper part of the turban represents the snake god Pak Hangba whom the Meities worshipped originally.

The Lai Haroba embodies the very essence of the Meitie cultural heritage. It has withstood the test of time; for even Bhagyachandra and his Vaishnavite descendants could not, for all their fanatic zeal, annihilate it. Its importance, however, did decline under the Vaishnavite rulers, who sought to replace it and fire the imagination of their subjects with a new type of dance, the Ras Lila.

THE RAS LILA

The love poetry of the Vaishnavite sages such as Chaitanya, Surdas, Jayadeva and others, was set to music and easily adapted for the dance. In Manipur, the Ras Lila of the Vaishnavites became very popular and soon acquired a significant place in the life and worship of the Meities. This may be attributed to the Meities' love for dancing and their natural interest in anything pertaining to God and religion.

The traditional Ras was of three varieties: the Tal Rasak, the Danda Rasak and the Mandal Rasak. In the Tal Rasak clapping was an important feature, while in the Danda Rasak the rhythmic effect was produced by sticks. Each dancer was provided with a pair of sticks and these were struck together as the dancers moved, weaving patterns as they danced. The Mandal Rasak consisted of a circle of female dancers representing the gopees and a male dancer, representing Krishna, in the centre. All three types of Rasak are found in Manipur.

Ras may be tandav or lasya. Of the seven generally accepted varieties five, Maha Ras, Vasanta Ras, Kunj Ras, Nitya Ras and Dija Ras — all of which relate to stories of Krishna and the gopees — are of the lasya type. Goshta Ras and Ulukhal Ras are of the tandav type and tell of the exploits of Krishna as leader of the youths of Vrindaban, of how he tended the cows, played games, rode horses and, even as a child, killed demons.

The Ras Lilas are performed at the appropriate times of the year in the Ras Mandals, or the specially erected halls adjacent to the temples. The performance usually continues from dusk to dawn and sometimes carries on for many days.

The predominant mood of the lasya variety of the Ras is shringar. Although each Ras Lila pertains to an incident in the Radha-Krishna theme, the action is not continuous. The drama is often interspersed with compositions like the Chalis and the Bhangi Parengs. The Chalis are short pure dance pieces which reveal the fundamental aspects of Manipuri dance technique and the Bhangi Parengs are dance compositions using a series of traditional dance poses. The Bhangi Parengs may be tandav or lasya and are used with the appropriate Ras Lilas. The Achouba, Vrindaban and Khrumba Bhangi Parengs, which are of the lasya variety, are used in the Maha Ras, the Vasanta Ras, the Kunja Ras, the Nitya Ras and

Manipuri Dance

the Dija Ras, while the Goshta Bhangi Pareng and the Goshta Vrindaban Pareng are used in the Goshta Ras and the Ulukhal Ras.

The sequence of each Ras Lila is strictly codified. Generally speaking the lasya types begin with short pieces such as the Krishna Abhisar (Krishna going to meet Radha), the Radha Abhisar (Radha on her way to meet Krishna secretly), the Krishna Nartan (dance of Krishna), the Radha Nartan (dance of Radha) and the dances of the chief gopees. These pieces are by way of introducing the main characters in the dance-dramas. The Chalis and Bhangi Parengs are also danced at this stage.

When the main theme of the dance-dramas is enacted the Bhangi Parengs serve as links between one scene and the next. The Ras Lila generally concludes with the Pushpanjali or the offering of flowers, and a prayer.

The story and significance of the Maha Ras, including the Antardhyan or the vanishing of Krishna, and his eventual re-appearance to complete the dance with the gopees, has already been described in Chapter 20.

The Vasanta Ras describes the Spring festival of Holi. Vasanta means Spring and Holi is the festival of colours, when the young men and women of the village spray each other with coloured water or powder. The general air of festivity leads to many practical jokes. Many songs have been written about Holi and most of them tell of Krishna having the upper hand. Radha is described as being shy and hesitant and afraid that Krishna might overstep the limits of propriety in the presence of the village folk.

The story of the Vasanta Ras is one of Radha's jealousy and anger at Krishna's neglect of her. We see Krishna and the gopees dancing and enjoying themselves. Suddenly Radha notices that her lord is flirting with the other gopees. She tries to draw his attention, but Krishna is so enraptured by the other gopees that he does not notice her, or perhaps he pretends not to notice her. Radha's jealousy knows no bounds and she leaves the Ras Mandal. When at last Krishna realizes her absence, he is filled with remorse and goes out to look for her. One of Radha's sakhis (girl companions) leads Krishna to Radha, but Radha has been hurt too deeply and refuses to see him. Krishna uses all his charm to persuade her and in the end melts her anger with his winning words. The two are reconciled and dance together in happiness.

The Kunj Ras is a delightful dance describing how Radha and

Lai Haroba and Ras Lila

Krishna set out to meet each other (the Radha and Krishna Abhisars), and later of their tryst in the 'kunj' or bower. The Nitya Ras again describes the Abhisar, and the Millan or divine union of Radha and Krishna. This Ras ends on a devotional note, with Radha surrendering her soul to her lord.

In the Goshta Ras, Krishna and Balaram are taught how to tend cows. They play ball with the other cowherds and, when they are hungry, Balaram takes them to a palm grove. The palm grove, however, is guarded by the ass-demon, Dhenukasur, who challenges the boys. Balaram is angry and seizes Dhenukasur by the legs and hurls him into a tall tree. Dhenukasur falls off the tree and dies.

We see more of Krishna's pranks in the Ulukhal Ras. His foster mother in exasperation ties him to a mortar so as to keep him out of trouble. Krishna wants to join his companions and so escapes with the mortar. But in his hurry Krishna and the mortar, to which he is still attached, get wedged between two trees. He pulls, heaves and brings down the trees with a great crash, and in doing so he releases two youths who had been imprisoned in them.

The stories of the Ras Lilas strive to bring out the divine nature of Krishna; and even when describing the most passionate meetings with Radha they do not neglect to remind one of his real self.

The Lai Haroba and the Ras Lilas have many similarities. The Lai Pou of the Lai Haroba is very similar to the Bhangi Pareng of the Ras Lila, and the love duets that find such an important place in both dances are so alike that one may be led to believe that only the names of the principal characters have been changed.

The prominent role of the Maibas and Maibis in the Lai Haroba can be compared to that of the Sabaja Panthis in the Ras Lila. The men dancers among the Panthis also dress like women and play female roles.

Many authorities believe that with the coming of Vaishnavism, the Lai Haroba became the Ras Lila with a few minor changes in the dance technique. The costume and music, however, were changed considerably.

23

Other Dances

Besides the Lai Haroba and the Ras Lila, three other dance-dramas have become important over the years. All three are associated with the Vaishnavite cult; but while the first two have mythological themes relating to the *Mahabharata*, in the one case, and the *Ramayana*, in the other, the third is based on the life of one of the celebrated Vaishnavite sages.

The Bharat Yuddha, or Battle of India, is a dance which recounts the story of the *Mahabharata* and is based on the war of succession between the Kauravs and the Pandavs. The Pandavs are generally regarded as the heroes of the dance-drama, as they were the eventual victors and the ones who were favoured by Krishna. Arjun, one of the Pandavs, had Krishna as his charioteer and counsellor during the decisive battle at Kurukshetra.

The Lanka Kand, the second dance-drama, is taken from the *Ramayana* and is the story of the saintly king Rama, whose wife was abducted by Ravana the king of Lanka. Rama eventually recovered his wife Sita after waging a fierce war against Ravana.

The Gouda Lila relates the story of Chaitanya the great missionary of Vaishnavism who came to be known as Maha Prabhu. It was he who instituted in Bengal the Goudiya form of Vaishnavism with its emphasis on Bhagti. Now Bhagti, or true adoration of God leading to ultimate union with Him, could be achieved in several different ways. Chaitanya believed that the most rewarding form of Bhagti was Sankeertan or community prayer, where the Lord's name was recited or sung in chorus. This form of worship, he maintained, would lead to 'the losing of one's self in rapture'. Chaitanya's disciples often reached a state of ecstatic delirium in which they would roll on the ground, embrace each other or burst into uncontrolled tears.

Other Dances

It was this highly emotional form of Vaishnavism that reached Manipur and took root there. Sankeertan, thus, became a part of community worship and today some of the most highly evolved Manipuri dances, such as the brilliant Pung Cholom and the Kartal Cholom are associated with the Sankeertan.

THE CHOLOMS

The Choloms are a tandav variety of dance belonging to the chalanam group. Both the Pung and Kartal Choloms are performed by large groups of well-trained dancers called Palas.

The Pung Cholom has rightly been called the king of the male repertoire. The dancers wear almost identical costumes consisting of white turbans, white dhotis and a folded shawl over the left shoulder. The pung or drum is secured in a horizontal position in front of the dancer by means of a strap which goes over the right shoulder and is then tied at the back. This leaves the dancer's hands free, either for playing the pung or for gesticulation.

The powerful rhythms of the pung match the dynamic grace of the dancers as they imitate several natural phenomena, such as thunder, rain, storms, or the beating of the human heart. The dancers produce the sounds with the pung and complement them with body movements. The dance includes some fiery drumming with high leaps and spins.

The Kartal Cholom is similar to the Pung Cholom, except that the rhythmic effects are achieved with cymbals or kartals. These are struck against each other to produce sounds which correspond with the syllables of the accompanying drum, the kartal marol. Although gestures are limited, for each performer has a pair of kartals, the dancers imitate the gaits of various animals and birds, at the same time exhibiting their mastery over the intricacies of rhythm.

The choreography of the Kartal Cholom is simple. The entire group of dancers and musicians forms one enormous circle and moves together in the same direction.

There is also a type of Kartal Cholom, the Mandilla Cholom, which is performed by women. This dance is used in a decorative way to accompany devotional songs about Krishna. Here, one cymbal represents Radha and the other, Krishna. Striking them, one against the other, denotes their playing together joyfully. Attached to these cymbals are long red tassels which make swirling patterns in the air.

There are two minor Cholom dances, both tandav in style. These are the Duff Cholom and the Dhol Cholom, the duff being a tambourine and the dhol a large drum used in folk music.

All the Cholom dances and the Sankeertans which form an integral part of them may be performed throughout the year, at births, deaths, or marriages and at the important religious festivals. They are also often danced as introductions to the Ras Lilas.

KUBAK ISHAI

The Kubak Ishai has sometimes been described as a variety of Tal Rasak. This dance stems from an ancient custom whereby a king's procession was accompanied by retainers who clapped rhythmically as they followed him. This tradition was absorbed into later Vaishnavite rites, so that the Kubak Ishai is now danced each year at the festival of Jagan-nath, when Vishnu is worshipped in all his splendour as the Sun God. Replicas of the god's chariot are taken out in procession to the singing of hymns and the chanting of sacred verses.

The Kubuk Ishai is dominated by the mood of viyog or separation. It is said that once, when one of the sages was watching the chariots being drawn through the city, he fell suddenly into a trance and saw himself as Radha torn with grief, as she watched her lord mount his chariot to leave for Mathura. This incident is now enacted as part of the Kubak Ishai.

Kubak Ishai may be tandav or lasya, but in either case the predominant mood is still viyog.

Other traditional dances include the Ougrihangal, or Dance of Shiva in the tandav style, the Chingkheirol, or dance describing the rising of Usha or the dawn in lasya style, and the Ke Ke Ke or Thavalchongbi which is sometimes performed as part of the Lai Haroba.

Some tribal dances also form part of the Manipuri dance style. It is because of this, and the fact that in many of the dances (Ke Ke Ke for example) the audience participates in the performance, that all Manipuri dancing was sometimes classified as a folk-art. Manipuri, however, contains a very rich variety of codified interpretative

India Tourist Office, Toronto

Uday Shankar

Sonal Mansingh in an Odissi pose

Marc Alexand
Indrani Rehman dances an item in Odissi style

Other Dances

movements and intricate rhythms and can, therefore, justly be regarded as one of the main classical dances of India.

Dancing in Manipur is often used in community worship so as to establish a close relationship between man and his Creator. The dancers are, as it were, at the High Altar, while the spectators by identifying themselves with the dancers, feel that they too are privileged to wait upon the Lord.

24

Sattra Dances of Assam

The Sattra dances originated in the Brahmaputra Valley region of Assam at the close of the sixteenth century. They were the direct outcome of a new religious upsurge that was slowly spreading throughout India in the form of Vaishnavism. It has already been seen that all the arts received a great stimulus during this period and that most of the leaders of the Vaishnavite school of thought were themselves artistes of merit. Sankardeva, who brought Vaishnavism to this part of Assam, was no exception. He was a talented poet and musician who sought to teach his followers the fundamental truths in simple similes that could be easily understood. It was to achieve this end that most of his dance-dramas were written and performed.

The dance technique used in Sankardeva's dramas probably owed a great deal to the existing dance styles in the neighbouring regions. But whatever the origin, it soon became a distinctive style capable of holding its own alongside the other classical dance styles of India.

Most of the dance-dramas of the Sattra school were written by Sankardeva and his chief disciple, Madhavdeva, and portrayed incidents from the lives of Krishna and Rama. These plays are collectively known as *Ankiya Nat* or simply *Anka*.

Perhaps the most striking feature of the Ankiya Nat is the lack of prominence given to Radha. Krishna is worshipped here as the Prince rather than the cowherd, as the destroyer of evil and hate, rather than the universal lover rousing the passions of the simple gopees. This is because the Sattra dances are based on the *Bhagavad Purana* and the *Bhagavad Gita*, which are the earliest works relating to Vishnu's incarnation as Krishna. Krishna's life in Vrindaban, although mentioned in these works, is not given the same importance as his life after he left home, because it was then that he accomplished his first mission of destroying evil in the person of the cruel king Kansa. He never again returned to Vrindaban or to his childhood companions. Also, Rukmini, is regarded as Krishna's wife and consort.

Radha, who is generally considered Krishna's favourite among the gopees, was not regarded as such in either the *Bhagavad Purana* or the *Bhagavad Gita*. The Radha-Krishna theme was emphasized by those who advocated the bhagti cult as a means of salvation for the soul. True bhagti demanded that the love for the Maker and Preserver be an all-consuming emotional experience, as is the love between a man and his beloved. A perfect example was found in Krishna. He was a god, and at the same time had been loved passionately by the gopees, who had forsaken their homes and husbands for him. Radha was later singled out as the most favoured of the gopees. She symbolized the soul while Krishna was the god. In loving him above all else, she was showing that God must always come first in one's life.

Unlike most of the other dance styles of India, the Sattra dances adhere to the earlier image of Krishna and even dances like the Gopee Pravesar Naach and the Sattra Ras, which relate to the love of the gopees for Krishna, conspicuously refrain from any mention of Radha.

The Sattra dance-dramas start with a musical prelude known as Dhemali, where one or more musical pieces may be rendered. These include solos on percussion instruments like the *khol*, or even vocal items. The leader of the orchestra sometimes interprets the verses being sung by the use of simple abhinaya.

The Dhemali is followed by the entry of the Sutradhara who conducts the rest of the performance. The Sutradhara has the key role in the dance-dramas, for he announces the play and sets the scene for the action to follow.

In order to make the first appearance of the Sutradhara dramatic, a screen is held up to shield him from the view of the audience. The suspense is heightened by the chanting of verses and the beating of drums. Suddenly, the screen is pulled away and the Sutradhara appears kneeling at centre stage with his forehead touching the ground. He begins his dance in a very slow tempo, moving his limbs slowly as he rises. As the dance progresses, the tempo increases and the movements become much more vigorous.

A notable feature of the dance of the Sutradhara is the occasional recitation of slokas. The syllables of these slokas are reproduced by the orchestra and rendered in dance by the Sutradhara. This manner of rendering the syllables of the verses may be compared to that of the chhands in Kathak. Similar slokas are found in the Dances of Krishna and the Dances of the Gopees, that follow. While dancing a sloka the dancer also interprets it, using appropriate gestures.

The costume of the Sutradhara is the result of the blend of Hindu and Muslim cultures. He is dressed in a white long-sleeved coat or *jama* with a full, gathered skirt, rather like that of a figure from a Mughal miniature. He also wears a white turban and elaborate ornaments.

After completing his dance the Sutradhara introduces the characters in the play. These introductions consist of a succession of short dances, known collectively as Pravesar Nritya. The name comes from 'pravesh' meaning 'to present'. Each character appears on the stage in order of importance, the first to dance being the hero, either Krishna or Rama. This dance is called Gosai Pravesar Nritya, 'the Dance of the Lord'.

As the Sutradhara announces the hero, the orchestra begins to play a suitable hymn or song from the text of the play. A screen is held up and an arch of lighted torches is made. The audience bows low as, by the removal of the screen, Krishna or Rama is seen for the first time. The short dances of the Gosai Pravesar Nritya describe the hero's deeds of valour. Some slokas also are recited and rendered in dance.

The gopees are next introduced in the Gopee Pravesar Naach. The dancers are usually young boys, as women are not allowed to take part in these dance-dramas. The movements here are soft and delicate and the gaits of the dancers are very important because they reveal the characters of the persons being represented.

This procedure continues until every character has been introduced to the audience. Then the play itself commences.

The main dance-drama can take several hours and is enacted without a break. It is made up of dances such as the Jhumuras, the Yuddhar Naach, the Nritya Bhangi, the Natuwa Naach and the Sattra Ras.

The Jhumuras were introduced by Madhavdeva and are divided into two sections, the Ramdani and the Ga-naach. The Ramdani is danced before the songs of the women characters and the Ga-naach with the songs. The Jhumura costume combines both male and female dress, a turban, a jacket, and a gathered skirt. Krishna was for each gopee, as it were, a crown on her head, and in this dance they wear turbans to symbolize the fact that they still cherish him as such, even though he has left them.

The Yuddhar Naach depicts scenes of battle, mostly the deeds of Krishna and Rama, and so its movements are strong and in a very quick tempo. Because of its heroic nature this dance is a favourite with the village audiences.

Since Nritya Bhangi uses songs from the Jhumuras, the division of the dance into Ramdani and Ga-naach is also found here. Its choreography is particularly pleasing for the dance is performed by a group of six dancers, three gopees and three gopas. The songs are not interpreted through any elaborate or stylized facial expressions. Only a few simple gestures are employed from time to time.

The word 'natuwa' means an actor and was originally applied to all dancers who took part in the dance-dramas. In later years the term Natuwa Naach came to mean the particular type of dance which was based on the lyrics of the *Ankiya Nat*. The songs used for the Natuwa Naach were those sung by women characters.

The natuwas are generally young boys who wear women's costumes consisting of a ghaagra and a tight fitting blouse, with a veil draped over the head.

The Sattra school also has its own variety of Ras dances which are based on the description of the Ras in the *Bhagavad Purana*. These dances are performed by Krishna and the gopees, but again there is no mention of Radha.

The dancers of the Sattra school start to train when still very young. Special exercises for the body and limbs ensure the delicacy required in playing female roles. The dancers are also taught the art of make-up. Masks are used quite often, especially for characters like Hanuman and Dhenukasur the ass-demon.

Although the Sattra dance style does not use any codified or systematic method in movement or abhinaya, the influence of the *Natya Shastra* is unmistakably present. The hastas used bear a resemblance to those prescribed in the shastra, and it also stresses the fundamental rule that the eyes must follow the hand if true representation is to be achieved. The Dhemalis too have their counterpart in the Purvaranga of the *Natya Shastra*.

PART FIVE

Odissi and Other Styles

25
Odissi

The Odissi dance of Orissa is considered one of the oldest in India. It was rediscovered comparatively recently and even then was thought to be an off-shoot of Dasi Attam and Kuchipudi. However, research has shown that there are many differences, not the least of which is the music, which in Dasi Attam and Kuchipudi is Karnatic and in Odissi Hindustani.

Orissa has been called the land of temples. The greatest of these are at Bhubhaneshwar and Puri, and it was these temples which were the centres of art and culture as well as of religion, and where dance took shape and grew. It follows therefore, that the development of dance was closely associated with that of religion. Shaivite, Buddhist, Jain and Vaishnavite temples, some dating from as early as the second century B.C. show sculptures and friezes of dance poses. Dancing girls have been dedicated for service in the temples from very early times, but there is evidence of an unbroken tradition of this in Orissa from the ninth century A.D. These girls, known as Maharis, together with their male counterparts, the Gotipuas, have preserved the art. The Maharis led chaste lives and had a high position in society. There is at least one instance of a princess who became a Mahari. The Gotipuas dressed and danced like the Maharis but had to leave the temple at the age of eighteen. They then usually became dance teachers. Because they had left the temple their style of dancing was open to outside influences and has, therefore, not come down in the same pure form as that of the Maharis.

One of the most celebrated temples of Orissa is the temple of Jagan-nath at Puri. Jagan-nath is another epithet of the god Vishnu and means 'Lord of the Universe'. The temple was built during the reign of Chodaganga Deva (1077–1147) when Vaishnavism was in the process of being established in Orissa.

Odissi and Other Styles

There are many versions of the story about how the three most sacred of the statues came to this temple. In one, Krishna is said to have been accidentally killed by the bird-hunter Jara. Arjun, Krishna's companion, tried to cremate the body but, unable to do so, floated it out to sea where it changed into a log. Now, King Indradyumna was forewarned in a dream about the true nature of the log which would be washed onto the shores of his kingdom. He therefore arranged for it to be retrieved and carved into the image of Vishnu. However, none was able to touch it until one Vishvakarma, an old carpenter, undertook the task on condition that he would not be disturbed until it was finished. One day the eager king, unable to contain his curiosity any longer, entered the room where the carpenter had closeted himself. He found to his surprise not one but three images, all half finished. Of the carpenter himself there was no trace. He then had these images of Vishnu, his brother Balaram and their sister Subhadra taken to the great temple.

Puri thus became a place of pilgrimage and during the great festival of Jagan-nath the statues were placed in gigantic chariots, called raths, which were drawn through the streets by pilgrims and devotees. In former times, the more ardent of the pilgrims used to throw themselves under the wheels of the chariots, in the belief that by this sacrifice they gained salvation. The English word 'juggernaut' derives from the name of the god. In all such processions the Maharis attended upon the gods with hymns and dances.

The temple was later extended by King Kapilendra Deva, who built the Nata Mandir especially for the devotional dancing of the Maharis. He also defined their duties which have since always retained the form laid down by him. They danced twice every day. At the time of the god's mid-day meal or Bhog, the Bahir-Jani Maharis danced in the Nata Mandir. The specially selected Bheetar-Jani Maharis danced before the deity in the inner shrine at the Barah-Shringar ceremony when the deity was adorned and made ready for the night. In addition, the dancers accompanied the gods on their periodic exoduses such as the Chandan Jatra when they were taken out in boats, and the Jhoolan Jatra when they were amused and entertained on swings.

One of the duties of the Maharis was to perform bhava to songs. From the fifteenth century these songs had been taken from the *Gita Govinda* and other books, but with the firm hold of Vaishnavism in the sixteenth century they were instructed to use songs from this work only to the exclusion of all others.

Odissi did not escape a decline any more than the other dances of India, but now the old gurus are helping towards its re-establishment. The Orissa State government and the Sangeet Natak Akademi are financing research and the translation of ancient texts. There are four institutes which now offer courses in Odissi, the Kalavikash Kendra, the Utkal College of Music and Dance, the Bhubhaneshwar Kala Kendra and the Orissa Sangeet Parishad.

The leading gurus of this dance style are Kelu Charan Mahapatra who was once a gotipua and now teaches at the Kalavikash Kendra, and Pankaj Charan who is from a Mahari family and teaches at Puri. Perhaps the most widely-known teacher is Deba Prasad Das who is the guru of Indrani Rehman.

Indrani Rehman is the first contemporary professional dancer to have studied Odissi seriously and to have performed it in other parts of India. Other dancers who have followed her are Priyambada Mohanty, Pratima Das, Ritha Devi, Yamini Krishnamurthi, Kum Kum Das and Sanjukta Misra.

TECHNIQUE

Odissi draws upon several ancient texts in Sanskrit and Oriya, most important of which are the *Natya Shastra*, the *Abhinaya Darpanam* and the *Abhinaya Chandrika*. Some of the works have illustrations and these, together with the temple sculptures, have been of great help in recreating certain postures and movements of the dance.

The training begins with eight *belis* or basic body positions and movements, each of which has many varieties.

The *uthas* are the positions used in rising and jumping. The various sitting positions are called *baithas*. The *sthankas* are the standing positions, and detail the varying distances between the feet and the positions of each knee, whether bent or straight. The gaits and walks are the *chaalis*. The quick movements, *burhas*, suggest joy and excitement. The alternate bending of the body from left to right is called *bhasa*. *Bhaunris* are spins executed on one spot, either clockwise or anti-clockwise and the *palis* are the stylized retreats on the stage which end short dance sequences.

Bhumi means the earth, but in this context it refers to the movement of the dancer on the stage and the patterns thus created.

Odissi and Other Styles

Usually the dancer moves round the outside of an imaginary circle or square and sometimes spins in one place. Also included here are movements in which the dancer comes forward, inscribing a small arc with each step.

Apart from the belis and the bhumis there are six foot positions called *pada bhedas*. Two of these are not found in other dances, the movement on the heels, and the *stambha pada*, which comes at the beginning of the dance. For this the feet are kept close together and the big toe of the right foot rests on that of the left one.

There are sixty-three hastas used in Odissi today. Some are identical with those in the ancient texts and have the same names, others are identical with those in the texts but have different names, yet others are unique to Odissi. A likely reason for the large number of hastas is that they were necessary in order to do justice to the ornate poetry of Upendra Bhanj, Surya Baladev Rath, Banamali Das and others whose works were especially favoured by Odissi dancers.

Some of the karanas used in Odissi are found in the *Natya Shastra*, but the majority are taken from the *Abhinaya Chandrika*. There are others which are recorded only on the temples of Orissa.

COSTUME

The *Abhinaya Chandrika* also lays down the details of costumes and ornaments to be worn by Odissi dancers. The women wear the patta sari, a brightly coloured silk sari which is nine yards long and a black or red blouse called the kanchula, which is embroidered with various stones and gold and silver thread. An apron-like piece of silk known as the nibi bandha is tied from the waist. The waistband itself, called the jhobha, is a length of cord with tasselled ends.

The kanchula of the Gotipuas is somewhat different as is the method in which their patta sari is draped.

The tendency of dancers nowadays, is to wear fewer ornaments than those prescribed in the *Abhinaya Chandrika*. Three ornaments are worn on the head, one along the hair-line of the forehead, one down the centre parting and one in the hair. There are two types of necklace, a choker and a longer one with a pendant. The ears are adorned with ornaments known as kapa. Decorative wristbands and armbands are also used.

There are three permissible hair styles; the pushpa-chanda with the hair coiled into the shape of a flower, the ardh-bathaka or semi-circular bun and the kati-beni which is a single plait down the back.

An elaborate design is made on the forehead with a vermilion mark in the centre. The eyes are made up with kohl and there is a small mark on the chin.

Some dancers do not use the authentic costume and ornaments and this has caused misgivings in Orissa.

AN ODISSI PERFORMANCE

Although Odissi recitals are nowadays given on the stage, they are nevertheless essentially a form of worship in which the dancer performs an act of adoration. She uses a balanced combination of nritta and nritya and although the style is lasya there are in it, some elements of tandav. There are no breaks between the different items which make up the whole dance but they do come in a set order.

The accompanying instruments have now been reduced to the mardal, a drum, the gini (cymbals), and a flute. A violin or veena may also sometimes be used. It was customary in former times for the dancer herself to sing but now a singer is usually included among the musicians.

The performance opens with the *bhumi pranam* which is a salutation to the earth or stage. With feet in *stambha pada* the dancer stands erect in the *sthai bhangi*. Trighanga poses then follow and the *vandana* commences. She touches the ground in an act of obeisance. This short invocatory piece was originally performed behind a curtain held up by two people.

The *bighnaraj puja* now begins and she performs bhava to a recital of slokas.

For the next item, Batu Nritya, there is neither song nor recitation and the mardal becomes the chief accompaniment. This is a very elaborate and difficult passage of dance dedicated to Shiva. It should show sixteen modes of prayer-offering but is now shortened to include only the last five. These are the offerings of flowers, incense, light, in the form of tiny earthenware oil lamps, food, and last of all pranam, or salutation.

To rhythmic syllables called *ukuttas* the dancer begins slowly with poses representing the playing of instruments to welcome the Lord. Between each mode of offering is an interlude of pure dance, where there is a fine interplay of complex rhythm patterns between dancer and drummer. Sometimes tals other than the basic ones are introduced so that the dancer is able to display her skill. Each consecutive nritta passage increases in tempo and complexity of footwork.

The dedication of Shiva is followed by the *ishtadeva vandana*, which is a devotion honouring the guardian deity of the dancer. Here the dancer interprets slokas through bhava.

Next comes the *swara pallabi nritta*, the structure of which is the same as that of the rendering of a raga and indeed, as the name implies, the stress is on the musical aspect. During the singing of the alap the dancer too sets the mood by using decorative poses and eye movements as in the thaat of Kathak. After this the dancer interprets the musical notation of the raga in movements. Occasionally ukuttas are danced in place of this, in which case the name *badya* is substituted for swara.

The same raga is used to provide the melody of the song or poem interpreted in the next item, which is the *sabhinaya*. Another name for this is *gita-abhinaya*. Each couplet or verse of the poem is punctuated with nritta, which becomes progressively more intricate, so that at the end it blends into the pure nritta of the finale. This is the *tarijham*, a dance of sheer joy. The excitement mounts as dancer and drummer play with different rhythms and the dance ends in a very fast tempo with long and intricate ukuttas.

In the past this was not the final item. Instead, the dancer bowed to the gods, the stage and the earth, and the audience. This triple leave-taking was called the *trikhandi majura*.

26

Santiniketan

Rabindranath Tagore represented in his life and work, the cultural renaissance of modern India. His rich liberalism drew its inspiration from India's ancient philosophy and, being a true traditionalist, he was always ready to accept the age and its challenges. Poet, novelist, playwright, philosopher, actor, painter and educationist, he also left his imperishable mark on the history of India's dance. Indeed, he was, with Vallathol, the pioneer of the revivalist movement that uplifted and restored the art to its proper place in the cultural life of the people. The task was by no means easy, for dancing had come to be regarded as synonymous with prostitution and loose living.

In 1901 Gurudev, the Preceptor, as he was known to his countrymen founded Santiniketan, the Home of Peace, where he experimented with his new educational methods. This school which later became a university was set in quiet surroundings away from the bustle and turmoil of Calcutta. The students led very simple lives and were encouraged to live in close communion with nature. The atmosphere was relaxed and there were no 'rules', as the poet insisted that the only discipline worth striving towards was the inner discipline which emanated from the soul. Santiniketan attracted some of the foremost thinkers and humanists from East and West and it was Tagore's inspiration which made it a great meeting place of the best minds. Although the curriculum included general academic subjects such as science and mathematics, great stress was laid on the arts. Painting, sculpture and music were taught, while Tagore himself wrote the plays which were regularly produced at Santiniketan and in some of the larger cities.

Tagore's plays were novel in that the dialogue was in blank verse and often set to music. Tagore had studied the classical ragas from a very early age and in composing the music for his plays he laid particular stress on raga-bhava, that is, he set the words to ragas that would best relate to the mood of the dialogue. A system of mixed ragas thus resulted. The actors were also the singers and remembering that his actors did not all have the same background in classical music as himself, he used only simple ragas together with popular Bengali folk melodies. Expressionistic movements and gestures were employed and dancing as such was not introduced till much later.

While on a lecture tour of Assam in 1919, Tagore saw the Goshta Lila or dance of the shepherd boys performed by a group in Sylhet. So impressed was he, that he invited the dance guru Budhimantra Sinha to come to his school and teach there. But even Tagore had to tread carefully and he could only introduce dancing as part of the physical education programme for the boys. In 1926, Tagore ventured further. With the help of the Maharaja of Manipur he brought Guru Naba Kumar to Santiniketan. This was a major breakthrough for now the girls too started their dance training. By this time the climate of opinion had begun to change and moreover, with Tagore's backing the girls had little fear of social stigma.

In the May of that same year he presented his first dance-drama in Calcutta with a cast composed wholly of girls. This drama, *Natir Puja*, is the story of a nati or dancing girl who becomes a Buddhist nun. The king, however, forbids the worship of Buddha and commands the nati to dance again. Much against her will the girl dresses herself in her most beautiful costume and dances at court. But as she dances she thinks only of Buddha. As the dance progresses she sheds her jewels one by one and finally throws off the costume as well. We see her, not naked, but in the humble habit of a nun. As she kneels in silence to worship Buddha, the king's soldiers close in and slay her for defying his orders. The princess who has been watching, is so moved by the nati's devotion and sacrifice that she too becomes a follower of Buddha's teachings.

Natir Puja was a great success and Tagore had at last brought home his message that dancing was a medium of expression like any other art. It could uplift the soul and was not necessarily a corrupting influence. Calcutta had been converted and many Bengali girls from the best families began to learn dancing.

Tagore composed other dance dramas; *Chitrangada*, *Shyama* and *Chandalika* are the best known. They were all based on ancient mythological tales and legends and he continued to use raga-bhava

Santiniketan

as the basic principle for the music. He took care to give the songs a well-defined rhythm which would lend itself to dancing. The tals generally used were the simple ones such as dadra, kaharwa, ektal and teental. The tempo was increased or decreased according to the mood, a slower tempo for the sad pieces and a faster one for joy or excitement. Sometimes, in order to heighten the dramatic effect, as in tragic scenes, the songs were sung without any rhythmic accompaniment. In *Shyama* for instance, the last few songs of the heroine are without tabla or dholak. She tells her lover how she had saved his life by sacrificing the life of her admirer Uttiya. She begs his forgiveness for any wrong that she may have done him and then finally tries to appease her guilt-stricken conscience by prayer and meditation.

Tagore, though not a dancer himself, devised the choreography for most of the dance-dramas. He was fortunate in getting the services of three more gurus, Senarik Singh, Nileswar Mukherji and Atomba Singh who came to Santiniketan to teach and assist with the ballets. He found, however, that Manipuri techniques alone could not do justice to his plays. Accordingly, he brought gurus from South India to teach his students the elementary movements and mudras of Kathakali. A new dance style was evolved which used simplified Manipuri and Kathakali techniques along with some folk dance movements. Now this style had obvious drawbacks arising from the dancers' limited foundation in any one classical dance. Moreover, the dancers were not required to interpret the text exactly so long as they were able to convey the general mood. This naturally led to a great deal of improvisation. Nevertheless, these compositions were colourful and light and brought new blood to rejuvenate the theatre of the time.

In recent years, when the classical dances of India are receiving increasing attention, the Santiniketan style has been criticized for its lack of a precise technical basis. Although this is largely true, it cannot eclipse the significance of Santiniketan's main contribution. Its greatest service lay in helping to change the attitude of the public towards dancing, and while it paved the way for modern ballet groups it also helped to rehabilitate the classical dance styles, especially Manipuri, which till then had never been seen outside Manipur. As Tagore toured India with his ballets giving his message through dancing, people began to set aside their prejudices and accept the art as part of their heritage.

27

Uday Shankar and His Dance

Uday Shankar, the pioneer of modern ballet in India, is well known to Western audiences. He rose to fame at a time when, because of dancers like Pavlova and Ruth St Denis, oriental dancing had already excited considerable interest in the West. Shankar, by his very presence on the stage, crystallized the popular image. His face and figure and the line of his hand and body movements seemed to be, in Western eyes, the quintessence of the mysterious dance of India. Even today there are many to whom Indian dancing is synonymous with his name.

His impact was somewhat different in India, where he was successful in the first instance because of his novel ideas, brilliant stagecraft and a kind of professionalism then almost unknown to the Indian theatre. At the same time he was misunderstood and even condemned by some critics because of the style of dance he had created. His dancing though basically Indian, was nevertheless his own personal creation, although it was influenced by European expressionist schools as well as the dances of the Far East. It was a combination of the many influences, both Eastern and Western, which were synthesized in, and had moulded, his own life.

Uday Shankar was only eighteen when he went to England as an art student under Sir William Rothenstein. Here he danced in a few charity performances organized by his father and was noticed by Anna Pavlova. Impressed by his dancing and magnetic stage presence, she asked him to help her to choreograph two oriental ballets, *The Hindu Wedding* and *Radha and Krishna*.

Shankar stayed with the Pavlova company for a year and a half and danced Krishna to her Radha. He then launched out on his own in Paris. This was the next formative stage in his career, for here he took advantage of the museums and art galleries to make a careful study of the art and culture of many countries, particularly the Far East. He also missed no opportunity of seeing the performances given by visiting international companies. All this influenced his dancing to some extent, but the style he developed was in no way imitative and matched his own personality.

For many years Shankar was based in England, where he rehearsed his company in the picturesque setting of Dartington Hall. He was assisted by his dance partner Simkie, a French girl who had been his pupil in Paris.

During his stay abroad, he had visited India several times and collected new material for his ballets. He made sketches of the dance sculptures in temples, filmed many Indian folk dances and learned the technique of the classical dances of India. Nevertheless, his dancing was not based on these classical styles any more than on foreign styles, although he incorporated movements, footwork and mudras with imagination wherever they served to enrich his own style of dancing.

Shankar also evolved a successful system of training. It was entirely his own and not in any way based on traditional Indian methods. The effect of this training was, that his corps de ballet earned a reputation for perfect harmony and co-ordination. All the exercises were classified as A, B, C, D and so on, and then numbered A_1, A_2, A_3, etc. For example, the exercises for the hands and wrists belonged to the 'A' group. There were many of these, such as those where both hands moved together, palms facing up and then down, or where the hands moved in opposite ways, right palm facing up while the left faced down. As the 'A' exercises became more complicated the wrists naturally played an increasingly active part in them.

Walking to rhythm was given great importance. A characteristic of Shankar's style was the way in which the dancers moved down and up between steps. This was referred to as the *dip* in the exercise count which went, 'one dip, two dip, three dip, and four dip'. As the tempo increased the shorter time lapse between counts meant that the body would have to move much faster. The second stage in these exercises used the double dip where, as the name implies, the dancers had to dip twice between beats.

In 1938 Shankar returned to India and opened his India Culture Centre at Almora. To this centre he invited gurus of the classical dance styles so that his pupils were able to learn the fundamentals of

Odissi and Other Styles

these, although the primary aim was always that they should learn the Shankar style of dancing. Kandappa Pillai was responsible for Bharata Natyam, Amubi Singh for Manipuri and Sankaran Nambudri for Kathakali. In addition, the great Ustad Alauddin Khan taught classical music.

Uday Shankar was very interested in the folk dances of India and adapted their simple rhythms and movements for the stage with great success.

His choreography was such that the existing classical ragas and tals would not have fitted it in their normal form. A certain amount of experiment was therefore necessary. He wanted music which was Indian, of a high quality without being too complex, and which would also allow for orchestration. The challenge was accepted by Tamir Baran, whom he commissioned to do this work. Baran used an orchestra of fourteen, which included various kinds of stringed as well as percussion instruments. The musicians were seated on the stage in full view of the audience. In terms of European music, fourteen instruments could hardly be said to comprise an orchestra, but for Indian classical music this is a very large number indeed, since this music is not based on harmony and so does not need a multiplicity of instruments which might easily endanger its particular unity. Since some of the ballets needed special sound effects as well, such as thunder, ploughing and harvesting, these too had to be devised. The experiment was successful and the audiences liked it, for the music skilfully complemented the choreography. Another successful composer and music director who worked with Shankar was Vishnudass Shirali.

When Uday Shankar first established himself in India his ballets were extremely popular. The themes were new for India, and based on contemporary situations. *Labour and Machinery* depicted the struggle of mill workers against the owner. *The Rhythm of Life* emphasized the need for a spirit of unity among Indians. It was at about this time that the classical dances were beginning to be revived and gaining popularity, so people were able to compare them with Shankar's ballets. The new-found love for the older styles showed itself in criticism of Shankar. He was accused of not restricting himself to one style and indeed, of not being classical, and of putting in movements from his own imagination. All these charges were, of course, quite justified, but these were the very things Shankar was trying to do. He wanted to forge a dance which

Uday Shankar and His Dance

would be relevant to modern conditions, in which contemporary problems could be expressed, and which would have meaning for his audiences. To do this he employed all the resources at his disposal irrespective of their origins, and still created an art which could not be mistaken for anything but Indian.

Quite apart from the quality of his work, Shankar is a turning-point in the history of Indian dance for many reasons. He was the first dancer to produce modern Indian ballets. His successful experiments in orchestration paved the way for those who were to use it later. Above all Shankar will be remembered for the finish and the professionalism of his productions. His programmes were carefully planned. The sets, lighting, costumes and make-up were given detailed attention at a time when all these had tended to be overlooked in the Indian theatre.

Shankar produced some brilliant dancers and directors among whom were Shanti Bardhan, Sachin Shankar, Kameshwar and Zohra Segal, Narendra Sharma, Debindra Shankar and his own wife Amala. Many of his pupils later formed their own troupes and carried on the tradition. The late Shanti Bardhan was particularly successful with his production of the *Ramayana*, and stories from the *Panchatantra*. *The Cranes* of Narendra Sharma is among the best of his many ballets. He also choreographed *Ramlila* for the Bharatiya Kala Kendra. The late Kameshwar Segal composed a ballet for human puppets and choreographed the beautiful *Lotus Dance*. Among Sachin Shankar's many ballets are *The Fisherman and the Mermaid*, *Utsav*, *Sanjh Savera* and *Jay Parajaya*.

In addition to dancers and directors Uday Shankar has trained many much needed technicians and stage managers.

Shankar is still active as a dancer and choreographer. In his recent ballet *Samanya Kshati*, he uses the latest technical innovations and shows no sign of stagnating.

APPENDIX

Gurus and Dancers

Amubi Arambam, like his father, the late Yaimabi Singh, specializes in the Lai Haroba dances. One of the younger generation of dancers, he has experimented considerably with presenting Manipuri dances on the modern stage. A talented choreographer, he has been associated with the Dance Department of Visva-Bharati University for some years.

Amubi Singh started his training under his mother who was a dancer at the palace in Manipur. He is now one of the leading gurus of the Manipuri dance and although his training was classical he is very receptive to new and creative work. He is famous for his grace and abhinaya and his rendering of lasya.

He has travelled widely in India and has taught at Uday Shankar's centre at Almora. He is now principal of the Dance College at Imphal and was awarded the Sangeet Natak Akademi Award in 1956.

Amudon Sharma comes from a family of illustrious gurus who taught at the Manipur palace. He is renowned for his classical drumming and his great knowledge of the technical aspect of the dance. According to him even the nritta movements are interpretative of the Radha-Krishna themes. He is a senior teacher at the Dance College at Imphal, is guru of the Govinda Palace Temple where Ras Lilas are performed, and is choreographer for the Manipuri Dramatic Union. In 1960 he was given the Sangeet Natak Akademi Award.

Ananda Shivaraman trained at the Kerala Kala Mandalam. His main interest has been in trying to adapt Kathakali to modern conditions. He has toured Japan, Australia and America. In America his dancing excited considerable interest, especially his peacock and lotus dances. His wife Janaki Devi is also a talented dancer.

Atomba Singh is one of the greatest exponents of the Ras. He studied dancing from an early age under the two great gurus Rudra Singh and Jhoolan Singh. His forte is the tandav aspect of the dance. One of his famous dance compositions is the Goshta Lila, in which the young Krishna and his cowherd companions ride on each others backs and play polo. This lively dance with its accompaniment of vigorous pung playing has won wide acclaim. This guru was head of the Dance Department at Santiniketan during Tagore's lifetime. He is now senior teacher at the Dance College at Manipur and is also a Sangeet Natak Akademi Award winner.

Balasaraswati is the greatest Dasi Attam dancer living today. Dancing seems to her as natural as breathing. This is not surprising for she is from a famous devadasi family which has produced musicians and dancers of the first rank for generations. Her mother is a very fine singer with an infinite store of padams, to which of course, Balasaraswati dances. Her grandmother, the great Veena Dhanam had a phenomenal knowledge of Karnatic music and was unequalled as an exponent of it. Her great-grandmother taught at the Tanjore Court and continued dancing till a very old age. Balasaraswati then, has inherited not only the very best that music and dance can offer, but also that delicate sensitivity and insight without which no art can be really great. When she walks on to the stage to dance, her very being seems permeated with an almost divine spirit, one which inspires respect and commands attention.

Balasaraswati's training started when she was four, under Kandappa Nattuvanar, the great-grandson of Chinniyah who was one of the four famous brothers at the Court of Tanjore. Her arangeetram or debut took place at the Ammanakshi Amman temple in Kanchipuram when she was seven. She first danced at Madras when she was fourteen and amazed the connoisseurs with her accomplished performance.

In later years Balasaraswati consulted Gauri Ammal and Chinnayya Naidu although her chief mentor was still Kandappa. Later still, she took further advice on abhinaya and padams from Lakshmi Narayana Shastri of Kuchipudi. Her career had been interrupted for some years because of an illness which made her gain far too much weight. But even though she is still on the heavy side she has at last come back to dancing. She has recently danced in Europe, Britain and America with great success.

Her particular forte is abhinaya. In this she never makes an unnecessary gesture, every movement has a purpose and even the most subtle change in the attitude of the fingers, head, or eyebrow adds to her exposition. Her mudras are incredibly eloquent and her understanding of human nature enables her to give every shade of meaning in a phrase. When, for example, she dances the complaining wife in a padam, we know exactly what kind of woman is saying the words because Balasaraswati goes beyond the words into the soul of the character. The effect is even more spellbinding when she herself takes over the singing of a padam, as a dancer should, for she has a beautiful voice and is a singer of considerable talent. Unlike some other dancers who adapt their programme to suit their audience, Balasaraswati makes no concessions, admits of no compromises. She wears simple costumes, uses the minimum of jewellery and does not need elaborate sets. At the moment, Balasaraswati is teaching at the Music Academy in Madras. She has received the Padma Bhusan and the President's Award.

Balasundari is a promising young dancer from Ceylon and comes from a distinguished family. She won the first prize for dancing in a national competition in Ceylon and then went to Kalakshetra for five years as a scholarship student where she danced the lead in a number of ballets. In 1966 she arrived in England and danced under the auspices of the British Council and the Asian Music Circle.

Bela Arnab is a well-known dancer in Bengal, and is at present teaching at the Bengal Music College in Calcutta. She has studied both schools of Kathak; the Jaipur school under Sohan Lal and Jai Lal and the Lucknow school under Shambu Maharaj.

Bharati Gupta is a young Kathak dancer of great promise. She has studied under Shambu Maharaj and Brijju Maharaj and danced the female lead in *Dalia*. She has partnered Brijju Maharaj on dance tours of America and Pakistan.

Bihari Sharma is a leading Manipuri dancer who started dancing at the age of three. He was trained at the Dance College at Manipur where he was an assistant teacher for some time. He is well known in the West since his first visit to the United States which was sponsored by Beryl de Zoete. He has now settled in America and has participated in several dance festivals with his wife Thambal Yaima.

Bipin Singh is an outstanding choreographer who brings out to great advantage the rhythmic beauty of the Manipuri Ras. He has also done much research into the theory of this dance. Bipin Singh's talents have been widely recognized and he divides his time between Manipur where he is now Hanjaba (Head) of the Palace Dance Troupe and the principal of the Sri Govindji Nartanalaya, and Bombay where he is the guru of the Manipur Dance Academy.

Brijju Maharaj, son of the late Achhan Maharaj, trained under his father until he was ten, when Achhan Maharaj died. His training was then taken over by his uncles, Lachhu Maharaj and Shambu Maharaj. He is an extremely accomplished percussionist and plays the tabla and the pakhawaj. His acquaintance with these two instruments has led him to experiment with new variations of rhythm in Kathak. His main interest at the moment is the challenge of presenting Kathak in the contemporary theatre. To this end he has devised and produced several full-length ballets, *Phag Lila, Govardhan Lila*, and *Kumara Sambhava* being notable amongst them. In all of these he danced the male lead for he dances both nritta and nritya with equal ease. Brijju Maharaj teaches Kathak at the Bharatiya Kala Kendra in New Delhi, and Partap Pawar, Tirath Ajmani and Rashmi Jain are among his pupils.

Champakulam Pachu Pillai comes from a family of Kathakali dancers. He was first trained by his uncle Sanku Pillai and then by Paramu Pillai and has since danced several times with this guru. He is tall and well built and so is able to play his favourite role of the red-beard types. Because of his excellent renderings he has been nicknamed Red Beard.

Chandralekha is a Bharata Natyam dancer who trained under Ellappa Pillai. She has danced abroad and is well known for her abhinaya.

Appendix

Chaoba Thangjam is a celebrated artiste of the Pala Cholom tradition. He is very much in demand during religious festivals and is particularly known for his abhinaya.

Charanji Lal was first trained by his father Hanuman Prasad of the Jaipur school of Kathak and later by the great Binda Din of Lucknow. He was attached to the erstwhile courts of Raigarh and Udaipur and later taught at the Gandharva Mahavidyala in Delhi. Among his notable pupils are the four sons of his brother, the late Narayan Prasad.

Chenganoor Raman Pillai was a versatile Kathakali dancer best known for his music and costumes. Among his disciples are Haripad Ramakrishna Pillai and Mankompu Sivasankara Pillai.

Damayanti Joshi is a purist of Kathak dancing, although she has shown a great interest in other schools as well. Trained under Menaka, Sitaram Prasad, Achhan Maharaj, Lachhu Maharaj and Shambu Maharaj, she has inherited a rich tradition of Kathak. Her first dance tour abroad was with Menaka whom she accompanied to Europe and the countries of South East Asia. In 1953 she went to China on a cultural mission and in 1958 to Japan. In 1964 she danced in London and other important European cities. She is extremely good in the portrayal of Nayika Bhedas.

E. Krishna Iyer is an important figure in the revival of Bharata Natyam, or Dasi Attam. As a young lawyer in Madras he had a promising future, but his great desire was to see the ancient art of Bharata Natyam flourish once again in India. This desire showed very little sign of ever being realized for this was the very height of the Anti-Nautch Campaign. However, in 1926 he decided to learn dancing himself. His teacher was the famous Natesa Iyer of Meratur. After being trained he tried to persuade young ladies from respectable families to learn the art, but his efforts produced only shocked misunderstanding of his motives. In spite of this he continued to campaign and went so far as to dress himself up as a woman and dance for anyone who would care to watch. This naturally aroused interest, as it was meant to, but it also aroused the Anti-Nautch groups to greater efforts against the 'nautch'.

For six years Krishna Iyer wrote books, contributed articles, and gave many lectures putting forward the case for the restoration of Bharata Natyam. The turning-point, by his own account, came in 1932 when he became involved in a heated debate in the press with a leader of the Anti-Nautch movement. This debate made people aware of the qualities of the dance and the result was that there were many more recitals which were well attended.

Krishna Iyer had by this time begun to 'collect and discover' the best dancers. They were all of the devadasi caste. In 1933 he arranged for the Kalyani sisters of Tiruvalaputtur to give a recital before the Music Academy in Madras and in the following year he took Balasaraswati to dance at the All India Music Conference at Varanasi. Other dancers such as Veralakshmi and Bhanumathi also began to give public performances. At last the battle was turning. The victory was complete when Rukmini Devi of Adyar and Kalanidhi of Mylapore, both from respectable backgrounds, took up Bharata Natyam as a profession.

Gauri Joshi started her dance career under Shanti Bardhan in the Little Ballet Troupe. In 1957 she trained as a kathak dancer under Shambu Maharaj and is now a senior member of the Bharatiya Kala Kendra ballet troupe.

Gauri Shankar was trained by his uncle Shiv Lal and later by Sunder Prasad. He made a great impression when he first danced in 1934 at the Allahabad Music Conference. He became Menaka's partner and danced at the International Dance Olympiad at Berlin in 1936 where he was awarded an honour prize. Gauri Shankar then joined Tagore at Santiniketan. In 1942 he rejoined Menaka's group and later started his own dance school at Bombay where he has trained some fine Kathak dancers.

Ghambini Devi studied Manipuri at the Sri Govindji Nartanalaya as a disciple of Guru Bipin Singh. She is well known for her rendering of Manipuri songs that accompany the dances at religious festivals. She has appeared in several concerts all over India and has a natural gift for abhinaya.

Gopi Krishan comes from a family of dancers and musicians. His father, who was a court musician in Nepal, took a great interest in his children's training and so five of Gopi Krishan's brothers and

Appendix

sisters are well-known artistes today. He studied Kathak under Shambu Maharaj and learnt Bharata Natyam from Govindaraj Pillai. Gopi Krishan's main interest is in the use of classical dancing in Indian films, which have not, unfortunately, received the benefit of this art form. His first success in this endeavour was with *Jhanak Jhanak Payal Baje*, a full-length feature film made by the enterprising producer Shantaram. The film was a milestone in Indian dance and Indian films, for it proved that classical dancing, when properly used by film makers, had its financial rewards.

Gopinath is a famous Katkakali dancer, both at home and abroad. He has a family background of Kathakali and his training began in a kalari when he was thirteen. His training continued under Kunju Kurup at the Kerala Kala Mandalam where he met Ragini Devi and later joined her troupe as her partner. They were the first to present scenes from Kathakali as independent items in a performance. Among Gopinath's most popular dances are Shiva Parvati, Shringar Lahari, and Dance of the Hunter. He now has his own school, Natana Niketan, in Madras.

Gopinath is married to Shrimati Thankamani who was the first girl pupil at the Kerala Kala Mandalam. She was trained in Mohini Attam by the late Kalyani Amma and has been her husband's dance partner for many years.

Hanuman Prasad of the Jaipur gharana was trained by his father Gangaram and later by Dhana Lal. Besides being an accomplished Kathak dancer he is a poet and composer of distinction. Although nritta is the speciality of the Jaipur dancers, Hanuman Prasad excels in bhava and the exposition of nritya.

Hazari Lal, also of the Jaipur gharana, was first trained as a Kathak dancer by his father Hanumantha Ram the sarangi player and his brother Satya Narain the tabla artiste. He later worked under Shiv Lal and Sunder Prasad. During the time of the Indian States he danced at the Courts of Gidhor, Raigarh and Paruna. He now teaches at Meerut.

Ibetombi Devi is a young artiste of exceptional merit. She has mastered all the main Manipuri styles but her greatest love is the Maibi dance of the Lai Haroba which she learnt from the renowned

Rajani Devi. She has her own dance centre at Manipur where she is assisted by her uncle Gourmani Singh, a research worker and scholar of the Maibi dances. Ibetombi Devi has toured many countries and her recent Australian tour was most successful.

Indrani Rehman is the daughter of Ragini Devi, an American who has dedicated her life to the dances of South India. Not only did Ragini Devi learn Indian dancing, particularly Kathakali, but she also learnt to play the sitar and tamboura and has written on both Indian music and dance. Indrani, then, grew up to the sounds of music and dancing. She became a pupil of Chokkalingam Pillai and has become a very able and well-known dancer. She has great beauty of face and figure which enhance her dancing, and enough stamina to carry her through the longest items with grace and charm. Her tours abroad, particularly in America have helped to develop a taste and understanding of Indian dancing in other countries. The Odissi style of dancing was more or less restricted to Orissa until Indrani Rehman popularized it wherever she went. Hitherto Odissi had been thought of as an advanced form of folk dance which had been influenced by Dasi Attam, but it is largely because of her efforts that it has now come to be recognized as a classical dance whose tradition stretches back to ancient times.

Jai Kumari is the daughter of the great leader of the Jaipur gharana, the late Jai Lal. She learnt to dance from her father who was successively Court dancer at Jaipur, Jodhpur, Sikri, Raigarh, Maihar, and Nepal. Until a few years ago no woman Kathak dancer could compete with her in rhythmic variations of footwork. Since the death of her father her public appearances have gradually decreased. She now lives in Calcutta where she coaches a few pupils privately.

Jayalakshmi Alva learnt Dasi Attam from K. N. Dandayuthapani Pillai and Swarna Saraswathi of Madras. She has toured Europe and South East Asia and with her husband, Rama Krishna Alva, founded the Chitrambalam Dance Centre in Bombay.

The Jhaveri Sisters, Nayana, Ranjana, Suverna, and Darshana, received their training under Guru Bipin Singh. Nayana the eldest and most famous is an extremely graceful dancer and the talented

Appendix

choreographer of several dance-dramas. The sisters run the Manipur Dance Academy in Bombay and have danced all over India and around the world in their mission to make this beautiful art known.

Kalavati and **Vinodini** graduated from the Sri Govindji Nartanalaya where they studied under Guru Bipin Singh. Both are extremely talented and have mastered the intricate rhythms of Manipuri dancing. They are well known to audiences in Bombay where they now live and often dance with the Jhaveri sisters.

Kamala Laxman became well known as a Bharata Natyam dancer at an early age and, therefore, was known as Baby Kamala. She is a student of Ramiah Pillai, who belongs to the brilliant family of Vazhuvur nattuvanars. She has great beauty and charm and her dancing is notable for its sculpturesque poses and the more than ordinary suppleness of her body and limbs.

Kartik Ram and **Kalyan Das** were first-rate dancers much in demand a few years ago. Their patron was that great lover of the arts, the Raja of Raigarh. He supervised their training and got the best gurus to teach them, Jai Lal of Jaipur and Achhan Maharaj of Lucknow. The pair benefited immensely from the teaching of these masters and the consistently high level of their Kathak earned them much respect and privilege at the Raja's court. After their patron's death, however, they have given up dancing altogether.

Krishan Kumar is the son of the dancer Pandit Gopal. Trained as a Kathak dancer by Hanuman Prasad and Ashiq Hussain, he is now working under Shambu Maharaj at the Bharatiya Kala Kendra, New Delhi.

Krishna Rao and his wife **Chandrabhaga Devi** run a school of dancing in Bangalore. Krishna Rao was trained by Kunju Kurup in Kathakali and later he and his wife learnt Dasi Attam from Minakshisundaram Pillai. Their translation of the palm-leaf manuscript *Lasya Ranjana* is a work of rare scholarship and their book *Dance in Modern India* is a prescribed text for dance examinations in Mysore State. Many of their pupils, Indian and foreign, have made a name for themselves as professional dancers. These include T. S. Bhat, Sonal Mansingh, Hari Das and Kama Dev.

Gurus and Dancers

In 1964 Krishna Rao and Chandrabhaga Devi received the Mysore State Award for dancing and in the following year were given a grant to conduct dance classes and give recitals and lecture-demonstrations in England under the auspices of the Asian Music Circle.

Krishnan Kutty began his training when he was seven. His teachers were Raghavan Pillai Asaan, Katchu Pillai Pannikar, and Guru Sankaran Nambudri. In 1937 he became a member of the Travancore palace Kathakali troupe. From 1939 to 1944 he was the Kathakali teacher at Menaka's dance centre at Khandala. After this he went to teach in Bombay where he also worked on such dance-dramas as *Prahlada Charitram*, *False Pride*, *Inspirations*, and *Birth of our Nation*. With Shirin Vajifdar he founded the Nritya Darpana Society and directed *Birth of Urvishi*, *Triumph of Life*, *Transposed Heads* and *Chitralekha*. In 1952 he and Shirin Vajifdar led their dance troupe on a tour of Europe. Later, Krishnan Kutty was sent by the government of India on a cultural mission to China.

Krishnan Nair teaches Kathakali in his home town of Alwaye. He was trained by Chandu Pannikar and at the Kerala Kala Mandalam, and has toured with Madame Stan Harding as her partner.

Kudamaloor Karunakaran Nair was trained by the late Rama Pannikar, the late Kavalapra Narayana Menon, and finally under Thottam Sankaran Nambudri. He has danced all over India and specializes in female Kathakali roles. He has won many awards and now teaches at Quilon.

Kumudini Lakhia was first trained by Radhelal Misra and then studied under Shambu Maharaj, Brijju Maharaj, and Sunder Prasad. Later, she joined the Ram Gopal troupe in London. At the Edinburgh Festival in 1956 she danced the role of Mumtaz Mahal in the Kathak ballet *Legend of the Taj Mahal*. She worked for a time with Brijju Maharaj and has danced opposite him in *Malati Madhav* and *Kumara Sambhava*.

Kundan Lal is a dancer of the Jaipur gharana. He has worked in the film industry in Bombay and is now a Kathak instructor in the Dance Department of Baroda University.

Appendix

Kunju Kurup, the grand old master of Kathakali, is now about 85 years old. Inspired by a performance when he was only twelve, he made up his mind to learn Kathakali, and immediately started lessons under Kochappi Raman Nair. He had his arangeetram two years later, and then became a pupil of Champakulam Sanku Pillai for the next seven years. He worked hard during this time not only at learning to dance, but also at acquiring the background and atmosphere of Kathakali and finding out as much as he could about the characters he danced. His early life as an artiste was difficult, for the troup had to travel long distances to give performances and even then their rewards, in practical terms at any rate, were meagre. However, his fortunes improved and he became the protégé of the Raja of Mantredathu Menekal. This allowed him time to study. He was encouraged in this by the Raja who was himself a scholar and musician. Kunju Kurup spent twelve years in the service of the Prince and then with the foundation of the Kerala Kala Mandalam was appointed the first musician there. He has danced all over India and has received the President's Award for his services to Kathakali. Among the many dancers he has trained, some like Gopinath, Ananda Shivaraman, Ram Gopal and Krishna Rao have reached the top of their profession.

Kuppaiah Pillai's family connection with Dasi Attam can be traced back to Venkatakrishna Nattuvanar who lived in the early part of the last century. He is the great-grandson of Venkatakrishna's sister. As happens in India, there were marriages within the caste so that relationships were doubled and are thus difficult to trace. Kuppaiah Pillai's father, Panchapakesa was a very famous nattuvanar, a dance master at the Tanjore Court and the Brihadeswara temple and honoured at the courts of Ramnad, Baroda and Mysore. He was a good scholar of Sanskrit and Telugu and himself wrote a treatise, *Abhinaya Navaneetham*.

In his time he trained many famous devadasis and naturally, his own son Kuppaiah. He died when his son was only fifteen, yet even at this age the boy had learnt a great deal. However, he completed his training under Kanniah Nattuvanar of Tanjore, and then settled down to teach in Tiruvidamaruthur. He has trained his cousin, himself the son of a well-known nattuvanar, as well as his own son Mahalingam. These two have a well-established school in Bombay, the Rajarajeshwari Bharata Natyam Kala Mandir.

Gurus and Dancers

Kurichi Kunjan Pannikar is now about eighty. He learnt Kathakali from his uncle Vehayaniya Pannikar. He has had a long and energetic career and was dancing, with great vigour, a wide variety of roles even in his seventies.

Lachhu Maharaj is the second of the three Maharaj brothers, older than Shambu and younger than Achhan who died in 1946. He is therefore, the most senior exponent of the Lucknow gharana. His training was severe under his father Kalka Prasad, and later his brother Achhan. He has his own dance school in Bombay and has choreographed a number of Kathak ballets, the most notable being *Malati Madhav*. In 1957 he won the Sangeet Natak Akademi Award for his contribution to Kathak.

Lokeshwar Singh is a noted Pala Cholom artiste. He learnt to play the pung from his father, Khomdol. He teaches at the Sri Govindji Nartanalaya in Manipur where he choreographs and composes.

Mankulam Vishnu Nambudri's father was an accomplished dancer. He started his Kathakali training early, for Guru Sankaran Pillai lived at their house. Later he trained with Thottam Sankaran Nambudri and Kochu Pillai Pannikar. He also learnt Sanskrit which was invaluable to him when he came to create new dances based on the ancient texts. His chief interest is in the paccha roles for which he is famous. He helped to arrange *Nalacharitha* in its present form.

Maya Rao has been trained in both the Kathak gharanas. Sohan Lal, Sunder Prasad, and Shambu Maharaj have been her mentors. She is a university graduate and has devoted herself to the research and literature of Kathak. In 1963 Maya Rao was invited to the Soviet Union to work with Madame Tangiva-Birznek on the choreography of Balasanyan's *Shakuntala*, a ballet based on the Sanskrit play. Her Natya Saraswati in Bangalore is a dance centre where interesting work is being done.

Minakshisundaram Pillai, who died a few years ago, came from an illustrious line of nattuvanars. His ancestry can be traced back to Subbaraya Nattuvanar of the Tanjore Court and father of the famous Chinniyah, Punniah, Vadivelu and Shivanandan. He was the great-grandson of Chinniyah. Minakshisundaram Pillai trained many devadasis and with the revival of Bharata Natyam he came to the fore again and was recognized as the greatest teacher of Dasi Attam. Among his favourite pupils was Shanta Rao who has given an account of his teaching methods. He was a devout man and Shanta tells of how she often had to wait for him to finish his puja before they could eat. He demanded hard work from his pupils but also showed understanding and concern for them. At one time he used to teach only the basic technique himself and leave the finishing off to Arunachalam Nattuvanar who was his cousin Kumaraswami's son. But with the death of Arunachalam this process was stopped. However, Guru Natesa Iyer used to spend two months every year with Minakshisundaram Pillai at Pandanallur when the two gurus would exchange ideas and Minakshisundaram would give some of his more able students permission to have further lessons in abhinaya from Natesa Iyer.

Contrary to the practice of many other teachers Minakshisundaram Pillai did not restrict his pupils to a comparatively small area in which to dance, but let them cover whatever amount of space they could use with comfort. Shanta Rao is an example. Due to her extraordinary agility she can fill a large stage without any kind of strain or apparent effort.

His choreography required dancers of vigour and stamina without which Dasi Attam loses its clarity and becomes merely pretty.

Some of the greatest dancers in India today have learnt their art from Minakshisundaram Pillai, and it is because of him that the Pandanallur school dominates the solo dancing of South India. His son-in-law, Chokkalingam Pillai, carries on the great guru's work.

Mohan Lal is the eldest son of the late Hanuman Prasad, his two other brothers being Charanji Lal and Narayan Prasad. He has danced at the Courts of Raigarh, Indore, Jaipur, Baroda and Gidhor, and is also well known as a vocalist of the dhrupad style. In spite of his advanced years he is still teaching Kathak.

Mohanrao Kalyanpurkar is head of the Dance Department at the Bhatkhande Music College, Lucknow. *Shakuntala*, *Meghdoot*, and *War and Peace* are some of the ballets he has directed. He has also composed many torahs and kavitas. Being an authority, he is an examiner and judge of Kathak examinations and competitions. His guru is Sunder Prasad.

Gurus and Dancers

Mrinalini Sarabhai is from a Brahmin family and was educated in Switzerland. There she studied Russian ballet and Greek dancing. On returning to India she spent three years at Santiniketan and toured with Tagore's company, playing leads in his plays and ballets. She spent a short time in Java where she studied Javanese dancing under its foremost teacher Prince Tedjoekoesoemo. She later joined Ram Gopal's centre at Bangalore and learnt Bharata Natyam from Ellappa Pillai, Chokkalingam Pillai and Minakshisundaram Pillai. As Ram Gopal's partner she danced in India and abroad.

In 1948 she founded Darpana, an academy of the arts in Ahmedabad. In her teaching she makes use of her wide experience, exploring the possibilities of the traditional forms while always being careful not to damage them. The Darpana troupe has toured Western Europe, Russia, Japan, South America and West Asia. In 1963 she directed *The Vision of Vasavadatta* in New York, and has herself written a play and a novel.

Mrinalini Sarabhai has been widely honoured. The honours include the medal of the French Archives Internationales de la Danse, the diploma of the American Academy of Dramatic Art, the title Natya Kala Kovida for Bharata Natyam, and the title Padma Shri from the Government of India. She is the first woman to receive the Veera Shrinkhala for her contribution to Kathakali.

Nirmala Ramachandran is a young Bharata Natyam dancer of talent. She has studied under Chokkalingam Pillai, Gauri Ammal and Balasaraswati.

Nodia Tourangbam was a famous pung player before he became a dancer. He trained under Guru Amubi Singh and the late Guru Mahavir. He teaches Manipuri for the West Bengal Sangeet Natak Akademi.

Padma Subrahmanyam comes from a talented family and was taught dancing from the age of five. Later she learnt from Ramiah Pillai. This young Bharata Natyam dancer is greatly interested in dance-dramas, her most successful being *Minakshi Kalyanam*. Under Dr Ramachandran she has worked on the problem of relating the karanas of the *Natya Shastra* with the sculptures and murals of South Indian temples.

Appendix

Premlata Rajkumari is a very successful Manipuri dancer who has visited many countries as a member of Indian cultural delegations.

Priyagopal Sana comes from a family of musicians. He is well known in India for his graceful and dignified dancing. He appears to be more partial to the Lai Haroba than to the Ras and most of his compositions have an unexpectedly dramatic ending.

Radha Krishan is the author of *Nrityakala Manjari*, a book on Kathak. He was trained by his father Jagan Nath Prasad who was a court dancer in Nepal. Radha Krishan teaches at the Birla College in Pilani.

Radhelal Misra has toured Europe a number of times and has taught Kathak in England. He now teaches at the Sangeet Bharati in Delhi. His guru was the great Jai Lal of Jaipur.

Raghavan Nair received his Kathakali training from Guru Karunakara Pannikar and Guru Ramunni Menon. He has danced all over India as well as in East Africa. Although he plays several roles extremely well, his most famous rendering is that of the she-demon Putana.

Raghavan Pillai's Kathakali training did not start until he had left school at sixteen. He was attached to a kalari where he trained under Guru Palliampil Velu Pillai, Kesava Pannikar Asaan and Mathur Kunju Pillai Pannikar, all famous teachers of that time. When he was twenty-three he began appearing in performances and became well known in southern Travancore. In 1929 he became Asaan, teacher, at a Kathakali kalari established by Iruppakkal Pannikar. He later started a school of his own and his troupe is called the Jayadambika Vilas Kathakali Yogam. Krishnan Kutty is the best-known product of this school. Raghavan Pillai is a keen social worker but his chief interest is the dance.

Rajani Devi is one of the most famous maibis today. She belongs to the Maibi Loisang of the Manipur palace and although she is now very old, her exquisite grace and rich abhinaya are remarkable. During the Lai Haroba season she is still invited to towns and villages to perform dances such as 'The Creation of the World' and 'Birth of the Divine Child'.

Gurus and Dancers

Rajkumar Singhajit Singh was trained at the Nrityashram and now teaches at the Triveni Kala Sangham in New Delhi. He has specialized in the Ras style and all his compositions reveal the innate grace of Manipuri.

Ram Gopal's father came from Ajmer and his mother from Burma. He was brought up in Bangalore and even though he had no family tradition of dancing — his father was a lawyer and discouraged him most vehemently — he showed a remarkable aptitude for dancing from a very early age. He started by teaching himself with the help of gramophone records and soon began holding private dance recitals. Luckily, he attracted the attention of the Yuvraja of Mysore who became his patron and encouraged him with financial support.

Ram Gopal went to Kunju Kurup to learn Kathakali and to Minakshisundaram Pillai for Dasi Attam. At about this time La Meri the American dancer was on a world tour. She visited Bangalore and met the young dancer who impressed her with his zeal and enthusiasm. La Meri signed him on and Ram Gopal accompanied her to the Far East. This tour completed his apprenticeship for he learnt stage management, decor, and modern publicity methods. Above all, for the first time, he tasted the very real hardships of a dancer's life.

He continued touring and danced in America, England, and Europe. Returning to India he started a dance school in Bangalore but this closed down after some time, and now with the coming of the war he toured the country for ENSA giving performances for the troops. After the war he again toured abroad and presented a ballet at the Edinburgh Festival.

Ram Gopal has now settled in London. His most famous presentations were 'Dances of India', *Legend of the Taj Mahal*, and 'Dance of the Setting Sun'.

Ram Gopal is the son of Jai Lal and he has earned the highest respect as a dancer and teacher of Kathak. He teaches at the Bani Bidhya Bithi in Calcutta, his father's old school.

Raman Kutty Nair was trained by Guru Ramunni Menon. He made his debut when he was eleven and after a period of training at the Kerala Kala Mandalam he was appointed a teacher there. His

Appendix

favourite roles are the powerful Kathakali characters, Ravana, Hanuman, Bhima and Kichaka. He has toured Eastern Europe, Russia, China and Malaya.

Ramiah Pillai is a renowned Dasi Attam teacher. He is descended from Nagappa Nattuvanar and Veerappa Nattuvanar. He started his training under his uncle Manicka, and later worked under Muthukumarappu. An excellent example of Ramiah Pillai's style is the dancing of his pupil Kamala Laxman. There is a great emphasis on sculpturesque poses and fluidity of movement that is both elegant and graceful.

Ramunni Nair received his Kathakali training from his father Krishnan Nair who was attached to the Kuttipuram Yogam. His father was an exacting teacher who insisted on precision and versatility. Before he was twenty Ramunni Nair had learnt to play all the leading roles. He had also acquired the addition of Kichakan to his name, after Kichaka one of the characters he played especially well. He is now Asaan at the Kadathnadu Yogam and in spite of his advanced years is still very active.

Rani Karna is a pupil of the late Narayan Prasad. She is a young Kathak dancer of great promise.

Ratan Shankar is a polished performer and his footwork is brilliant. He was trained by his father Gyan Shankar, a teacher of the Lahore school of Kathak.

Rina Singha studied Kathak under Shambu Maharaj. After completing her training she joined the Bharatiya Kala Kendra ballet troupe and danced many important roles including the female lead in *Kumara Sambhava*. She joined Ram Gopal in 1961 and partnered him on European tours, and later taught at his dance school. She has appeared on British television and choreographed some short ballets. She has now settled in Canada and divides her time between her dance engagements and her dance school, 'Jhankar', in Toronto.

Ritha Devi is an extremely versatile dancer from Bengal. Among her forbears are poets, musicians, scholars and saints. She trained in Manipuri under Guru Atomba Singh and Guru Yaimabi Singh and is the first woman dancer to have presented the sacred Sattra Dance of Assam to the general public. This rare dance form had hitherto been the preserve of male dancers who had taken the vows of poverty and celibacy. Ritha Devi has also studied Odissi, Mohini Attam, Kathakali and Dasi Attam. Her European tours in 1958, 1962 and 1964 were highly praised by the critics.

Rohini Bhate runs her own Kathak centre in Poona. She is a competent dancer and has worked with Sohan Lal, Mohanrao Kalyanpurkar and Manna Lal. She has written on Kathak, and in 1952 was a member of an Indian cultural delegation to China.

Roshan Kumari's father is Fakir Mohammed the tabla player and her mother Zohra Jan the singer. She learnt her Kathak from Sunder Prasad and K. S. Moray and her Bharata Natyam from Mahalingam Pillai and Govindaraj Pillai. A brilliant dancer, she is much in demand for films, conferences and festivals. Her performance in Satyajit Ray's film *Jalsaghar* (The Music Room) is one of the better examples of Kathak in films.

Roshan Vajifdar, sister of Shirin, has a large public in India. She has beauty and grace and her abhinaya is exquisite. Her Bharata Natyam gurus are Chokkalingam Pillai and Kittappa.

Rukmini Devi is a dancer whose name will always be linked with the regeneration of Bharata Natyam. She is from a highly respected Brahmin family of Tanjore and grew up in an atmosphere both cultured and liberal. At a young age she came under the influence of Theosophy. In 1920 she married Dr George Arundale overriding much opposition from orthodox South Indian society.

Rukmini Devi began dancing under the supervision of Pavlova and then went to the finest guru, Minakshisundaram Pillai. She was an enchanting dancer and has been compared with the apsaras. It is said that at times she became so absorbed in her dancing and was so much at one with her art that it was difficult to say where body left off and soul began.

Her flexibility and her sense of line and grace of movement served to enhance even more the inner impetus she gave to her dancing. Her approach to dancing has always been one of intellectual discipline and total dedication. She was in fact, one of the first women

Appendix

from a respectable home to become a professional dancer — this at a time when dancing was regarded as one of the lowest of occupations and inextricably associated with prostitution. It must have required great courage to ignore the slighting remarks of the puritanical, the genuine concern of those who knew her, and even perhaps the sympathy of those who must have regarded her as, at the very least, misguided.

She searched for old and very often forgotten gurus, who lived neglected lives in remote villages. She travelled the world with her husband, exciting curiosity about Indian culture. Gradually the interest grew and she founded Kalakshetra, an international arts centre, at Adyar. The centre has now moved to new and extended premises at Tiruvanmiyur in Madras.

The aim of Kalakshetra is to resuscitate the arts of India and more particularly the various types of dancing in South India. Many first-rate dancers have been trained here but the main contribution of Kalakshetra has been in the production of Kathakali ballets for the contemporary theatre.

Rukmini Devi still travels widely, lecturing on dance, vegetarianism, and theosophy. Bharata Natyam owes a very large debt to this great lady.

Savita Mehta is a disciple of Guru Amudon Singh. She and her sister Nirmala have toured Europe giving Manipuri recitals.

Shambu Maharaj is today the most celebrated Kathak guru. He learnt his dancing within the family, from his father, uncle, and eldest brother. His classical music he learnt from Ustad Rahimuddin Khan. Shambu Maharaj excels in bhava and has done much to revive the nritya aspect of the dance through the use of thumris and bhajans. He is head of the Dance Department at the Bharatiya Kala Kendra in New Delhi, and his pupils include some of the best Kathak exponents. He has been honoured with the Sangeet Natak Akademi Award and the title of Padma Shri.

Shanta Rao is from a Brahmin family of Bombay which had no previous connections with dancing although the atmosphere in the home was conducive to artistic pursuits. At an early age Shanta decided she wanted to become a dancer and her parents gave in to her wishes with some reluctance. In 1939 she joined the Kerala

Kala Mandalam and trained in Kathakali under Guru Ravunni Menon. She undertook the full discipline, learning even the extremely masculine roles of the dance-drama. So inspired was her technique that Vallathol composed a Tandav Nritya for her. She also learnt Mohini Attam from Shri Pannikar and is one of the finest exponents of this form today. Shanta then went to Pandanallur to learn Dasi Attam from Minakshisundaram Pillai. Her repertoire is very wide and includes over twenty padams, nine varnams, eight tillanas, and seven jatiswarams.

Shanta has many devoted admirers but there are some critics who say that her style is far too masculine, characterized as it is by her wide leaps and springs. Her defenders counter this by saying that she is always in complete control of the space she uses and her movements, even when strong, are always in proportion to the space. She has, moreover, a personality that holds the attention of her audience even during the longest recitals. Her dance tours in India and abroad have always been very successful.

Shiv Lal taught Kathak for many years. He was a disciple of the late Binda Din Maharaj and was court dancer in Mysore and Nepal. Old age forced him to retire many years ago.

Shrimati Tagore was trained by Rajkumar Surjaboro of Manipur. Her approach to dancing is mainly devotional and she has done considerable research on the Lai Haroba.

Sita Pooviah is the eldest of three sisters who were trained by Sunder Prasad and the late Jai Lal. The sisters have made a name for themselves as Kathak dancers.

Sitara is the daughter of Sukhdev Misra and sister of Gopi Krishan. She was trained as a Kathak dancer by her father, and later by Achhan Maharaj. Her dancing is noted for its vivacity and brilliance. She has toured abroad many times and has danced in numerous films.

Sohan Lal teaches Kathak in Calcutta. Among his pupils are Leela Desai, Jharna Saha and Ram Dhan. He belongs to the Jaipur gharana and was trained by Jai Lal.

Sonal Mansingh comes from a distinguished family. She studied

Appendix

Odissi under Kelu Charan Mahapatra and Dasi Attam under Krishna Rao and Chandrabhaga Devi. She has danced widely in India and Europe.

Sudhershan Kumar has learnt Manipuri, Bharata Natyam and Kathak. His main interest now lies in Kathak in which style he was trained by Hazari Lal.

Sudhir Singh is well known for his dancing in the Khamba-Taibi sequences of the Lai Haroba. He is a patient researcher into the classical Ras.

Sunder Lal is a dance instructor at Baroda University. He has composed a number of torahs and is a tabla player of great virtuosity. He belongs to the Jaipur gharana, having learnt most of his Kathak from Shiv Narain and Jagan Nath Prasad.

Sunder Prasad is the younger brother of the late Jai Lal and is the present guru of the Jaipur gharana. He has also been trained in the traditions of the Lucknow gharana and his dancing combines the best of both schools. He teaches at the Bharatiya Kala Kendra and his pupils include some very well-known dancers. In 1959 he received the Sangeet Natak Akademi Award for his services to Kathak.

Suryamukhi was trained at the Mahavir School of Dance and later joined the Little Ballet Troupe. She has toured Russia, China and the Far East. Her Ras dancing is much admired and in 1961 she was acclaimed for her role in Tagore's *Chitrangada*.

Tarun Kumar and his wife **Vilasini Devi** are talented dancers and teachers. He started his career as a drummer but later turned to Manipuri dancing. His dance compositions hint at his experiments with other styles.

Thambal Angoubi is a well-known dancer and actress who is associated with the Manipuri Dance College. She studied Ras and Lai Haroba under Guru Amubi Singh and Pala Cholom under the late Guru Thambal Angon.

Thambal Sharma concentrates on folk dances and some of his compositions such as the Mahou Dance have been very well received. He has also choreographed a few dances in the tandav style. He teaches at the Manipuri Dance College.

Thambal Yaima is one of the very few foreigners who have specialized in Manipuri dance. In 1958 she attended the Manipuri Dance College and studied under the gurus Amubi Singh, Amudon Sharma and Atomba Singh. She also learnt the Maibi dances from Ibetombi Devi. She dances with her husband Bihari Sharma and has given many brilliant performances in Europe and the United States.

Thourani Shabi's abhinaya and singing are exceptional. She was trained in Manipuri by Guru Bipin Singh at the Sri Govindji Nartanalaya and often dances with Ghambini Devi.

Tombi Kshetri is a leading artiste who started dancing with the Manipur Palace Troupe. She excels in abhinaya and has a voice of rare quality. Tombi Kshetri still performs at religious ceremonies where she uses her wide knowledge of keertan music. She teaches at the Sri Govindji Nartanalaya.

Tombinou trained at Nrityashram. Her forte is the tandav style of Manipuri and the rendering of complicated rhythms. She has toured abroad on various cultural missions.

Tondon Devi is a charming Manipuri dancer who trained under Guru Amubi Singh.

Uma Sharma is a Kathak dancer of great vivacity. She is a pupil of Shambu Maharaj and is at present working under Brijju Maharaj at the Bharatiya Kala Kendra. She has danced in America and Russia and in early 1967 she had a very successful tour in Britain with Indrani Rehman's dance company.

Vazhenkata Kunchu Nair was trained in Kathakali by Koppan Nair, Govinda Pisharoti and Ramunni Menon. His best roles are Bahuka, Kichaka, Ravana and Parasurama.

Yamini Krishnamurthi was first trained at Kalakshetra at Adyar,

Appendix

and was later coached by Ellappa Pillai and Gauri Ammal. She has developed into an excellent dancer and performed at the 1965 Commonwealth Arts Festival in Britain. Besides Dasi Attam she also dances Odissi, Kuchipudi and Mohini Attam.

Zohra Segal comes from an aristocratic family of Uttar Pradesh. She studied eurhythmics in Germany under Mary Wigman and later trained at Uday Shankar's dance centre at Almora where she became a leading artiste. She toured the world with the Shankar troupe and then she and her husband, Kameshwar Segal the choreographer, started their own dance school at Lahore. She is a brilliant actress, has the certificate of the British Drama League, and for fourteen years was the leading lady of Prithvi Theatres. Zohra Segal now lives in London where she does work for the BBC, acts, and teaches dancing. In 1963 she received the Sangeet Natak Akademi Award.

BIBLIOGRAPHY

A Forgotten Empire, Robert Sewell, Swan Sonnenschein & Co. London. 1900
A History of Urdu Literature, Ram Babu Saxsena, Ram Narain Lal, Allahabad. 1940
Abhinaya Darpanam, Nandikesvara, trans. Manomohan Ghosh, Metropolitan Printing & Publishing House, Calcutta. 1934
An Idealist's View of Life, Radhakrishnan, Allen & Unwin, London. 1932
Anatomy of Ballet, Fernau Hall, Melrose, London. 1953
Ancient Art and Ritual, Jane Ellen Harrison, O.U.P. 1951
Arthashastra, Kautilya, trans. R. Shamasastry, Mysore.
Ballet, Arnold Haskell, Pelican Special. 1945
Bhagavad Gita, trans. Juan Mascaro, Penguin Classics. 1962
Buddhist Scriptures, trans. Edward Conze, Penguin Classics. 1959
Classical and Folk Dances of India, ed. Mulk Raj Anand, Marg Publications, Bombay. 1965
Classical Dance Poses of India, Gopinath and S. V. Ramana Rao, Natana Kiketan, Madras. 1955
Classical Dances and Costumes of India, Kay Ambrose, Adam & Charles Black, London. 1952
Dance in India, G. Venkatachalam, Nalanda Publications, Bombay.
Dances of India, Ragini Devi, Susil Gupta, Calcutta. 1962
De Syria Dea, Lucian, trans. A. M. Harmon, Harvard University Press & Heinemann, London, 1953
Discovery of India, Jawaharlal Nehru, Meridian Books, London. 1946
Folk Plays and Dances of Kerala, M. D. Raghavan, Rama Varma Archaeological Society, Trichur. 1947
Geography, Strabo, trans. H. L. Jones, Harvard University Press & Heinemann, London. 1923–30
Gita Govinda, Jayadeva, trans. Sir Edwin Arnold, Trubner.
Hindu Manners, Customs and Ceremonies, Abbé Dubois, O.U.P. 1906
Hindu Scriptures, Nicol Macnicol, Dent, London. 1938

Bibliography

Hinduism, K. M. Sen, Pelican Books. 1961
Hindustani Music, An Outline of Its Physics and Aesthetics, G. H. Ranade, Sangli. 1938
History, Herodotus, trans. George Rawlinson, Harrap, London.
India, A Short Cultural History, H. G. Rawlinson, Cresset Press, London. 1937
India's Heritage, Humayun Kabir, Meridian Books, London. 1947
Kama Sutra, Vatsyayana, trans. Sir Richard Burton and F. F. Arbuthnot, Panther Books, London. 1963
Kathakali, K. Bharata Iyer, Luzac, London. 1955
Life and Works of Amir Khusro, M. W. Mirza, Panjab Univ. 1935
Loves of Krishna, W. G. Archer, Allen & Unwin, London. 1957
Mahabharata, trans. P. C. Roy, Luzac, London.
Marg, ed. Mulk Raj Anand, Marg Publications, Bombay.
Melodic Types of Hindustan, N. K. Bose, Jaico Publishing House, Bombay. 1960
Music and Dance in Indian Art, Edinburgh Festival Society. 1963
Mysticism in World Religion, Sidney Spencer, Penguin. 1963
Natya Magazine, ed. B. Naaraayan, New Delhi.
Natya Shastra, Bharata, trans. Manomohan Ghosh, Royal Asiatic Society of Bengal, Calcutta. 1950
Nayars of Malabar, F. Fawcett, Madras Govt. Museum. 1901
Northern Indian Music, vol. I, Alain Danielou, Christopher Johnson, London, & Visva Bharati, Calcutta. 1949
Nritta Manjari, Leela Row, Indian Society of Oriental Art, Calcutta.
Prehistoric India, Stuart Piggott, Cassell, London. 1962
Prostitution and Society, Fernando Henriques, Macgibbon & Kee, London. 1962
Ramayana, trans. Rajagopalachari, Luzac, London. 1962
Rig-Veda, trans. Aurobindo, Luzac, London. 1952
Sangeet Natak Akademi, Dance Seminar Papers (1958):
    Dance Traditions in Assam, Maheshwar Neog
    Kathakali, Gopinath
    Manipuri Dancing, Atombapu Sharma and Amubi Singh
    Manipuri Dancing, Nayana Jhaveri
    Music in the Dance-Dramas of Tagore, Santidev Ghose
    Ritual Dances of South India, Mohan Khokar
    Shaivism and Vaishnavism in Indian Dance, Mohan Khokar
Tagore, Poet and Dramatist, Edward Thomson, O.U.P. 1962
The Ajanta Caves, Benjamin Rowland, Collins, U.N.E.S.C.O. 1963

Bibliography

The Art of Hindu Dance, M. Bhadhury and S. Chatterjee, S. K. Chatterjee, Calcutta. 1945

The Art of Kathakali, A. C. Pandeya, Kitabistan, Allahabad. 1961

The Dance in India, Faubion Bowers, Columbia University Press, New York. 1953

The Dance of Life, Havelock Ellis, Constable, London. 1923

The Dance of Shiva, Ananda Coomaraswamy, Asia Pub. House, Bombay. 1956

The Erotic Sculpture of India, Max-Pol Fouchet, trans. Brian Rhys, Allen & Unwin, London. 1959

The Indian Theatre, Mulk Raj Anand, Dennis Dobson, London. 1950

The Indus Civilization, Ernest Mackay, Lovat Dickson & Thompson, London. 1935

The Makers of Civilization — In Race and History, L. A. Waddell, Luzac, London. 1929

The Meaning of Art, Sir Herbert Read, Faber & Faber, London. 1951

The Mirror of Gesture, A. Coomaraswamy and G. K. Duggirala, E. Weyhe, New York — also O.U.P. 1917

The Music of India, H. A. Popley, Y.M.C.A. Publishing House, Calcutta. 1950

The Other Mind, Beryl de Zoete, Victor Gollancz, London. 1953

The Rise of Music in the Ancient World — East and West, Curt Sachs, Dent, London. 1943

The Sanskrit Drama, A. B. Keith, Clarendon Press, Oxford.

The Story of Indian Music, O. Goswami, Asia Publishing House, Bombay. 1961

Theatre in India, Balwant Gargi, Theatre Art Books, New York. 1962

The Wonder That Was India, A. L. Basham, Sidgwick & Jackson, London. 1954

Vishnu Purana, trans. H. H. Wilson, John Murray, London. 1840

Yoga, Ernest Wood, Penguin Classics. 1959

GLOSSARY

abhinaya expression
adavu dance unit (Bharata Natyam)
adbhuta (ras) wonder
aharya abhinaya costume, make-up and jewellery expressing the dramatic element, sentiment, or mood
alap introductory passage in music which establishes the atmosphere
amad entry (Kathak)
angik abhinaya gestures of the body expressing the dramatic element, sentiment, or mood
apsara divine nymph
arangeetram debut of a dancer
ashtapadi hymn
asura demon

bhagat devotee, one who is dedicated to the truth (North India)
bhagta devotee of Vishnu
bhagvata devotee of Vishnu (Bhagvata Mela Nataka)
bhagvatulu devotee of Vishnu (Kuchipudi)
bhajan hymn
bhangi pareng dance embodying the traditional Manipuri poses
bhava mood
bhayanaka (ras) terror
bibhatsa (ras) disgust
boles rhythmic dance syllables (Kathak)

chaal a Kathak walk or gait, also called *gati*; called *chaali* in Odissi
chakkar a turn or pirouette in Kathak
chakkiyar reciter of sacred texts in the temples of Kerala
chali a pure dance piece (Ras Lila of Manipur)
chari foot movement (Manipuri)
charita history
charnam final part of a song, verse, or poem

Glossary

chela disciple, follower
chenda upright cylindrical drum (Kathakali)
chhand form of ancient religious poem
cholom a masculine variety of dance (Manipuri)
chutti rice paste used for beard (Kathakali)

daru introductory dance for important characters (Kuchipudi)
desi (dance) for the pleasure of humans
devadasi woman servant of the gods, temple dancer (Dasi Attam)
dhoti loin cloth
dupatta veil, also called *orhni*

gath dance in which a story is told (Kathak)
gati a Kathak walk or gait, also called *chaal*
ghaagra long gathered skirt
gharana school or style
ghungurus ankle bells
gopee milkmaid, young woman

hasta hand gesture
hasya (ras) humour

jati complex rhythm pattern in footwork of Bharata Natyam
jhanki tableau

kalari Kathakali training school
kalasam short piece of pure dance (Kathakali)
karana a unit of dance including poses and hand and foot movements
kartal small cymbals used in Manipuri
karuna (ras) pathos
keertan devotional song
khandas four-line stanzas which make up the text of the Kathakali dance-drama
kriti dance-song
kumil costume used in Manipuri
kumin long skirt stiffened at the bottom (Manipuri)

lasya feminine aspect of the dance
layakari the dancer's mastery of the variations of rhythm within the time measure (Kathak)

Glossary

lehra single phrase of music played repeatedly (Kathak)

maddalam mridangam-like drum (Kathakali)
mahari female temple dancer (Odissi)
margi (dance) sacred to the gods
mridangam South Indian drum with two striking surfaces, one bigger than the other
mudra hand gesture
mukhabhinaya facial expression

nattuvanar musician, dance master
natya the dramatic element
nayaka young man, hero
nayika young woman, heroine
nayanabhinaya expression through the eyes
nritta pure dance
nritya the expression of sentiment and mood in dance

orhni veil, also called *dupatta*

pada love lyric
padam that part of a Bharata Natyam performance where the padas are interpreted through abhinaya
pakhawaj North Indian drum with two striking surfaces, one bigger than the other
palta a pure dance figure involving a turn (Kathak)
phanek sarong-like costume (Manipuri)
puja service of devotion
pujaree person taking part in a service of devotion
pung drum (Manipuri)

raga musical mode, melody archetype
rajasik character with particular flaws or vices (Kathakali)
rakshasa demon
ras sentiment, emotional state
rudra (ras) anger

sahitya literature, literary content
sakhi confidante
sambhoga union in love

Glossary

sankeertan communal prayer
satvik heroic, virtuous character (Kathakali)
satvik abhinaya physical manifestation of mental or emotional states (Natya Shastra)
shanta (ras) serenity
shringar (ras) love
sloka short religious verse in Sanskrit
sollukuttus rhythmic dance syllables (Bharata Natyam)
sum the first and key beat of the time measure
swara musical sound, note

tal time measure in dance or music
tamasik evil character (Kathakali)
tandav masculine aspect of dance
tatkar footwork (Kathak)
therissila the curtain held up by two people (Kathakali)
tirmana a short brilliant succession of adavus (Bharata Natyam)
torah short dance piece, similar to a *tukra* (Kathak)

vipralambha separation in love
vir (ras) heroism
viyog separation from the loved one (Manipuri)

INDEX

All names in capitals are those of dancers and gurus dealt with in detail. Italics are reserved here for book, manuscript, ballet and similar titles

Abdul Hassan Tahnisha, Nawab of Golconda, in Kuchipudi history, 63
Abhanga (body posture), 25
Abhinaya element of dance, 24-6; of Dasi Attam, 42-3, 46, 47; of Kathakali, 85, 95; of Krishna Attam, 87; of Kuchipudi, 64-5; of Manipuri, 182; of Mohini Attam, 115; of Yakshagana, 121; *Abhinaya Chandrika* as Odissi source, 203, 204; *Abhinaya Darpanam* of Nandikeshvara as source material, 24, 149, 203; *Abhinaya Navaneetham* (Kuppaiah Pillai), 224
Abhinava Gupta, 22
Abhishekams of Kuchipudi, 65
Achhan Maharaj, 135, 217, 218, 222; 225, 233
Achouba Bhangi Pareng (Ras Lila), 176, 187
Achutappa Nayak, king of Tanjore, 68
Achutapuram village (now Melatur), 69
Adavus (dance units), 39; aspect of Dasi Attam, 41; evolved from karana, 41; succession of, as tirmana, 42
Adbhuta (wonder) ras, 26
Adivasis (children of the forest), 82
Aharya abhinaya, 24, 25
Ahmedabad, theatre performances at, 161
Akbar the Great, and golden period of Kathak 130, 131
'Akhtar' (Wajid Ali Shah), last Nawab of Avadh, and the Lucknow culture, 133, 134

Akhtar Piya (court musician), 134
Alampur village, in Kuchipudi history, 63
Alankaradasis, *see* Dancing girls
Alap (opening item of music), 150
Al-Barauni, Arab historian, 54
Alexander the Great, in India, 126
Allahabad Music Conferences, 142, 219
Allarippu of Dasi Attam, 39, 44, 45, 46
Almora, Uday Shankar's India Culture Centre at, 211-12, 214
Alokita (glance) of Kathakali, 95
Amad (opening item), 142, 150; in Kathak training, 159
Amaiba and Amaibis (dancers of Meities) and ameebah (*Rig-Veda*), 184, 185
Amala Shankar, wife of Uday Shankar, 213
Ambalapuzha, Raja of, in history of Ottan Tullal, 117
Ammanakshi Amman temple, Kanchipuram, 215
Amrita (elixir of life), 132; in Mohini Attam, 114
AMUBI ARAMBAM, 214
AMUBI SINGH, 175, 178, 212, 214, 227, 234, 235
Amudon Sharma, 178, 214, 235
Amudon Singh, 232
Ananda (tandav expressing joy), 22
ANANDA SHIVARAMAN, 91, 214, 224
Andhra; dance-dramas, *see* Kuchipudi; Andhra dancers in Tanjore as

244

Index

Brahmin refugees, 69; Telugu language of, 63, 65, 69
Angarkha, modern versions of, 137, 138; Mughal dress, 130
Angik, gestures of, analysed, 24, 25; Angik abhinaya of Manipuri, 181
Anka (*Ankiya Nat*) plays of Sattra school, on Rama and Krishna, 194, 197
Ankle-bells; Kathak, 141; Mohini Attam, 116; *see* Ghungurus
Anti-Nautch campaign, 218
Anuvritta (glance) of Kathakali, 95
Apsaras, creation of Brahma, 20 34
Ardh-bathaka (hair-style), 204
Ardha Nari Nateswara, *see* Dasi Attam
Arjun, 100, 101
Arti ceremony, devadasis' right to perform, 59-60
Arthshastra, *see* Kautilya
Arunachalam Nattuvanar, 226
Arundale, Dr. George, 231
Aryans; arrival of, in Indian subcontinent, 18; profound influence of, 31, 53; and Kathakali, 84; and Kathak, 125; gods, legends, scholars, 19
Asamyuta and samyuta (hand-gestures, Kathakali), 93
Ashiq Hussain, 222
Ashoka, king, Buddhism under, 33, 125
Ashta kalasam of Kathakali, 93
Ashtapadis (hymns, nritya items), 64, 152
Asian Music Circle, England, 216, 223
Asvathi, Prince, plays of, in history of Kathakali, 89
Assam, Sattra dances of, 194-7; Tagore's 1919 lecture tour in, 208
Atharva-Veda, 19, 20
Atibhanga (body postures), 25
ATOMBA SINGH, 178, 209, 215, 230, 235
Atombapu Sharma, 175
Avadh, Nawabs of, transfer Delhi's cultural pre-eminence to Lucknow, 133-4
Avalokita (glance) of Kathakali, 95

Azhagar (a Kuravanji danced for Vishnu), 75

Bactrians, invaders of North India, 34
Badya, in Odissi performance, 206
Bahir-Jani Maharis, 202
Bahubhedas (hand movements, Manipuri), 181
Bahurupa tandav (dance with facial expression), 22
Baithas (sitting positions) of Odissi, 203
'Balagopala Tarangam', section of *Krishna Lila Tarangini* (on Krishna's childhood), 64
Balaram (in Goshta Ras), 189
Balaram, brother of Vishnu, 202
Balarama Varma, *see* Karthika Tirunal
BALASARASWATI, 67, 215, 219, 227
Balasubramania Shastri, 69
BALASUNDARI, 216
Balatripurasundari, goddess of the Kuchipudi temple, 66
Bali, dances of (Dasi Attam-inspired), 33; make-up for, 101
Ballets, Kathak, 161; *see* Menaka
Banamali Das, poet, and Odissi, 204
Bani Bidhya Bithi (dance school, Calcutta), 229
Banya (a Kathak drum), 139
Barah-Shringar ceremony, 202
Baroda (University, dance department) as centre for Kathak training, 164, 223, 234
Basava sub-caste, devadasis from, 56
Bhatkhande Music College, Lucknow, 226
Batu Nritya (of Odissi), 205
Bayalata, local name for Yakshagana, 121
Bearded characters of Kathakali, 100, 105
Behag (raga) in Dasi Attam, 42
BELA ARNAB, 216
Belis, basic body positions (Odissi), 203
Bells, of Kathakali dancers, 106
Belur (Vaishnavite) temple, in history of Dasi Attam, 35, 38
Bengal, Kathak survivals in, 131-2; Bengal Music College, 216

Index

Berlin 1936 International Dance Olympiad, 219
Bhagavad Gita, 86, 195; Krishna in, as new concept of a personal god, 62
Bhagavad Purana, 195, 197; Ras Lila described in, 165
Bhagtas, Bhagti movement, 62, 127; and the Krishna-Radha story, 195; Sankeertan as form of Bhagti, 190
Bhagvata Mela Nataka (Tamil Nad form of Kuchipudi), 62, 68-72
Bhagvata Purana; as Sattra source, 194, 195; in the Kuchipudi, 64; as sacred work, 88
Bhagvati, Great Mother Goddess, worshipped by Dravidians of Kerala, 81, 82, 83
Bhagvati Pattu (dance, Kathakali), 82
Bhagyachandra, King of Manipur, 175, 176, 186; contribution of, to Manipuri dance, 175-7; hastas codified in reign of, 180
Bhajan (nritya item), 148, 152
Bhama Kalapam (dance-drama), 67
Bhangi Parengs (Manipuri), 176, 182, 187, 188
Bhanuji, a founder of Jaipur school of Kathak, 133
Bharat Yuddha (Battle of India) dance, 190
Bharata Natyam dance, and its revival, 218-19, 226, 231-2; (modern threat to Bharata Natyam, 38)
Bharata Natya Shastra, 20-1; roots of Dasi Attam in, 31; describes the 108 dance units, 40-1; on the two meanings of love, 48-9; role of, in Hindu drama, 21; date, authorship, manuscript of, 21-2; interpretations of 'Bharata', 21; defines natya, 23; on six parts of drama, 23; on gestures, tempos, rasas, 25-6
BHARATI GUPTA, 136, 216
Bharatiya Kala Kendra (New Delhi), 133, 135, 136, 140, 156, 213, 217, 219, 222, 232, 234; training at, 157-61; ballet troupe of, 161, 230, 235
Bharatram Nallur Narayanaswami, 69
Bhargava, Aryan warrior (an avatar of Vishnu), 80

Bharmari (foot movements, Manipuri), 182
Bhasa (of Odissi), 203; plays of, 85
Bhaskara Ravi Varma, King, patron of Kudiyattam, 85
Bhasmasura Vadham (dance-drama), 69
Bhat, T. S., 222
Bhatkhande Sangeet Vidyapeeth, music college, Lucknow, 164, 226
Bhaumichari (foot movements, Manipuri), 181-2
Bhaunris (Odissi), 'spins on one spot', 203
Bhava (mood), 24, 49, 159; of Ras Lila, 167; bhava dikhana (Kathak), 94
Bhayanaka (terror) ras, 26, 27, 96
Bheetar-Jani Maharis, 202
Bhikshinis (Buddhist order of nuns and almswomen), 54
Bhima, 109; make-up (Kathakali), 102
Bhima-Dushasana combat, in Kathakali, 112-13
Bhubhaneshwar Kala Kendra, school, 203
Bhubhaneshwar temple, Orissa, 201, 203
Bhumi (Odissi), 203-4; Buhmi pranam opening performance, 205
Bibhatsa (disgust) ras, 26; in Kathakali, 96
Bighnaraj puja (Odissi), 205
Bihar State, Dravidian survivals in, 82
BIHARI SHARMA (*see also* THAMBAL YAIMA), 216, 235
Binda Din Maharaj, 135, 147, 218, 233
BIPIN SINGH, 178, 179, 217, 219, 221, 235
Birla College, Pilani, 228
Birth of our Nation (dance-drama), 223
Birth of Urvishi (dance-drama), 223
Boles (dance-syllables), 129, 141
Bombay, as training centre, 164, 219
Brahma; and Natya Veda, 20-1; creates apsaras, 20; as deity associated with wonder ras, 26; hand gesture denoting, 94; Brahma Melas, 62
Brahminism, rise of, and Manu's

246

Index

functions of four castes, 55; intellectual leadership from, 18, 19; Buddhism's retreat before revived Brahminism, 33-4

Bratya religion of early Meities, 171; Vaishnavism ousts, 174

Brihadeswara temple, 224

BRIJJU MAHARAJ, 135, 136, 156, 160-1, 216, 217, 235

Buddhism, birth and spread of, 125-6; as proselytizing religion, 33; and Brahminism (in south), 33-4; irrelevance of dancing and other arts to, 54, 126; is absorbed into Hinduism, 34

Budhimantra Sinha, 208

Burhas (of Odissi), 203

Calcutta; Bengal Music College in, 216; Kendra troupe visits, 163

Cambodian dances, 33

Caste system, 18, 31-2; break-up of, 18-19, 126, 156; reasons for success of, 18, 32; dancers' castes, 27, 58, 59; Bhagti movement mitigating inequalities of, 127; missionaries challenge, 36; some cultural benefits of, 155

Chaal (gait); of Kathak, 144, 151; of Ras Lila, 166

Chaali (gait); of Odissi, 203

Chaitanya, Vaishnavite sage and missionary, 187, 190

Chakkar (pirouette), 142-3, 157, 159

Chakkardhar tukra of Kathak, 142

Chakkiyar caste, 84, 85, 117

Chakkiyar-kuttu (recitation of Sanskrit shastras of Brahmins), 84, 118; in history of Ottan Tullal, 117-18

Chakpa, present-day type of Lai Haroba, 186

Chakradhar Singh of Raigarh (Raja), last great patron of Kathak, 135, 222

Chalanam, type of tandav, (Manipuri), 181

Chalis (short dance pieces) of Ras Lila, 187, 188

Champa tal (Kathakali), 93

CHAMPAKULAM PACHU PILLAI, 217

Champakulam Sanku Pillai, 224

Chandalika (dance-drama by Tagore), 208

Chandan Jatra (Orissa), 202

Chandidas (poet-musician), 129

CHANDRABHAGA DEVI (*see also* KRISHNA RAO), 222, 234

Chandra Kriti Singh, 177

CHANDRALEKHA, 217

Chandu Pannikar, 223

CHAOBA THANGJAM, 218

Chapka (head ornament), 138

CHARANJI LAL, 218, 226

Charis (leg movements), 25; four Manipuri types, 181

Charnam, in Shabdam, 43; as climax of Varnam, 47

Chaturang (short musical composition, Manipuri), 183

Chelas, disciples of gurus, 21

Chenda (drum accompanying Kathakali), 82, 86, 87, 108

CHENGANOOR RAMAN PILLAI, 218

Cheraman, King, patron of Kudiyattam, 85

Chidambaram, Temple of (South India), the 108 karanas on gateways of, 25, 34, 41

Chilmén bharna (novices' attitude to guru), 155

Chingkheirol, old Manipuri dance of rising of Usha (dawn), 172, 192

Chinnaya Naidu, 215

Chinniyah Pillai of Tanjore (and brothers), Dasi Attam redefined by, 36; preserving art of dance music, 58, 215, 225

Chinta Krishna Murti, 67

Chitralekha (dance-drama), 223

Chitrambala (Kuravanji dance), 75

Chitrambalam Dance Centre, Bombay, 221

Chitrangada (dance-drama by Tagore), 208, 234

Chodaganga Deva, ruler of Orissa, 201

Chokanna Tadi (red-bearded, demonic character in Kathakali,) 100, 101

Chokkalingam Pillai, 221, 226, 227, 231

Index

Choli (garment), 130
Chollus (jatis played on drums), 42
Choloms (tandav of Chalanam group), 181, 191-2
Chust pajama (garment), 130
Chutti (rice paste used in make-up), 100, 101, 106
Chuttipuvvu (pith knobs used in make-up), 100
Coimbatore district (South India), devadasis of, 55
Commonwealth Arts Festival (G.B.), 1965, 236
Conch shells, in Manipuri, 183
Conjeevaram, murals of temple near, showing devadasis, 56
Costume conventions, 25, 102-5, 106-7, 116, 119; *see* named styles of dance
'Creation by sound', 32

Dadras; as poetry set to music, 134; as six-beat measure, 140; as nritya items, 135, 146, 152
Dagar brothers; as music directors of Kathak, 164; as exponents of Dhrupad style of music, 136
Dalia (ballet), 136
DAMAYANTI JOSHI, 136, 218
Damru (small drum), symbol of creation, held by Shiva 32
Dance: and religions, 37; classifications of, 22-3; three main components of classical (natya, nritya, nritta), 23-4; the four main aspects of abhinaya, 24-6; the four ideal postures, 25; regional differences, 27; 19th century decline of, 27
Dancing girls, two main classes of, 58-9; method of retirement, 60-1; dancing caste, 27; *see* Devadasis, Domnis, Hansinis, Hourkinis, etc.
Dance of Modern India (Krishna Rao and wife), 222
'Dances of India' (Ram Gopal), 229
Danda Rasak (of Ras Lila of Manipur), 187
Darpana, academy of the arts (Ahmedabad), 227
Darshans (divine visitations), 86

Dartington Hall, Uday Shankar at, 211
Daruka, king of demons, in Kathakali, 82
Darus (introductory dances), 66, 67
Dasavatara, in Kuchipudi, 64, 70
Dasi Attam, classical dance, history of, 31-8; as dance for women only, 39; technical terms, movements of, 39-43; a performance of, 44-50; at courts of Deccan Sultans, after 16th century, 35; reasons for decline of, 36-7; elements of pre-Aryan dances in, 74; the allarippu of, 39, 42; tandav and lasya aspects of, 40; celebrating Shiva as Ardha Nari Nateswara, 40; sollukuttus in, 40
Deba Prasad Das, 203
Debindra Shankar, 213
Deccan plateau, as division between south and north, 31
Delhi: as declining cultural centre, late 18th century, 133; Gandharva Mahavidyala in, 218; International Centre for Kathakali in, 91
Devadasis, devadasi caste (servants of the gods), 31, 51-61; wide recognition of role of, 59-60; of great temples of South India, 55-8; morals of, 33; late 19th century disrepute of, 36, 48; modern descendants of, 61
Deva Vijaya Nritya (Kathak ballet), 132
Dhana Lal, 220
Dhemali, prelude to Sattra dance-dramas, 195
Dhenukasur, the ass demon, 189, 197
Dhol Cholom (a minor Cholom dance), 192
Dhoti (garments), types of, 138
Dhrupads (15th century music for Kathak), 139, 146; dhrupad style today, 131, 136, 146, 156
Dhruva Charitram (dance-drama), 69
Dija Ras (Ras Lila, Manipuri), 187, 188
'Dip' in Shankar's dance style, 211
Divas (earthenware oil-lamps), 67, 70
Domnis (dancing girls), 129
Donne, John: invocations of, compared with bhajans, 148
Dravidians, of South India, 18, 32-3,

Index

74; influences of, on dance, *see* Kathakali
Dubois, Abbé (*Hindu Manners, Customs and Ceremonies*) 57; on devadasis, 60
Duff Cholom (a minor Cholom dance), 192
Dupatta (garment), 130
Dushasana, make-up (Kathakali), 101, 102

Ear-rings (worn in Kathakali), 106
E. KRISHNA IYER, 218; and revival of dance, 27, 37
Ektal (measure of twelve beats), 140
Ellappa Pillai, 217, 227, 236
Elwin, Verrier; studies by, of Dravidian survivors of Aryan invasions, 82
Evil eye, 73
Eyes, importance of, in Kathakali, 94, 97, 98

Fakir Mohammed (tabla player), 231
False Pride (dance-drama), 223
Fatehpur Sikri, capital of Akbar the Great, 130
Fertility cults, Mother goddesses, 51

Gambhir Singh, Maharaja (Manipur), 177
Ga-naach section of Jhumuras, 196, 197
Ganapati (Ganesh, elephant-headed god), *see* Ganesh
Gandharvas (heavenly musicians), 172
Gandhi, on devadasis, 61
Ganesh (elephant-headed idol), 56, 149; role of, in Bhagvata Mela, 72; in Kuravanji, 75; invoked at start of Ottan Tullal, 119; 'Ganesh Vandana', salutation at opening of Kathak recital, 149
Gangaram Prasad, 220
Garuda, hand gesture denoting, 94
Gaths (dancers' delineation of stories), 143-5; three sections of subject-matter of, 145; in Kathak training, 160; gath bhavas, 145, 146, 151, 152; gath nikas, 144, 145-6, 151
Gatis (chaals), *see* Chaal

Gauri (tandav danced by Shiva with consort Gauri), 22
Gauri Ammal, 215, 227, 236
GAURI JOSHI, 219
GAURI SHANKAR, 219
Ghaagra (garment) with choli and dupatta, 167; with orhni (Hindu Kathak costume), 136-7
GHAMBINI DEVI, 219
Gharana defined, 132, 156
Ghazals (poems set to music), 134, 135, 146, 148
Ghuncha-e-raag (describing gaths), 145
Ghungat gath, in Kathak, 144-5
Ghungurus, in Kendra training, 141, 143, 144, 153, 157
Gita Govinda, 64, 66; as Mohini Attam source, 115; as source of Maharis' dance-songs (Orissa), 202
'Glances' of Kathakali mukhabhinaya, 95
Golconda (Muslim kingdom), dancing girls of, 57
Golla Bhama (dance-drama), 69
Gopee Pravesar Naach (in Sattra dances of Assam), 195, 196
GOPI KRISHAN, 136, 219, 233
GOPINATH, 220, 224
Gosai Pravesar Nritya ('Dance of the Lord'), 196
Goshta Bhangi Pareng, 177, 188; Goshta Lila (Atomba Singh), 178, 208, 215; Goshta Ras (Ras Lila), 187, 188, 189; Goshta Vrindaban Pareng, 177, 188
Gotipuas, male counterparts of Maharis, 201
Gouda Lila (Manipuri dance-drama), 190
Govardhan Lila (ballet), 217
Govinda, *see* Krishna
Govinda Palace temple, 214
Govinda Pisharoti, 235
Govindaraj Pillai, 220, 231
Govindasangeet Lila Vilasa (ancient text, Manipuri source), 177, 180, 181
G. Swaminathan, 69
Gourmani Singh (scholar of Maibi dances), 221

249

Greek drama, three points of resemblance with natya, 23
Greek invaders of North India, 34
Grosset, 22
Gunthanam tandav (Manipuri), 181
Gurava Raju, tyrant of Siddhavattam, 62
Guravayur temple, Krishna Attam still performed in, 86
Gurjaras, invaders of North India, 126
Gurudev, the Preceptor, *see* Rabindranath Tagore
Guru, defined, 21, 27-28
Gyan Shankar, 230

Halebid (Vaishnavite) temple, 50; in history of Dasi Attam, 35, 38
Hall, 22
Hand ornaments (for back of hand), 137-8
Hansinis (dancing-girls), 129
Hanuman, monkey-god, 100, 145, 197; make-up and costume for, 100-1, 103, 105
HANUMAN PRASAD, 218, 220, 222, 226
Hanumantha Ram (sarangi player), 220
Harappa civilization of Indus valley, 17; possible role of dancing in, 53
Harding, Mme. Stan, 223
Hari Das, 222
Harikatha (a devotional singer), 69
Haripad Ramakrishna Pillai, 218
Hari Prasad (and brother Hanuman), 133
Harishchandra (dance-drama), 69
Harmonium, in Indian music, 71
Harsha, plays of, 85
Hasta Lakshana Deepika (text on Kathakali mudras), 93
Hastas (hand-gestures; *see also* Mudras), 25; Kathak, 144-5; of Odissi, 204; of Sattra dances, 197; hasta-abhinaya, 87; Manipuri, 181
Hasya (humour) ras, 26
Hasyagadu, role of in Kuchipudi, 66
HAZARI LAL, 220, 234
Head-dress types, Kathakali, 104-5
Herodotus, on temple-gods of Assyria, 51-2

Heymann, 22
Hinduism: and Muslim invasion of North India, 35; absorbs Buddhism, 126; in Manipuri, early 18th century, 174; four root sentiments of, 47; drama of, compared with Greek, 23-4; major role of devadasis in Hindu society, 58
Hindustani music, in Odissi dance, 201
Hiranyakasipu (demon) in *Prahlada Charitram*, 70-1
Holi, festival of, 133, 167-8; Holika-krida, Manipuri festival dance, 183
Hourkinis, dancing-girls, 129
Hoysala power, Muslims destroy, 35
Huien Tsang, Chinese Buddhist pilgrim, 54
Huns, invaders of North India, 34
Hunter, Dance of the, 220
Hyderabad, theatre performances at, 161
Hypnosis, dance inducing, 71

IBETOMBI DEVI, 220, 235; dance centre of, Manipur, 179
Idangai, 'left-hand' caste of dancing-girls, 58-9
Immadi Narasa Nayaka, King (Siddhavattam), 62
Imphal; dance college at, Manipuri centre, 178-9, 214; temple of Govindji at, 175, 177
India Culture Centre, Almora, 211-12
Indra; Banner Festival of, 20; as deity associated with vir (heroism) ras, 26; and the *Natya-Veda*, 20; in the Parijatapaharana legend, of Kuchipudi, 63
Indradyumna, 202
INDRANI REHMAN, 203, 221, 235
Inspirations (dance-drama), 223
Irayimman Thampi, Kathakali plays of, 89
Iruppakkal Pannikar, 228
Israj (musical instrument), 183
Ishtadeva vandana (Odissi), 206

Jagan-nath festival (Orissa) and temple, 192, 201, 202
Jagan Nath Prasad, 228, 234

250

Index

Jagoi (early Meitie and Manipuri dance), 171, 184, 185
JAI KUMARI, 221
JAI LAL of Jaipur (Kathak), 133, 135, 221, 222, 228, 233-4
Jaipur gharana of Kathak, 132-3, 142, 156, 220, 221, 223, 234; nritta hastas of, 144; thaat of, 151; of today, 133
Jalsaghar (film, Satyajit Ray), 231
Jal-tarang (musical instrument), 161
Janaki Devi, 215
Janamashtami, festival of, 167-8
Janki Prasad, of Jaipur gharana, 133
Japanese dance, theatre (cf. Indian), 33-4
Jatis (rhythm patterns), 42, 45-6, 153
Jatta, coil of hair identifying Rama 145-6
Jayadambika Vilas Kathakali Yogam (dance school), 228
Jayadeva (Vaishnavite sage and poet), author of *Gita Govinda*, 64, 85-6, 129, 187
JAYALAKSHMI ALVA, 221
Jay Parajaya (ballet), 213
Jehangir, son of Akbar, 130
Jewellery of dancers, 106, 116, 137-8; see named dances
Jhanak Jhanak Payal Baje (film), 220
Jhankar dance school, Toronto, 230
Jhankis (tableaux) of the Ras Lila of Braj, 165-6, 167
Jharna Saha, 233
JHAVERI SISTERS, Darshana, Nayana, Ranjana, Suverna, 178, 179, 221-2; Nayana at Manipuri Dance Academy, 179
Jhobha (part of costume), 204
Jhoolan Jatra (Orissa), 202
Jhoolan Singh, 215
Jhumar (head-ornament), 138
Jhumuras (dances in Sattra dance-dramas), 196-7
'Juggernaut', origin of word, 202

Kabir (famous Bhagat, 15th century), 127
Kadar Piya (19th century court musician), 134
Kadathnadu Yogam (dance-school), 230
Kafi (raga) in Dasi Attam, 42
Kala, deity associated with bhayanaka (terror) ras, 26
Kalahantarita (example of Nayika bheda), 144
Kalakshetra (international arts centre, Adyar), (also Tiruvanmiyur), 75, 232, 235
Kalanidhi, of Mylapore, 219
Kalaris (sunken gymnasia of Nayar warriors), 83
Kalasams of Kathakali, 92-3, 110
KALAVATI (and VINODINI), 222
Kalavikash Kendra, courses in Odissi at, 203
Kali (goddess), 83
Kalidasa, author of *Malavikagnimitram*, etc., 85, 132, 161
Kalika (demon), Shiva tandav for, 22
Kaliya, serpent subdued by Krishna, 145, 152; *Kaliya Mardana* (a Krishna gath), 145
Kalka Prasad, 135, 225
Kal sadhakam (Kathakoli foot exercises), 92
Kalyani Amma, 220; as exponent of Mohini Attam, 115
Kalyani sisters, Tiruvalaputtur, 219
Kama Dev, 222
KAMALA LAXMAN, 37, 222, 230
Kama Sutra, see Vatsayana
Kameshwar Segal, 213; see ZOHRA SEGAL; dance school of Kameshwar Segal, Lahore, 236
Kammaladasis (idangai), 'left-hand' caste of dancing girls, 59
Kamsavadha (dance-drama), 69
Kanchula, in Odissi costume, 204
Kandappa Nattuvanar, 215; Pillai, 212
Kanduka Khel (Manipuri dance, Krishna and cowherds), 183
Kannakole, pure dance of Kuchipudi, 65
Kanniah Nattuvanar, 224
Kansa, King, destroyed by Krishna, 195
Kapa (ear-ornament), 204
Kapilendra Deva, King (Orissa), 202

Index

Kappatralla village (Kuchipudi), 63
Karana (unit of dance), 25, 41; source of Odissi, 204
Kari make-up, 101; head-dress with, 105
Karnatic music (Dasi Attam, Mohini Attam, Kuchipudi), 65, 115, 201, 215
Kartal Choloms, 183, 191; kartals (cymbals), 183, 191; kartal marol (drum), 191
Kartarimukha mudra (Kathakali hand gesture), 94
Karthika Tirunal, Maharaja of Travancore, plays of, 89; treatise on dance by, *Balarama Bharatam*, 89
Kartik Purnamashi, festival of 164
KARTIK RAM (and KALYAN DAS), 222
Karuna (pathos) ras, 26
Karunakara Pannikar, 228
Karuppu Tadi (black-bearded characters, Kathakali), 100, 101, 105
Kashinath Pandurang Parab, Pandit, 22
Kati-beni (hair-style), 205
Kataka mudra (Kathakali hand gesture), 94
Katchu Pillai Pannikar, 223
Kathak; history of, 125-38; a performance of, 149-54; techniques of, 139-48; training for, 155-64; 'nautch' as debased form of, 131; ballet (film and stage), 135, 136, 138; footwork as specially notable, 140; element of in Kuchipudi, 65; Jaipar and Lucknow layakari of, 65; (*see* Jaipur, Lucknow); relations with Ras Lila of Braj, 165-8; costumes on Persian model, 130-1; costumes today, 136-7; two main branches of modern, 132; Kathak Kendra, *see* Bharatiya Kala Kendra
Kathaks, as wandering instructors, 125
Kathakali; history of, 79-91; techniques, training, 92-8; costume, make-up, etc., 99-107; stories of dance-dramas, 108-13; related dances, 114-21; four groups of dancers' exercises, 92; correct posture for, 96

Kathaprasangam Manthrakam (solo performance in Kathakali), 85
Katti (Knife make-up, Kathakali), 100
Kautilya's *Arthshastra* (references to courtesans in), 54
Kavalapra Narayana Menon, 90, 223
Kavita (poem in Sanskrit), 148; kavita torah of Kathak, 144, 148
Keertans (devotional songs), 129, 139, 146, 174
Ke Ke Ke, or Thavalchongbi, Manipuri dance, 192
Kelikottu (drumming to open performance), 109
Kelu Charan Mahapatra (Odissi), 203, 234
Kerala; home of Kathakali, 33, 79; nature of caste system of, 82-3
Kerala Kala Mandalam (Institute of Arts), 90-1, 115, 214, 220, 223, 224, 229, 232-3
Kesava Pannikar Asaan, 228
Khali (unstressed beat), 141, 144
Khamba-Taibi story, 173, 174; in Moirang Lai Haroba, 186
Khamboji (raga), 43
Khandala, *see* Menaka
Khandalawala, Karl, in Kathak revival, 132
Khandas (4-line stanzas) of Kathakali, 92
Kharé rehné ké tariqué defined, 158, 159
Khol (percussion instrument) in Sattra dance, 195
Khomdol, father of Lokeshwar Singh, 225
Khowai Tampak, King, in history of Manipuri, 173
Khrumba Pareng of Manipur, 177
Khrumba Bhangi Parengs (Ras Lila), 187
Kirata the hunter (Shiva), make-up for, 101; head-dress, 105
Kiritam, head-dress of Kathakali, 104-5
Kittappa, Bharata Natyam Guru, 231
Kirti prabhand (short musical composition) of Manipuri, 183
K.N. Dandayuthapani Pillai, 221

252

Index

Knee-bells, in Kathakali and Ottan Tullal, 119
Kochappi Raman Nair, 224
Kochu Pillai Pannikar, 225
Kodanda Rama Iyer, 69
Konglei, present-day type of Lai Haroba, 186
Koppan Nair, 235
Kottarakkara, Raja of, and initiation of Raman Attam, 87, 88
Kottayam, Raja of, 87, 88; four plays of, based on *Mahabharata*, 89
Krishna: and Arjun (*Mahabharata*), 128-9; as avatar of Vishnu, 35, 62, 175; and Bhagyachandra, King of Manipur, 175, 176; as the Dark One, 147; gaths of (Kathak), 152; and gopees of Vrindaban, 23, 182, 187, 188; see also Ras Lila of Braj, Vrindaban; as Govinda, 128; as Murli Manohar, 128; as Natwar 152; and Radha, symbolism of, 128; in Sattra dance-dramas, 194, 195; as synthesis of Aryan and Dravidian cultures, 128; ways of identifying, 151-2; by costume, 103, 104
Krishna Attam, see *Krishnapadi*
Krishna Jayanti, festival of, 86
Krishna Lila (ballet), 132
Krishnapadi, 86, 88
Krishna Rasasangeeta, ancient text laying down Manipuri dance rules, 180
Krishna-Rukmini story, in Kathakali, 111
Krishna-Sudama story, in Kathakali, 111-12
Krishna-Vrindaban, 175
KRISHNA RAO (and CHANDRA-BHAGA DEVI), 222, 223, 224, 234
KRISHNAN KUMAR, 222
KRISHNAN KUTTY, 91, 223
KRISHNAN NAIR, 223, 230
Kshatriyas (warrior caste), 82; role of, in caste system, 18; as princely caste in Manipur, 176-7
Kshetrayya of Muvva, writer of padams, 64
K.S. Moray, 231
K. Subramania Iyer, 69
Kubak Ishai, variety of Tal Rasak, 192

Kuchelapuram village, in Kuchipudi history, 63-4
Kuchipudi, 62-7; performance described, 66-7
KUDAMALOOR KARUNAKARAN NAIR, 223
Kulasekhara, King, patron of Kudiyattam, 85
Kudiyattam, forerunner of Kerala dance-drama, 85
Kumara Sambhava (dance-drama), 136, 162, 164, 217, 223, 230
Kumbesara (Kuravanji dance), 75
Kumil (costume of Manipuri Ras), 176
Kumin (long skirt of Manipuri costume), 176
Kum Kum Das, 203
Kummi (of Kathakali, introductory dance of female characters), 110
KUMUDINI LAKHIA, 136, 223
Kunda flower, 26
KUNDAN LAL, 133, 164, 223
Kunj Ras, of Manipur, 175, 187, 188-9
KUNJU KURUP, 90, 220, 222, 224, 229
Kunju Pillai, 95
KUPPAIAH PILLAI, 224
Kuravanji, 73-5
Kuravas (hill tribe), 73-5
KURICHI KUNJAN PANNIKAR, 225
Kurmakis (temple dancers), Vizagapatnam temple, 59
Kusa, son of Rama, 104
Kushans, invaders of North India, 34, 126
Kuthambalam (temple platform for Chakkiyars' use), 84
Kuttipuram Yogam (school), 230
Kyamba, King of Manipur, 174

Labour and Machinery (ballet), 212
LACHHU MAHARAJ, 135-6, 164, 217, 218, 225
Lahore, 133, 230, 236
Lai Haroba, dances of Maibi (priestesses, Manipur), and 'Merrymaking of the Gods' (Manipuri dance), 173, 174, 176, 179, 184-6, 214, 220-1, 228, 233, 234; described, 184-6;

253

Index

costume for, 185; three modern types of, 186
Laihunba and Lai Pou (of Lai Haroba), 185, 189
Laithak Leikha Jagoi, ancient text, Manipuri source, 180
Lakshmi Narayana Shastri, Kuchipudi exponent, 67, 215
Lallan Piya (19th century court musician), 134
La Meri (American dancer), 229
Lanka Kand (dance-drama), 190
Lasya and tandav, of Manipuri, precise definition of, 180-1
Lasya Ranjana, palm-leaf manuscript, and translation, 222
Lava, son of Rama, identified by head-dress, 104
Laya, three categories of, 140
Layakari, 65; defined, 142
Leela Desai, 233
Legend of the Taj Mahal (dance-drama), 223, 229
Lehra (refrain), 131, 132; in Mughal courts, 139-40
Lila, 109, 166-7
Little Ballet Troupe, 219, 234
Loisangs (art guilds) of Manipur, 173
LOKESHWAR SINGH, 225
Lolonis (dancing-girls), 129
Lotus and bee decoration on Manipuri costume, 176
Lotus Dance, choreographed by Kameshwar Segal, 213
Lucian, on temple girls of Byblos, 52
Lucknow gharana, for Kathak training, 132, 156

Machupalli Kaifiat, on Kuchipudi and related dance-dramas, 62
Mackay, Professor, quoted, 53
Madan-ul-Musiqui, describing gaths, 145
Maddalam (elongated drum) of Ottan Tullal, 108, 118
Madhavan, 91
Madhavdeva, disciple of Sankardeva, 194, 196
Madras in 1927, 61; Madras Music Academy, 216, 219

Madurai, devadasis of temple of, 60
Mahabharata epic, 19, 88, 125, 190; as Kathakali source, 98; Sutas of, 84; Yakshagana plays based on, 121
Mahalingam Pillai, 224, 231
Maharaj Binda Din, 147, 148
Maha Ras of Ras Lila, Manipur, 175, 187, 188
Maharis (dancing-girls of Orissa), 201, 202
Mahavir, and Mahavir School of Dance, 227, 234
Mahou dance (Thambal Sharma), 235
Maibas, Maibis: cosmic dances of, 180-1; role of, in the Lai Haroba, 189
Mai sadhakam (body exercises, Kathakali), 92
Malabar coast (historic), 79, 102-3
Malabar Raman Nair, exponent of Ottan Tullal, 119
Malati Madhav (dance-drama), 135, 223, 225
Malavikagnimitram (ballet), 132
Malayalam, the vernacular of Kerala, 84, 85; as language of Ottan Tullal, 118; of Mohini Attam, 115
Make-up described (Kathakali), 99-101; the 5 main types of, 100-102
Mandal Rasak of Ras Lila of Manipur, 187
Mandapetta village, in Kuchipudi history, 63
Mandilla Cholom, type of Kartal Cholom, 191
Mantredathu Menekal, Raja of, 224
Maneshi De, in Kathak revival, 132
Manicka, uncle of Ramiah Pillai, 230
Manipur; paucity of historic records, 172-3; valley, 171; as 'Gandharvadesa', 172; Manipuri dance, 171-9; traditional Lai Haroba, 184-6; Ras Lila and related dances, 187-9, 190-3; music and techniques, 180-3; Manipur Palace Dance Troupe, 217; dance college, 217, 234, 235; Manipuri Dance Academy in Bombay, 179, 217, 222; Manipuri Dramatic Union, 214; see also Meities
Manjutara (songs from *Gita Govinda*) in Kathakali, 109

254

Index

Mankompu Sivasankara Pillai, 218
MANKULAM VISHNU NAMBUDRI, 225
Manna Lal (dancer), 231
Mannarsala, centre of snake worship, 81
Manomohan Ghosh, 22
Mantras, Brahmins' repositories of knowledge, in verse, 19
Manu, the laws of, 74; and caste system structure, 126
Marampali village, in Kuchipudi history, 63
Mardal (musical instrument), 205
Margi, *see* Dance, classification of
Marich gath (golden deer episode, Sita), 146
Markandaya (dance-drama), 69
Masks, 71, 81, 197
Massage, in Kathakali training, 95-6
Mathura, 48, 168
Mathur Kunju Pillai Pannikar, 228
Matras (musical beats), 140
Mattuswami Dikshitar (musician), 58
Maya (illusion) symbolized in Kathakali, 109
MAYA RAO, 136, 225
Mayo, Katherine, *Mother India* and *Slaves of the Gods*, 61
Meelita (glance) of Kathakali, 95
Meghdoot (ballet), 226
Mehfil (select company of connoisseurs), 136
Meities of Manipur, 171; converted to Vaishnavism, 182; Meitie Jagoi, early Manipuri dance, 174-5
Melatur village, 69, 71
Menaka (reviver of Kathak), 37, 132, 218, 219; dance centre of, Khandala (1938), 132, 223; dancing *Deva Vijaya Nritya*, 114
Menaka Lasyam (ballet), 132
Menkup, a Manipuri tal, 183
Methwold quoted, on devadasis of Golconda, 57
Mian Tansen (saint-musician), and Hindustani music, 131, 156
Minakshi Kalyanam (dance-drama), 227
MINAKSHISUNDARAM PILLAI, 222, 225, 227, 229, 231, 233

Minukku, type of make-up, 102; costume associated with, 103-4
Mira (poet-musician), 129
Misra, mudras of Kathakali, 94
Mizhavu (large copper drum), 85, 117
MOHAN LAL, 133, 226
MOHANRAO KALYANPURKAR, 164, 226, 231
Mohenjo Daro civilization (Indus valley), 17, 53, 176
Mohini Attam, 90, 114-16; decline of, 115
Moirang, modern type of Lai Haroba, 186; Moirang School (Manipuri dancing), 174
Moirang Parba (a Manipuri epic), 173, 174
Mongpokhong gate, the Manipuri legend of, 172
Mridangam (musical instrument), 66, 168
MRINALINI SARABHAI, 91, 115, 227
Mudali, surname taken by some nattuvanars, 58
Mudi, a Kathakali head-dress, 104-5
Mudras (symbolic hand gestures), 33; Kathak, 144; of Kathakali, built on 24 basic, 93, 97-8; of Mohini Attam, 115; Mudra sadhakam, study of gestures, Kathakali, 92
Mughal empire, 129-30, 131, 133
Mukhabhinaya (Kathakali) 87, 95; sadhakam, facial expressions, exercises for, 92, 94
Mundaka shabda (among shabdams of Kuchipudi), 65
Murli Manohar, *see* Krishna
Muslims; invasions of India, 35; and Hinduism, 63, 127; condemn sacred dance as sacrilegious, 127, 129
Musti mudra of Kathakali, 94
Muthukumarappu, 230
Mutti-yettu, dance, 82
Mysore: Yuvraja of, as patron of the young Ram Gopal, 229; as home of Yakshagana dance-drama, 121

Naba Kumar, 178, 208

Index

Nagaloka, the snake people, 81
Nagappa Nattuvanar, 230
Nagaraja, king of the cobras, make-up of, in Kathakali, 102
Naghmat-ul-Hind, (describing gaths), 145
Nails, silver, on left hand of Kathakali dancer, 106
Nakara (musical instrument), 153
Nala-Damayanti story, in Kathakali, 111
Nalacharitha (dance-drama), 225
Nallur village, 72
Nama mudra (Kathakali), 94
Namashkar, greeting (joined palms), 44
Nambiar, 85; and Ottan Tullal, 117-18; Nambiar caste as mizhavu players in Chakkiyar-kuttu, 85, 117
Nambudri Brahmins of Kerala, 80; and Raman Attam, 87
Nangiar, Nangiar-kuttu (Kathakali), 85
Narada-Ravana-Bali story, in Kathakali, 111
Narada Muni (sage) in Parijata-paharana legend, 63
Narasimha, the man-lion, an incarnation of Vishnu, 70, 112; make-up of, 102; Narasimha Jayanti festival, 69
Narayana, deity associated with Shanta (serenity) ras, 26
Narayan Prasad, 218, 226, 230
Narendra Sharma, 213
Nartana Ras (of Manipur), 177
Natana Niketan dance school, Madras, 220
Natanathi Vadya Ranjanam (South Indian treatise on dancing), 39
Nataraj, *see* Shiva (Lord of the Dance)
Natesa Iyer, 69, 281, 226
Natir Puja, Tagore's first dance-drama, 208
Nattuvanars (musicians) and devadasis, 35, 58, 66
Natuwa, 197; 'Natuwa Naach', 196, 197
Natwari, tukras, 152; boles, 153
Natya Saraswati, Bangalore (dance centre), 225

Natya Shastra, 165, 181, 185, 227; violence on stage, 23, 113; as Odissi source, 203, 204; mudras enumerated in, 97; influencing Sattra dance style of Assam, 197
Natya-Veda, origin of, 20
Nautch, as debased form of Kathak, 131; of Tanjore, 36
Nawal Kishore, 133
Nayika and nayaka (beloved and lover) in padams, 47; Nayika bheda technique, indicating emotional state of hero and heroine, 144
Nayanabhinaya, emotion shown through eyes (Kathakali), 94, 95
Nayar warrior caste, Kerala, 27, 82, 83, 84
Nibi bandha (garment), 204
Nigah (glance), 159
Nileswar Mukherji, 178, 209
Ninadi, *see* Rani Ripjit Singh
Nirmala Joshi, 136
Nirmala Mehta, 178, 232
NIRMALA RAMACHANDRAN, 227
Nitya ras (of Ras Lila), 166, 187, 189
NODIA TOURANGBAM, 227
Nokki-kanuka (stanza theme expressed by eyes) of Kathakali, 94
Nongpokningthou, incarnation of Shiva, 174, 186
Nritta aspect of dance, *see* Dance classification; in Dasi Attam, 41, 42, 47; Kathak, 139; Kuchipudi, 65; nritta hastas of the Jaipur gharana, 144
Nritya aspect of dance, *see* Dance classification; of Dasi Attam, 46; of Kathak, 127, 143-4, 146-8, 152; of Kuchipudi, 65; of Mohini Attam, 115
Nritya Bhangi, in Sattra dance-dramas, 196, 197
Nritya Darpana Society, 223
Nrityakala Manjari (Radha Krishnan), 228
Nrityashram, 229
Nuniz, Fernao, (on devadasis of Vijayanagar), 56
N. Venkataraman, 69

Index

Oberammergau Passion Play, comparison with Bhagvatas, 70
Odissi of Orissa, 201-3; costume for, 204-5; a performance of, 205-6; techniques, 203-4; popularized by Indrani Rehman, 221
Oothkadu village, 72
Orhni (garment), 130, 136, 137
Orissa, *see* Odissi; dancing-girls tradition in, 201; Orissa Sangeet Parishad, courses in Odissi at, 203; Dravidian survivors in Orissa State, 82
Ottan Tullal, 90, 117-20; as 'poor man's Kathakali', 118
Ougrihangal (tandav dance of Shiva), Manipuri, 192

Paan (betel) addiction, 68
Paccha, light-green make-up (Kathakali), 100, 104
Pada bhedas (foot positions), of Odissi, 204
Padams, 43, 47, 48, 49, 64, 65; Kathakali, 89
Paes, Domingo, quoted on devadasis of Vijayanagar, 56
PADMA SUBRAHMANYAM, 227
Padmapurana, on prostitutes of temple of Surya, 54
Padmasini Bai, daughter of Natesa Iyer, 69
Pagati Veshamu, (Kuchipudi) snatches of comic relief, 67
Pak Hangba, snake-god of ancient Meities, 186
Pakhawaj (long drum for Kathak), 133, 139, 150, 152, 153, 161, 217
Palaloisang (guild for Manipuri dancers), 173
Palas, (groups of dancers of Choloms), 191
Palis (stylized retreats from stage) of Odissi, 203
Palliampil Velu Pillai, 228
Palta (pure dance figure) of Kathak, 145, 146, 152
Pamheiba, King of Manipur, 174
Pampin Tullal ceremony (Kerala), dance of the snakes, 81
Panchapakesa Pillai (nattuvanar), 224
Panchatantra, dance-dramas from, 213
Panchayat (caste court), 59
Pandanallur school of dancing, 226
Pandit Gopal, 222
Pandita Radhya Charita, 62
Pankaj Charan, 203
Panthoibi, incarnation of Parvati, 174, 186
Paramelu, part of Kathak recital, 142, 153
Paramu Pillai, 217
Parans, 133, 142
Parasaranam, a Manipuri tandav type, 181
Parasurama, legend of, 80-1
Parayan Tullal, a variety of Tullal, 119
Parijatapaharana legend (Krishna and Rukmini), 63
'Pariyon ka Khana', Wajid Ali Shah founds, 134
Parmuls (rhythmic pieces) of Ras Lila of Braj, 166
Partap Pawar, 217
Parvati, consort of Shiva, 149, 172; instructs Usha in lasya, 23; marriage of, symbolized in devadasis' marriage to idol, 56; with Shiva in dance contest, 41
Pataka mudra in Kathakali, 93-4
Pathakam, in Kathakali background, 85
Patta sari (garment), 204
Patukaran, make-up artist (Kathakali), 99
Pavlova, 27, 210, 231; Menaka's friendship with, 132
Pena (musical instrument), 183
Persian and Central Asian influences on Kathak, 129-30
Perumal dynasty, as patrons of Kudiyattam, 85
Phag Lila (ballet), 217
Phanek (early Meitie dance costume), 176, 186
Pillai, as nattuvanar surname, 58
P.K. Subbier, 69
Pong, King of Burma, 174
Poona, as centre for Kathak training, 164, 231

Index

Prabhand style (religious songs), 139; Prabhand-kuttu (solo performance), 85
Prahlada Charitram (dance-drama), 69, 70, 71, 223
Prakashji, lost work on gaths by, 145
Pralokita (glance) of Kathakali, 95
Pramatha, deity associated with Hasya (humour) ras, 26
Pratima Das, 203
Pravesar Nritya, short dances in Sattra dances of Assam, 196
Prekashani tandav (danced without facial expression), 22
PREMLATA RAJKUMARI, 228
Prithvi Theatres, 236
PRIYAGOPAL SANA, 228
Priyambada Mohanty, 203
Prostitution (sacred), 51-4; possible connection with dance before Aryan invasion of 2000 B.C., 53-4; after 4th century rise of Brahminism, 55; 19th century decline of, 36
Pulluvan caste, 81
Pung (Manipuri drum), 183; pung dances of Manipur, 177; Pung Choloms (Manipuri dance compositions), 183, 191, 192
Punniah Pillai, preserving art of dance music, 36, 58, 225
Puranas (legends concerned with gods), 19
Purappad of Kathakali (first appearance of hero and partner), 109
Puri, Orissa, as place of pilgrimage 202
Pushpa-chanda (hair-style), 204
Pushpanjali hasta described, 150
Putana-Krishna story (Kathakali), 109, 112; make-up for Putana, 101-2

Qaisar Bagh palace, Wajid Ali Shah founds, 134
Quarles, Francis, invocations of, compared with bhajans, 148

Rabindranath Tagore; in cultural renaissance, 207-8; revives Manipuri at Santiniketan (*q.v.*), 177
Radha, 35, 182, 186, 188; ways of characterizing, 152; in Maha Ras of Manipur, 175; in Ras Lila of Braj, 166; minor role of, in *Ankiya-Nat*, 194, 195; *Radha and Krishna* (ballet), 210
RADHA KRISHNAN, 228
RADHELAL MISRA, 223, 228
Raga; 42, 43; raga-bhava, stress on in Tagore's plays, 208
Raghavan, Dr., in Kathak revival, 132
Raghavan, M.D., 75
RAGHAVAN NAIR, 228
RAGHAVAN PILLAI, 223, 228
Ragini Devi, 220, 221, 25, 91
Ragmalikas, 43
Rai Bahadur Daya Ram Sahni, dancing-girl figurine found by, 53
Raigarh, Raja of, as patron of the arts, 135, 222
Rajadasis, *see* Dancing girls
RAJANI DEVI, 228
Rajaraja, Chola king, *see* Tanjore
Rajarajeshwari Bharata Natyam Kala Mandir (school), Bombay, 224
Rajasik (characters of Kathakali drama with particular vices), 99, 100
Rajasthan, Kathak survivals in, 131-2, 133
Raj Kumar, 163
RAJKUMAR SINGHAJIT SINGH, 229
Rajkumar Surjaboro, 233
Rajniel (a Manipuri tal), 183
Ram Chandra Gangooly, 312
Ram Dhan, 233
RAM GOPAL, 91, 223, 224, 227, 229, 230
RAM GOPAL, son of JAI LAL, 229
Ram Narain Misra, 132
Rama, spouse of Sita, 94, 104, 145-6; in the Lanka Kand, 190; in Sattra dance-dramas, 194
Rama Krishna Alva, 221
Rama Pannikar, 223
Ramachandran, Dr., 227
Raman Attam, in Kathakali background, 87-8
RAMAN KUTTY NAIR, 229
Ramayana epic, 19, 98, 121, 125, 145,

258

Index

172, 190; Yakshagana plays based on, 121; production by Shanti Bardhan, 213
Ramdani section of Jhumuras, 196-7
RAMIAH PILLAI, 222, 227, 230
Ramiah Shastri; *Golla Kalapam* (play), 64
Ramlila (ballet), 213
Rampur, Kendra troupe's visit to, 163
Ramunni Menon, 228, 229, 235
RAMUNNI NAIR, 230
Rang manj ki puja ('offering to the stage'), 150, 158, 159
RANI KARNA, 230
Rani Rijpit Singh (Ninadi) ballet troupe administrator, 162-3
Ras; in Kathakali, 111; eight rasas enumerated by *Natya Shastra*, 26; dancer's method of evoking, 26; seven accepted Manipuri, 187; and rasak, as described in *Natya Shastra*, 165; ras mandal as dance area, 166, 168
Ras Lila, 134, 178, 187-9; composing of ras varieties, 175; costume and performance described in *Govindasangeet Lila Vilasa*, 180; strictly codified sequence of, 188; of Braj, Kathak elements of, 165-8
Rasak, 165; three types of, Ras Lila of Manipur, 187
Rashmi Jain, 217
RATAN SHANKAR, 230
Ravana, demon king of Lanka, 95, 100, 111, 145, 146; hand gestures denoting, 94; sister of ,102
Ravana Vijayam (dance-drama), 95
Ravunni Menon, 90, 233
Rechakas of Dasi Attam, 44
Rig-Veda, 19, 20, 125, 184, 185
RINA SINGHA, 230
RITHA DEVI, 178, 203, 230
R. Nagarajan, 69
Rodin, on the Nataraj, 32
ROHINI BHATE, 164, 231
ROSHAN KUMARI, 231
ROSHAN VAJIFDAR, 115, 231
Rothenstein, Sir William, 210
Rudra (anger) ras, 26; deity Rudra associated with, 26; character types of Yakshagana, 121
Rudra Singh, 215
Rugmangada, a king of Ayodhya, in Kathakali drama, 114-15
Rukmangada (dance-drama), 69
Rukmini, 63, 195
Rukmini, consort, *see* Krishna
RUKMINI DEVI, 37, 75, 91, 219, 231-2
Rukmini Kalyanam (dance-drama), 69
Rupa Goswami; *Ujjavalanilamani* (on abhinaya of Manipuri), 182

Sabaja Panthis, in Ras Lila of Manipur, 189
Sabhinaya, gita-abhinaya, in Odissi performance, 206
Sachin Shankar, 213
Sahitya, 46
St. Denis, Ruth, 210
Sakhi (confidante) in songs of varnam (Dasi Attam), 47
Salaami, Muslim salutation, 142, 150; salamu concluding part of shabdam in Dasi Attam, 35, 43, 46
Saliyamangalam village, 72
Sama (glance) of Kathakali, 95
Samabhanga (body posture), 25
Samanya Kshati (ballet), 213
Sambhoga (union aspect of love), 48-9
Samhara, Shiva's tandav dance of death, 23
Samurai war dances, Japan, and other combats, as entertainment, 84
Sam-Veda, 19, 20
Sanchi (glance) of Kathakali, 95
Sandhya, Shiva's evening tandav, 22
Sangeet, didactic piece of Ras Lila of Braj, 166
Sangeet Bharati, Delhi, 228; Sangeet Natak Akademi, India's national academy of music and drama, 91, 135, 203
Sangeet Sara, 149
Sanis, temple dancers (Telugu districts), 59
Sanjh Savera (ballet), 213
Sanjukta Misra, 203

Index

Sankaran Pillai, 225
Sankardeva, brings Vaishnavism to Assam, 194
Sankeertan, feature of Manipuri Vaishnavism, 181, 190, 191, 192; highly evolved dances associated with, 191
Sanku Pillai, 217
Santala, Queen, sculptures of (Vishnu temples), 35, 38
Santiniketan (Home of Peace), 115, 207-9, 215, 219, 227; criticisms of style of, 209
Sarangi (stringed instrument), 139, 158
Saraswati, goddess of learning, invoked at start of Ottan Tullal, 119
Sari, for dance, 137; patta sari, 204
Sarode (musical instrument), 161
Sattra dances of Assam, 194-7, 231; faithful to early image of Krishna, 195; Sattra Ras, 195, 196; the Pravesar Nritya of, 166
Satvik, abhinaya, 24, 25-6 characters as virtuous beings of drama, 99; make-up of satvik characters, 100
Satyabhama (a beloved of Krishna), 63
Satya Narain, tabla player, 220
Saut-ul-Mubarak (describing gaths), 145
Savaal-javaab (duets) of Kathak, 162
SAVITA MEHTA (and sister NIRMALA), 178, 232
Sayed Agha Hassan Amanat (poet), 134
Scythian invaders of North India, 34, 126
Seetankan Tullal, a variety of Ottan Tullal, 119
Senarik Singh, 178, 209
Shabdam (song of praise) in Dasi Attam, 42-3, 46
Shakti (primal energy) symbolized in Kathakali, 109
Shakuntala (ballet), 225, 226
SHAMBU MAHARAJ, 135, 136, 140, 145, 147, 148, 156, 157-60, 216, 217, 218, 219, 220, 222, 223, 225, 230, 232, 235

Shan-é-Avadh (ballet), 136
Shanta (serenity, ras), 26
Shantaram, film producer, 220
SHANTA RAO, 37, 75, 91, 226, 232; dancing Kuravanji, 75; dancing Mohini Attam, 115
Shanti Bardhan, 213, 219
Shasta, son of Shiva, 114
Shastras, books embodying Aryan learning, 19
Sheigonnabi, Manipuri (a dance composition), 183
Shirbhedas (head movements) of Manipuri, 181
Shirin Vajifdar, joint founder of Nritya Darpana Society, 223, 231
Shiv Lal, 219, 220
Shiv Narain, 234
Shiva, 56, 46, 47; as Ardha Nari Nateswara in Dasi Attam, 40; as god of Aryan Brahmins, 32; as possibly pre-Vedic deity, 171; in the Bratya religion, 171; and Ganesh, 149; in lingam form, 33; Khamba regarded as incarnation of, 173-4; as Lord of the Dance (Nataraj), 32, 41; as Mahakala, deity associated with bibhatsa (disgust) ras, 26; and Mohini, 114, 132; name of, in Manipur, 174, 186; Odissi dedications to, 205, 206; and Parvati, 174, 220; loss of religious fervour for, 36; seven tandavs of, 22-3; as Thirukudanthar, 75; ways of characterizing, 152; hand gesture denoting, 94
Shivadatta, Pandit, 22
Shiva-Lila Natyam (earliest dance-drama of South India), 62
Shivanandan Pillai, 36, 58, 225
Shiva Purana (sacred work), 88
Shivarathrivaibhavam (dance-drama), 69
Shortt, Dr. R., on devadasis, 58, 60
SHRIMATI TAGORE, 233
Shrimati Thankamani, 220
Shringar (love) ras, 26, 150; Shringar Lahari, 220; as predominant ras of Manipuri, 182, 187
Shri Pannikar, 233
Shudras, role of in caste system, 18

Shyama (dance-drama), 208, 209
Siddharta, Prince (Sakya tribe), founder of Buddhism, 125
Sidhyendra Yogi (Telugu Brahmin), founder of Kuchipudi, 63
Sikandar Piya (19th century court musician), 134
Sikkim, King of, 44
Silappadikaram, epic ('Epic of the Anklet'), 84
Simkie, dance partner to Uday Shankar, 211
Singers in Kathakali, 86-7, 108
Sita, wife of Rama, 88; Sita Harana gath, 145-6
Sita Kalyanam (dance-drama), 69
SITA POOVIAH, 233
Sitar (musical instrument), 161
SITARA, 136, 138, 233
Sitaram Prasad, 218
Slokas; defined, 65; 149; padas evolved from, 43; in the Sattra dances of Assam, 196
Snake groves of Kerala, 81
SOHAN LAL, 133, 216, 225, 231, 233
Sollukuttus (dance-syllables), 40, 44, 45, 64; allarippu of Mohini Attam, 115
SONAL MANSINGH, 222, 233
Soolamangalam village, 72
Sri Govindji Nartanalaya (Manipuri dance college), 179, 217, 219, 222, 225, 235
Stambha pada (special Odissi movement), 204
Sthankas (of Odissi), standing positions, 203; of Manipuri, 182
Strabo quoted, on temple girls of Comana and Corinth, 52, 53
Subbaraya Nattuvanar, 225
Subhadra, sister of Vishnu, 202
Subramanya, son of Shiva, in Kuravanji, 75
Suchindram temple, South Travancore, devadasis of, 56
SUDHERSHAN KUMAR, 234
SUDHIR SINGH, 234
Sufism, rise of, in Islam, 127
Sukhdev Misra, father of Sitara, 233
'Sum' in Kathak, 140, 141, 143, 151, 154

Sumya (gentle) character types of Yakshagana, 121
SUNDER LAL, 164, 234
SUNDER PRASAD, 133, 156, 219, 220, 223, 225, 226, 231, 233, 234
Surdas (sage, musician, poet), 129, 187
Surpanakha (Kathakali), make-up of, 101-2
Surya, sun-god, cult of, 53-4
Surya Baladev Rath, 204
SURYAMUKHI, 234
Sutradhara, role of, in Sattra dances of Assam, 195; dance of the, 195-6; costume for, 196
Swara (musical sound) and Swarajati, 42, 43; swara pallabi nritta of Odissi, 206
Swarmala (short musical composition, Manipuri), 183
Swarna Saraswathi, 221
Swathi Rama Varma, Maharaja of Travancore, composer of Kathakali padams, 89
Sword dances of Nayars, 83

Tabla (upright drum), 133, 139, 153, 158, 161, 217
Tagore (Rabindranath Tagore), and revival of dance, 27, 28, 115; *see* Santiniketan, *also* Rabindranath Tagore
Taibi and Khamba, love story of (Manipuri), 173, 174; in Moirang Lai Haroba, 186
Tal (time-measure), 140-2; in Manipuri dance, 183
Tal Rasak (Ras Lila), 187
Tali (wedding necklace), tying ceremony, 55-6
Tamasik, evil characters of drama, 99
Tamboura (musical instrument), 183
Tamir Baran, 212
Tanchep (a tal of Manipuri), 183
Tandav, *see* Dance classifications; three Manipuri types of, 181
Tandu, disciple of Shiva, 22
Tangiva-Birznek, Mme. (Russian choreographer), 225
Tanjore, Court of, 215, 224, 225; devadasis of temple, 55, 60

Index

'Tanjore nautch', 36
Tansen, exponent of Dhrupad style, 131, 156
Tapas Sen, lighting technician, 162
Tapasya (meditation), 132
Tarijham (Odissi performance finale), 206
TARUN KUMAR (and wife, VILASINI DEVI), 234
Tatkar (footwork in Kathak), 140-1, 153; of Jaipur gharana, 142
Tattooing of face, 73
Tavaifs (dancing girls, Agra, Lucknow, Delhi), 57
Tedjoekoesoemo, Prince, teacher of Javanese dancing, 227
Television, Kathak profiting from, 138
Telugu language, 59; combined with Tamil in Bhagvata Mela Nataka, 70
Thaat, of Kathak, 150-1
Thabalchong, a Manipuri dance, 182
Thakur Prasad, 134
THAMBAL ANGOUBI, 234
THAMBAL SHARMA, 235
THAMBAL YAIMA, 178, 217, 235
Thankachi, daughter of I. Thampi, plays by, 89
Thavalchongbi, a Manipuri dance, 192
The Cranes (ballet), 213
The Fisherman and the Mermaid (ballet), 213
The Hindu Wedding (ballet), 210
The Rhythm of Life (ballet), 212
The Vision of Vasavadatta (dance-drama), 227
Theperumanallur village, 72
Therissila ('stage' curtain, Kathakali), 108, 109
Thirukutrala Kuravanji (dance), 75
Thottam Sankaran Nambudri, 223, 225
THOURANI SHABI, 235
Thumris (in Kathak, nritya items), 134, 135, 146, 152; Thumri andaaz, 65, 146-147
Thurston, *Castes and Tribes of Southern India*, 60
Thyagaraja, dance-songs of (kritis), 64
Tika (forehead jewel), 137

Tillana of Dasi Attam, 42, 49-50
Tiranokku ('curtain-look'), introducing Kathakali demon, 109-10
Tirath Ajmani, 217
Tiray-attam, dance, 82
Tirmana, *see* Adavus; in Dasi Attam, defined, 42; 46, 50
Tirtha Narayan Yati, *Krishna Lila Tarangini* of, 64
Tiya-attam, dance, 82
Todayam, a Kathakali devotional dance, 109
Todi (raga) in Dasi Attam, 42
TOMBI KSHETRI, 235
TOMBINOU, 235
TONDON DEVI, 235
Torah (short dance piece), 143
Transposed Heads (dance-drama), 223
Travancore, Princely State of, 61, 223; Malayam-speaking dancers of Southern, 59; Maharajas of, as patrons of Kathakali, 89
Tribhanga (body posture), 25, 150
Trikasta, rule of the, 176-7
Trikhandi majura (triple leave-taking, Odissi), 206
Tripura-Shiva combat, tandav of, 23
Trital (16-beat measure), 140, 142
Triumph of Life (dance-drama), 223
Triveni Kala Sangham, New Delhi, 229
Tukras (short items in Kathak), 142, 144, 160, 161; slow, medium and fast (named), 142; of natwari type, 152
Tulsidas (poet-musician), 129

Uday Shankar, 210-13; dance centre of (Almora), 236; and Dasi Attam revival, 27, 37; and Kathakali, 91
Ujjain, birthplace of Kalidasa, 161, 164
Ujjavalanilamani, Manipuri text, 182
Ukuttas (rhythmic syllables, Odissi style), 205, 206
Ullokita (glance) of Kathakali, 95
Ulukhal Ras (Ras Lila), 187, 189
Uma (tandav of Shiva and consort Uma), 22
UMA SHARMA, 235
Untouchables, 59

Index

Upavishta (foot movements, Manipuri), 182; upavishta sthankas (sitting poses), 182
Upendra Bhanj (poet), work of, in Odissi dances, 204
Urus; bull, cult of, 53
Urvishi (heavenly nymph) in Kathakali, 102
Usha, and the Parvati dance, 23, 172
Usha Parinayam (dance-drama), 69
Ustad Alauddin Khan, teacher at India Culture Centre, 212
Ustad Rahimuddin Khan, 232
Uthas (rising, jumping positions, Odissi), 203
Utkal College of Music and Dance, 203
Utpluti (foot movements, Manipuri), 182
Utsav (ballet), 213
Uttariyam (stole) worn in Kathakali, 106

Vachik, vachik abhinaya, 24, 25
Vadivelu Pillai, 36, 225; and art of dance music, 58
Vaishnavism (*see also* Vishnu), 34, 85-6, 166; as stimulus to art, music, etc., 174; influence of, on Kathak, 127; becomes religion of Manipur, 175; in Assam, 194-7; in Orissa, 201; the nine forms of Bhagti in, 174; furnishing themes of Bhagvata Mela dance-dramas, 69
Vaishyas, role of, in caste system, 18
Valangai ('right-hand' caste of dancing girls), 58-9
Valia Kalasam of Kathakali described, 93
Vallathol Narayana Menon (poet), 90, 115, 233; and dance revival, 27
Valli, *see* Subramanya
Varadaraja Perumal temple, 71
Varanasi, 133; All India Music Conference at, 219
Varnam of Dasi Attam, 43; described, 46-7
Vasakasajja (example of nayika bheda), 144
Vasant, festival of, 167-8; Vasanta Ras (Ras Lila, Manipuri), 175, 187, 188
Vatsayana; *Kama Sutra* (*c.* A.D. 100), 54
Vatta mudi (head-dress), 105
VAZHENKATA KUNCHU NAIR, 235
Vazhuvur nattuvanars, 222
Vedas, the four principal, 19; Vedic religions (ancient) of North India, 125
Veena (musical instrument), 205
Veena Dhanam, grandmother of Balasaraswati, 215
Veerappa Nattuvanar, 230
Vehayaniya Pannikar, 225
Veluppu Tadi (white-bearded characters of Kathakali), 100
Venkatakrishna Nattuvanar, 224
Venkatarama Shastri, dance-dramas by, 69
Veralakshmi, 219
Victorian age, and Indian culture, 90
Vidyapati (poet-musician), 129
Vijayanagar Empire, 35, 62; temple dancing girls of, 56
VILASINI DEVI, 234; *see* TARUN KUMAR
Vinayaka Kavita (among shabdams of Kuchipudi), 65
VINODINI, 222; *see* KALAVATI
Vipralambha (separation) aspect of love, 48-9
Vir (heroism) ras, 26, 27, 96
Virginity, as offering to deities, 51-2
Vishnu, 26, 70, 75, 104; as Bhargava, 80; Buddha as an avatar of, 126; as Krishna, 127-8, 194; as Krishna, in Manipur, 174; as Mohini, female form, 114, 132; new art forms in wake of Vishnu's replacement of Shiva, 62; as 'the Preserver' (Manipur), 174; as Sun God (festival of Jagan-nath), 192; ten avatars of, 34, 35, 64-65 (in Kuchipudi)
Vishnu Shirodkar, in Kathak revival, 132
Vishnudass Shirali (composer, music director), 212
Visva-Bharati university, dance department of, 214

263

Index

Visvamitra (sage) in *Menaka Lasyam* ballet, 132
Vivida, monkey character, 100
Viyog (aspect of shringar ras), 182; dominating Kubuk Ishai, 192
Vizagapatnam temple, 59
Vrindaban, Krishna's life in, 128, 174, 194-5; Vrindaban Bhangi Pareng (Ras Lila), 187; Vrindaban Pareng of Manipuri dance, 177

Wajid Ali Shah, gaths described by, 145
War and Peace (ballet), 162, 226
West Bengal Sangeet Natak Akademi, 227
White Huns (invaders of North India), 126
Wigman, Mary, 236

Yaimabi Singh, 214, 230
Yajur-Veda, 19, 20
Yakshagana, 121
Yama, deity associated with Karuna (pathos) ras, 26
YAMINI KRISHNAMURTHI, 203, 235
Yamuna river, 128; in the Ras Lila of Braj, 165
Yasoda, foster-mother of Krishna, 128
Yuddhar Naach (dance in Sattra dance-dramas), 196, 197

Zamorin of Calicut, 87; *Krishnapadi* of, 86; introduces dance-dramas based on *Gita Govinda*, 86
de Zoete, Beryl, 217
Zohra Jan (singer), 231
ZOHRA SEGAL, 213, 236